SLIM

Memories of a Rich and Imperfect Life

SLIM KEITH

WITH

ANNETTE TAPERT

SIMON AND SCHUSTER

NEW YORK • LONDON • TORONTO • SYDNEY •
TOKYO • SINGAPORE

Simon and Schuster

SIMON & SCHUSTER BUILDING

ROCKEFELLER CENTER

1230 AVENUE OF THE AMERICAS

NEW YORK, NEW YORK 10020

COPYRIGHT © 1990 BY THE ESTATE OF NANCY KEITH

DESIGNED BY EVE METZ

MANUFACTURED IN THE UNITED STATES OF AMERICA

1   3   5   7   9   10   8   6   4   2

LIBRARY OF CONGRESS CATALOGING IN PUBLICATION DATA

KEITH, SLIM, 1917–1990

SLIM: MEMORIES OF A RICH AND IMPERFECT LIFE/SLIM KEITH WITH

ANNETTE TAPERT.

P.   CM.

1. KEITH, SLIM, 1917–1990—FRIENDS AND ASSOCIATES.

2. KEITH, SLIM, 1917–1990—RELATIONS WITH MEN.

3. CELEBRITIES—UNITED STATES—BIOGRAPHY.

4. UNITED STATES—BIOGRAPHY.   I. TAPERT, ANNETTE.   II. TITLE.

CT275.K4314A3   1990

973.9′092—DC20

[B]   90-31452

CIP

ISBN 0-671-63164-0

*The photographs in this volume
are all part of the Slim Keith collection.*

FOR MY MOTHER
FROM HER DAUGHTER

AND

FOR MY DAUGHTER
FROM HER MOTHER

ACKNOWLEDGMENTS

My gratitude:
—to Sonny Sloan, who got me into the whole ugly mess at the outset;
—to Hal Hinson, currently of *The Washington Post*, who began with me, and whose kindness during a very big sickness never flagged; transcripts from our voluminous conversations are impressive and a marvelous mirror of his superior intelligence;
—to Irene Selznick, who sees this effort for the first time, my thanks for her encouragement and interest, which helped me stay alive during the dry, dead periods;
—to Tom Guinzburg, my neighbor and dear friend, whose criticism and judgment were sound and productive;
—to Jerome Robbins, who is tough, wise, and honest, and most of all, my enduring friend;
—to Dr. Shervert Frazier, for support, faith, and patience during barren and dusty times;
—to Annette Tapert, who picked up the tattered banner, and bolstered my sagging resolve with order, diligence, and progress; hers has been a most rewarding contribution, from every point of view, and I look upon her as a new and gifted daughter;
—and to Marie Arana-Ward, dazzling editor and friend, who came late to the battlefield, and guided the troops to the end, with tact, intelligence, and great skill, a very deep bow.

AUTHOR'S NOTE

The material in this book is from a 72-year-old memory—a rickety contraption at best, but one that works quite well still. It is about the truth, the way things really were through all these years. There is a lot left out, for a variety of reasons, but what is here is how it happened.

CONTENTS

PROLOGUE

In 1938, when I was twenty and there seemed no place better in the world to be than San Simeon, I met a marvelous, lusty, open, funny girl called Patricia "Honeychile" Wilder. She had a deep southern accent, and in the sometimes staid environment of William Randolph Hearst's California "ranch," she was very, very good company. Thirty years later, she reappeared as Princess Hohenlohe. It does seem a delicious coincidence that the second time I saw her she was emerging from a special room reserved for the royals at Windsor Castle on the occasion of a party that the Queen of England gave before Princess Alexandra's wedding to Angus Ogilvy.

Honeychile Wilder, a.k.a. Princess Hohenlohe, had had a goodly share of the royal champagne and, I should suspect, very little of the royal supper. Her tiara was slightly askew, just a hair to the left, and her walk had a perceptible list, but she wore a big smile as she spotted me. "Hiya, Slim-honey," she crooned. "Look around here —how about this place? Beats San Simeon any day. Listen, baby, I can sure tell you one thing: We've made it."

I never quite found out how Honeychile had made her social

ascent. I can't, for that matter, tell you how I made mine—if an ascent is what I'd made. But if credentials are anything, I had some, and Honeychile, as a dedicated follower of matters social, knew what they were: I had been married to the film director Howard Hawks; I had been married to the great literary agent and impresario Leland Hayward; I was now, thanks to my marriage to Sir Kenneth Keith, bearing a title, the Lady Keith. Along the way, I had "discovered" Lauren Bacall, and Howard Hawks had used my image to create hers in *To Have and Have Not*. I had made the best-dressed list innumerable times, I had shot with Hemingway, traveled with Capote, and been wooed by Gable. To Honeychile, I was a celebrity.

Perhaps I was. But it was a very accidental celebrity, with none of the social engineering you see these days. I never made a plan or had a design or gave ten million dollars to a museum. My celebrity was born less from me than from others' perception of me. It was about good looks, brains, taste, and style. I can't take any credit for the good looks and brains, that was heredity. And I really can't take credit for taste and style; that was mostly instinct. The only ingredient I brought to this recipe was the recognition that, while you have to be natural, you also have to be different. If, that is, you want to make an impact.

In my day, different meant not having your hair done in a pompadour and adorning it with a snood, or not trying to hide your intelligence behind a sea of frills. I somehow knew there was a glut in that market. I opted for a scrubbed-clean, polished look. I thought it was more important to have an intelligence that showed, a humor that never failed, and a healthy interest in men.

The character that came to be Slim was really, in the end, a mixture of those attributes, with the help of good luck and good timing. But a perfect image rarely goes with a perfect life. By the time I saw Honeychile Wilder, I'd had my share of disappointments: a childhood filled with storms and insecurities, two failed marriages, miscarriages, and sick children. And yet Honeychile Wilder was right: I had, like her, come a long way.

EAST
OF
EDEN

I was born "east of Eden," in Salinas, California, in John Steinbeck's "Long Valley"—that beautiful green-carpeted fertile piece
of California which now feeds most of the country its artichokes and
lettuce. I came into this world on July 15, 1917, as Mary Raye Gross,
second daughter of Raye Nell Boyer and Edward Gross. My mother
soon thought better of my name and changed it to Nancy.

From the time I was born until my teenage years, my family lived
in Pacific Grove, one of the small towns on the Monterey Peninsula.
The peninsula was divided into sections. Monterey was the commercial section and the home of all the sardine canneries. Pacific
Grove started out to be—and I don't think it has ever become much
more—a conservative, middle-class, middle-priced seaside resort.
People came and rented little beach houses for a few weeks in the
summer, swam in the sea and took the scenic seventeen-mile drive
that girdled Pebble Beach, a large and exclusive compound. Off
season, it was just another quiet town tucked between two other
quiet towns.

For this child, Pacific Grove was a magic kingdom. It was where
I learned to swim and have wonderful childhood adventures on the

beach: playing hide-and-seek among the rocks, collecting shells, and draping myself in seaweed. All this set against an almost total Steinbeck backdrop. My father owned several of the fish canneries Steinbeck wrote about in *Cannery Row*. And the Hopkins Marine Laboratory of Tortilla Flat was my playground.

My family knew John Steinbeck's parents, and often I had to be removed from the roof of their summer cottage—it was covered with an insanely rampant passion vine which made for the best jungle climbing in the neighborhood. My mother would come to fetch me after a call from the patient Mrs. Steinbeck, and, like a fireman retrieving a stuck cat, would pull me out of the network of roots and take me home a block away.

I don't have any vivid childhood memories of John Steinbeck. All I really remember of him was that he was a burly, rather strong-looking man in his early twenties who lived in a funny house that he'd built with his father. He still lived with his well-spoken, elderly parents. And then suddenly when I was about eighteen he was the famous author of *Tortilla Flat*. I met him much later, in my life in New York, where I would see him sometimes on the cocktail party circuit. He would say, "I remember you, you were that pretty little girl with the long legs who was always crawling around my mother's roof."

When I grew up and read Steinbeck, it was as if I were walking through my childhood. The shabby districts of Tortilla Flat and Cannery Row with their drunks, hobos, and ladies of the night were, by my parents' decree, strictly forbidden places. The reckless side of my nature always got the better of me and I would make what I thought were dangerous forays into these neighborhoods. I would casually say to Mother that I was going to play at the beach, but would discreetly take a right turn instead of a left and the next thing I knew I was down on Cannery Row. Or, on the daily walk home from school, I'd drift out of my zone. As I was a curious child, I consistently managed to make friends with the "worst" children at school—and would proudly drag them home. My mother in her firm but gentle way would explain to me that I mustn't bring them back —my father wouldn't approve.

I had a friend called Patsy. As I look back, I'm sure her mother was a dope addict—she was always sleepy or invisible. But the rest of the family was nice to me. They'd always invite me in

Me, age six.

In lace.

and I'd sit in the house with its dead, dusty smell, thinking, "I'm glad I don't live here, but I'm awfully glad I have a friend."

Then I made real friends with a girl whose name I can't remember, but I certainly remember her grandmother's name. The grandmother was Flora Woods, who was the model for Dora, the madam of the brothel in John Steinbeck's *Cannery Row*. My friend was probably not Flora's granddaughter at all, but the child of one of the ladies who worked there. I was totally captivated by this girl. She was full of life and had all sorts of filthy things to say, which just fascinated me. I didn't know what she was talking about, but I certainly wanted to find out. Mother got wind of this friendship and said to me, "Enough is enough. You can't bring this child home with you. I'm sure she is a perfectly nice girl, but she's just not the right sort of company for you." I didn't know what business her grandmother was in, or if I ever saw her. I certainly remember snooping around the whorehouse sneaking surreptitious looks, hoping someone would go in or out. I wasn't absolutely sure about what went on there, but I knew it couldn't be good.

The only time I was allowed to venture outside my neighborhood was when my father would take the family for dinner in the Italian section of Monterey. He would often bring us to the home of Mr. Cardinelli, who captained the fishing fleet my father leased for his

18

cannery business. For my father these were courtesy dinners, but I adored them. Mrs. Cardinelli would cook what I still think of as the best Italian food I've ever had. Marvelous bouillabaisse, or cioppino, as they called it. You sat at a great big long table alongside a lusty, noisy group of mostly sailors and their children, and platter after platter after platter came out of the tiny kitchen, each one more glorious than the dish before. The meal was accompanied by loaves of bread that they would cut at the table and wash down with what my father called "Dago Red."

It wasn't just the fascinating dinners like those at the Cardinellis' or the small decadences of Tortilla Flat that captured my interest. My curiosity extended to simpler things. I loved to go down to the edge of the bay in the early morning when the boats came in with their night's catch. I could tell how good their haul was by how low the boats were in the water. Before docking, they would stop at a floating tank attached to a big pipe and the fish would be sucked out of the boat, down through the pipe, and into the cannery. There, they would go up on a conveyor belt to a row of female scalers and then off to the girls who opened and gutted them. (It was probably from watching this so often that I developed my somewhat renowned and lifelong talent for fish gutting.) The fish were then washed and moved to the packers to be canned. The cans were sealed, put on enormous trollies, and rolled into the ovens to be cooked. Then they shuttled along the conveyor belt that crossed the street and into another building where they were labeled and boxed. I was fascinated by all of that. I would pick one fish, tell myself it was my fish, and follow its progress all the way.

Steinbeck documented the unconventional lives of the colorful denizens of Monterey, its bums and its workers, but its bawdy

Cannery Row. (Photo courtesy of the Pat Hathaway Collection)

fables did not in any way correspond to the life I knew behind the front door of my family's house. My family was something else. We were sheltered and insular, and almost thoroughly isolated.

We lived in a typical white frame turn-of-the-century house, a block from Monterey Bay. The place had a large front porch, its roof held up by large stone pillars. My mother preferred to call it the veranda. Her pride and joy was a plate-glass wall on one side of this porch which she kept so spotless that it seemed invisible. So clean, in fact, that kamikaze hummingbirds claimed their death daily during the summer. The living room had a fireplace, the dining room looked out to the Monterey Bay. Sliding doors between all the main rooms, usually pushed back in their invisible position, gave the space an open feeling. At the back of the house was a small garden with a goldfish pond. And beyond that was an open space reserved for my father, who in autumn would haul in barrels of grapes and large vats and attempt to make his own wine—an endeavor that never worked. The closest we ever came to tasting it was the year all the bottles he laid down exploded in the basement.

For another family, it would have been a wonderful place—warm, inviting, filled with friends. The house couldn't have been too small, because everyone had his own room: my parents, my sister, my baby brother, and I. And my maternal grandmother. My father hated having her there, perhaps with some justification. I don't think mothers-in-law were in demand then any more than they are now.

Not having to share a room was the one way my childhood was fair. I was the middle child, the skinniest, the least likely to succeed at anything. My sister Theodora (Teedie) was five years older than I. She was blond and beautiful and mean as a snake, but she seemed to get everything she wanted. Buddy, the sole boy and heir apparent, was the only one of us my father seemed to love; he got all my father's attention and was said to be the hope of the family. I got what was left. Precious little.

Of my siblings, I could most easily have resented my brother, who was three years younger than I. He was tow-headed, and that thatch of unruly hair grew in independent directions all over his head. His bright blue eyes and round cherubic face combined with a winning nature. I adored him. And he loved me back. We spoke to each other in a private language. Even when he was an infant I could understand what he was trying to communicate. And strangely enough, I could communicate right back in his own little language. Mother would say, "What does he want?" And I'd say, "He wants to sit in another chair," or, "He wants to go to another room." It was baby talk, but I could understand it. I was like a nanny to him. And for me, he was my best playmate. When he grew a little older, we would climb into bushes and trees, make houses in the tops, hide from the world, and maybe we were gone only fifteen minutes, but it seemed as though we were spending a lifetime there.

Like many children, we essentially made our own fun. The difference—for me, anyway—was that I needed no paraphernalia. I lived totally in my head. Not only did I have imaginary friends, I had imaginary worlds. I lived in palaces, plied the seas in great boats with silken sails, and ate mostly grapes. I wore emerald overshoes and diamond wraps and life was full, rich, and perfect. I needed an imagination. It was all I had to protect me from a household dominated by a patriarch beyond any measure.

My father's method, hardly original, was to rule through fear. Strong, sturdily built, and very masculine, he possessed the most piercing light blue eyes I've ever seen. It was as if a pale fire burned in them. Rimless glasses increased their incandescence. I can't remember his smile, as I don't think I ever saw it. He was a rigid, bigoted, dogmatic German with great drive, diligence, and will. He worked hard and succeeded and became a force in the community, but I should imagine he was an unpopular man. I can't remember that he ever had a close friend. He never understood why we wanted friends and playmates, and he was very clear that none of our friends were to be around when he got home—this was a man who believed everyone conspired against him, his family as well as his business associates.

The Catholics—he was a non-practicing one—were his special enemies, and he theirs. He accused them of inventing Christmas as a personal plot against him. He hated Christmas not only because it cost him money but because plum pudding gave him indigestion.

The Jews he looked upon as a band of scurrilous merchants who sat about thinking of ways to lure unsuspecting shoppers into buying things they didn't need.

Democrats were the worst villains of all: not only were they Democrats, but they could be Catholic or Jewish as well. He couldn't accept the fact that it was possible to be a Protestant and a Democrat at the same time.

My father did, however, like Herbert Hoover—liked him a lot. If there had been a John Birch Society in his day, he would have been to the right of that.

Mother was our buffer. Her calmness began with her appearance: thick auburn hair—so long she could sit on it—pulled into a giant knot at the back of her head, huge soft blue eyes, a ready smile, and a warm sense of humor. She was always the peacemaker. She never voted, and eventually became a Christian Scientist. By keeping her children quiet and her mother closed in her room while my father was in the house, she managed a moderately tranquil atmosphere. We were to be silent while in the back of the car for the obligatory Sunday drive, and we were to keep in order at the table, because a dropped fork or a spilled glass of milk or being unable to finish what was on one's plate meant punishment, not only for the offender but for all three children. When my father wasn't complaining or punishing us for something, he ignored us. I can't remember him acknowledging a birthday, a good school report, or even bestowing so much as a pat on the head for a task well done.

In some miraculous way, my mother made up for what he denied us. I remember I would sometimes come home from school and tell her about some awful child who had been unkind to me. She would say, "Darling, feel sorry for her, don't be angry. She's just jealous of you." I found this hard to believe—I couldn't understand how anyone could be jealous of me—but Mother's goodness had a way of making me feel things weren't as bad as they really were.

Certainly, it helped that her own mother was always there. That was wonderful for us children, too. Auntie Rydie, as we called her, was a sweet old lady whose lap was a warm, safe place to be. Her chair was a place to hide behind if the posse was out. She spent most of her time in her room and very seldom came to meals, but she was a wonderful hostess in her own small domain, providing for us endless entertainment. She taught me and my sister how to sew, knit, and crochet. She told us stories about her youth that were like illustrated lectures, with side trips through all her boxes, trunks, and dresser drawers.

I loved these explorations best of all. She had only to open a

Mother.

cedar trunk for my imagination to fly around the world and back. Then came the exotic oddments: fur, silk, ribbon and lace, shining jet buttons, a mother-of-pearl shoehorn, pieces of string, a length of China silk, little gauze bags filled with lavender of long-lost fragrance, books, a scrap of worn velvet, brown photographs of gone people. Each little oddment had a story with a cast she either invented or that really existed in an ancient past.

None of this fantasy obscured what I perceived to be the fundamental failure of my parents' marriage. I never saw them touch or show one another any kind of affection. Nor did they argue in our presence. Whatever happened between them happened behind closed doors. On the outside, my father treated my mother as he treated his children—with indifference. I think Mother stayed on because she thought she had no alternative. Like us, she was scared of my father. She loved us all with a fierce gentleness and did what she could to make a happy life for us. The wonder was how she managed, with all the restrictions put upon her, to provide for us what was essentially a good childhood.

Our treats were few. But there was one we got every evening. While my father was still at work, my mother gave us our dinner. Then, in the sweetest moment of our day, she'd tell us a story before we were put to bed. The three of us vied to sit in Mother's lap as she invented wonderful tales in which we children were all principals with marvelous roles.

One winter evening that changed forever. My father was blissfully absent, the fire was dying out on the hearth, and we all lounged together in the living room dressed for bed—my sister and I in flannel nighties, Buddy in a long miniature old man's nightshirt. The storytelling was over, and my eight-year-old brother stood with his back to the open fireplace. He was warming his little bottom, and as he leaned back toward the warmth, the hem of his nightshirt brushed the live embers that lurked under the dead ash.

The nightshirt caught fire. Flames licked up the garment like red snakes. He screamed and screamed, racing about the room to get away from the enveloping terror and pain. None of us could catch him. Mother finally made a grab for him, threw him on the floor, and rolled him up in a carpet—Buddy screaming in mummified agony all the while.

Mother unrolled him, gathered up his now silent but still living body, and carried him upstairs. Guilt engulfed us. We all felt we should have caught him sooner. We all felt we could have done something more than we had done.

My father was called. The doctor was called. And a blanket of gloom, silence, and terror settled over the house. The bumbling old Dr. Sandholt recommended a blood transfusion. In those days, there was no such thing as blood typing or any knowledge of the Rh factor. Naturally my father insisted on giving his own blood to save his son. The transfusion was done. But Buddy could not withstand the trauma and, perhaps, the wrong type blood. His little heart stopped beating.

During Buddy's deathwatch, I hadn't been allowed to see him. After he died, I waited until no one was on that floor of the house, then crept into his room. I pulled down the blanket to look at his face; the only part of him that wasn't burned. I sat with his body for a while—not to study or examine him, but simply to feel his presence. It somehow made it possible for me to accept the fact that he was dead.

After Buddy's funeral, my father commissioned a small white marble mausoleum on the site of the family burial plot, and had "Gross" carved on the pediment. Buddy was removed from the ground and placed in the upper-left-hand corner, his name and dates chiseled in.

My grief was such that it took me a while to notice that the face of the mausoleum was divided into four. Whenever we visited Buddy, I always wondered who of our family of five was going to be the odd man out. Only later did I realize that Father had decided the person to be excluded was my mother. He would be alone there with his three children.

From then on, my father turned all the rage and despair that he felt over Buddy's death on one target—my mother. He blamed her for the accident, never believing that she couldn't have saved Buddy. His anger at Mother became a force so strong that it destroyed whatever they had between them. And as she became his psychic punching bag, life in the house as I had known it dissolved, then disappeared altogether.

LITTLE
GIRL
LOST

The first few years after Buddy's death in 1928 were the blackest, most hopeless of my life, and I struggled, like the rest of my family, to deal with his loss. My father became more guarded and more inexplicable than ever. My mother came through the devastation even kinder and more compassionate than before. My sixteen-year-old sister, whose grief must have been great, chose to hide those feelings. Instead, she became meaner and more selfish.

Being only eleven, I dealt with Buddy's death in the only way I could—by creating an illusion. I wrote a letter to my mother in which I told her that Buddy's death was like my going off to school. If she watched me leave, she'd see me walk along the hedge and turn to the right, and although I was out of her sight, I still existed, I was just going on about my life. My brother was, too. It made absolute sense to me, and my mother took great comfort from this idea. It made her feel that Buddy wasn't just burned-up ash.

None of this relieved the strain on the family unit, which reached such a pitch a year after Buddy's death that Theodora and I were sent as boarders to the Sisters of Notre Dame, a convent school one hundred miles north of Monterey. This was worse than living at

home. I now had to figure out the loss of my brother by myself—
and somehow get used to being without my mother at the same
time. I was in the sixth grade, away from home for the first time, on
the cusp of adolescence and, as a result of my grief, very tentative
about making friends or opening up in any way.

My loneliness should have been relieved by the presence of my
sister, but she was now a bright, good-looking teenager—a glamorous big wheel in the school's hierarchy and a distant relation indeed. For some inexplicable reason, Teedie chose to ignore me. If
I passed her in the hallway during school hours or in the dining
room she wouldn't speak to me or look at me. When our eyes did
lock, it was in a long, icy stare. Which turned into disgust on her
part, for I was going through my ugly stage—tall, gawky, much too
skinny. I assumed she was embarrassed by my ungainly appearance. I knew that if I told my mother, she would ask Teedie to be
kinder to me, but I also knew Teedie would have responded by
becoming more abusive.

I could have coped with Teedie's indifference. What destroyed
me was her chastising me for a problem over which I had no control
—bedwetting. I had developed the habit only after my brother's
death and there was no way to keep it a secret. Along with perhaps
twenty other little girls, I slept in a dormitory cubicle that contained
only a bed, a chair, a dresser, a small hanging cupboard, a mirror
over the dresser, and Jesus over my head. Sheets were changed
once or twice a week, and I could not ask for new ones each day.
So in the mornings I simply made my bed, wet sheets and all, and
got back into my wet sheets at night. My nightie would have dried
out by hanging in the locker all day, but at night I would climb back
into those clammy sheets, pull the covers tight around my neck so
that the telltale reek could not escape, and go to sleep praying that
I wouldn't move and that it would not happen again.

God did not hear me. There was no one to help me disguise or
remove the pungent evidence. It was my sole burden and disgrace.
And looming over me all the time was the specter of my sister. She
would wait until she had a sufficient gallery of friends, then, feigning surprise and disgust, take the lead and announce that I was a
bedwetter—a sixth-grade bedwetter. She would ask me, in front of
whomever she had gathered, if I had wet my bed again last night.
And then she would glare at me until she had her answer.

All this humiliation could have turned into self-hatred. But I was lucky. Instead of hating myself, I began to hate my sister. Luckier still, that hatred took the form of strength and determination. I was determined not just to get even but to excel. I would be better, brighter, more beautiful; I would become someone who would scale heights and realize all the dreams my sister and I both must have had. I knew I would realize them, and I knew she wouldn't.

After Teedie's graduation, we both returned to Monterey. Only then did we learn that our father had moved out of our house and was living in a hotel, carrying on his business as usual. He was away from whatever reminded him of what he had lost and what he had never had.

That summer, my sister also began to spend more and more time away from home; in her case, the lure was a middle-aged woman with a man's haircut and lots of tweed jackets and brogues. I never did know where she came from, but she grew to have total control over—and the full attention of—my sister.

One morning, a moving van drew up in front of our house. A man got out, came to the front door, and asked to see Miss Theodora Gross. My mother asked what he wanted. He said, "I have come to remove Miss Gross's possessions, as ordered." And on that morning, my sister—who had, unbeknownst to my mother or anyone else in the house, packed her things—moved out. Her furniture, her clothes, and her books were crated up and taken away within an hour's time.

It was cold, lethal, and final. My mother just stood at the door with tears pouring down her face, unable to understand. Teedie offered no explanation whatsoever. She simply said, "I'm leaving." And out she went to her friend's car, which was waiting behind the van, and drove away. As far as I know, she never saw my mother again.

As the years went by and I was old enough to attend social functions in Monterey, I occasionally would see her across a crowded room, but I never spoke to her and I made sure our eyes never met.

A few years later, my sister got married in a small rustic chapel in Carmel. Mother and I were not asked to the ceremony, but she did so want to see her first-born in her wedding dress. I drove her to the little church after the ceremony had started so that she could watch, unseen, as Teedie left the church in a cloud of silk and white

Teedie.

Mother and Teedie in front of our house in Pacific Grove.

tulle on the arm of her new, but soon-to-be short-term, husband. Mother wept. I boiled. Teedie later remarried and had two daughters. Although I have no contact with my sister, news occasionally trickles back to me. I know she is a grandmother and, maybe by now, even a great-grandmother.

With Teedie's rejection of our mother, she gained our father's respect. Whether her lady friend pushed her to do it or whether the idea was her own, the result was the same—by rejecting our mother, she became, in my father's eyes, our brother's replacement. She had always been, or pretended to be, interested in my father's businesses, which were now quite extensive; in addition to his canneries, there was considerable real estate. He made her a partner in these businesses and gave her a great deal of money up front. I think Teedie thought that gradually he would turn the operations over to her and eventually leave her his considerable fortune—for, as he now saw things, she was his only heir.

For me, the real wonder was, once again, my mother. Here was a woman who had obviously lived an almost loveless life—she had lost her only son, been blamed continually for his death, and been abandoned by her firstborn child for reasons never explained. How she could have endured the pain and loss that she did and remain

SLIM

sane, kind, and compassionate is a miracle. My admiration and
respect for her now and my love for her then have provided me, all
my grown-up life, an example I have tried to emulate. I don't maintain for a moment that I have the goodness, the forgiveness, the
patience, or the constancy she had, but her example is responsible
for the best part of me.

That fall, when I was thirteen, I was sent to the Dominican convent in San Rafael, a constructive and helpful school where I began
to have the first really happy schooldays I can remember. I was
older, independent, and agreeable enough to do well socially, and
bright enough to excel academically, particularly in English. Words
began to fascinate me and it was here that I developed my lifelong
love of literature. And, for the first time since Buddy's death, I
made friends. I had a teenage beau—not serious really but a beau
all the same, who constantly wrote me letters on writing paper he
had engraved with both of our names. He sent flowers and built up
my ego, and slowly I began to believe I was someone of worth.

Best of all, my mother and I began to enjoy a more peaceful
existence. She came to see me every Wednesday, which was my
day off. It was a day's journey each way, but she did it. She would
take me out to lunch, letting me bring friends along. Most of all, she
made me feel normal—she did all the little things parents do for
kids off in boarding school.

Independence doesn't exist until tested. In my case, the test
came during my first year at the Dominican convent, when I received a surprise visit from my father. He came on a school day,
not a visitor's day. The nuns called me out of class and said,
"You're wanted in the parlor," which was like being told you're
wanted by the warden. It had to be bad news.

A chill went up my spine. "What for?" I asked.

"Your father has come to see you."

I was puzzled that he was there; he never had come to see me
before. There he sat, in a stiff-backed chair in that spare, highly
polished, immaculate reception room which smelled of wax and a
trace of incense from the chapel down the hall. I seated myself
across from him and we looked at one another.

He asked a few questions about my health and my studies and
then said, "You know your mother and I are going to be divorced."

I said, "Yes, I know that and I'm sorry."

30

My father, Edward Gross, in later age.

"I'm here to ask you to come and live with me," he said. "You see, your mother is responsible for the death of her son. Your sister has already made her choice. If you also leave your mother's house, it will prove to the court that she's an unfit parent—and I won't have to provide any support for her."

I was absolutely appalled, even at my young age, that anybody would do such a thing.

He saw this, so he sweetened the offer. "If you live with me, you'll have many advantages you've never had before. I'll give you a horse, a little boat, a car when you are ready." He made a long list of enticing things.

I said, "It's very nice of you . . . but I don't think it's fair."

"What do you mean?"

"Well, there are only two of us left, and there are only two of you, and you should each have one of us. So I'm going to stay with my mother."

He was shocked. "You don't mean that," he said.

"Yes, I do," I replied, holding my ground. "I absolutely mean it. I love my mother, she's been wonderful to me. I see no reason to punish her for something she didn't do. I'm staying with her."

My father got up without a word. He walked out of the room, down those big, long gray stairs, and never looked back. I never spoke to him, never saw him again until very near the end of his life.

LIFE
BEGINS

After my father had gone and my sister moved away, there was no one left but my mother, my grandmother, and me. In the summer of 1934, Mother decided to sell the house and move to a hotel, so we moved across the hill from Pacific Grove into an apartment at the La Playa Hotel in Carmel. The La Playa was a comfortable, rather simple but civilized resort hotel in a fancier, more upwardly mobile town. My mother was able to afford for us to live here thanks to the comfortable divorce settlement she had been awarded by the court; when my father's plan to have me come and live with him backfired, my mother took him to court and fought for her fair share. I don't know what Mother received exactly—whether it was a portion of his real estate holdings or child support income—but the money afforded us a civilized though not extravagant life. Mother saw to it that I got everything I needed, even if it meant she had to deprive herself to give it to me.

Mother probably would have stayed on in Pacific Grove, but she thought Carmel was better for me. Life there consisted of tennis lessons, swimming, horseback riding, and parties, all at the Del Monte Hotel, which was the social center for the Monterey Peninsula's younger upper-middle-class set.

This move definitely put me on an upward spiral, but I hardly noticed. At seventeen, I was too busy working through adolescence —and what a time that was! For one thing, I saw that I wasn't an understuffed rag doll. I was on the brink of my life, and I sensed that something perfectly marvelous was just around the corner.

It began to dawn on me, rather late in the day, that I had some qualities that were attractive to other people. I had a good sense of humor, a happy spirit, and a certain charm that seemed to work for me. I was good-looking, and could do a number of social activities quite well—ride, swim, dance. As a result, there was always a fellow or two in pursuit. I became very skillful at juggling them so there would be someone onstage and one or two in the wings. All of this was very innocent—necking, but no bed work.

The juggling and flirting were short-lived. That summer of my eighteenth year, I fell deeply in love for the first time—not a crush or a flirt, but an overwhelming, breath-stopping, heart-pounding love. He was beautiful, elegant, highly intelligent, deeply sensitive, and to me absolutely irresistible.

We met on a tennis court at the Del Monte Hotel. Thank God, my lesson preceded his, so he never really knew how bad I was. We were introduced by the pro, and I asked if he minded my watching his lesson. He had a carved, lean beauty that was impossible to ignore, regardless of whatever else was going on around him.

I learned that he'd been raised in New York and San Francisco. At twenty-one, he had received an inheritance that made working unnecessary. For a young man, he used his money in the most sophisticated way: he built himself a splendid house, and lived there alone with a very good servant and two Dobermans. He read voraciously and deeply, not the popular writers of the day, but Proust, Nietzsche, and Mann. He listened to classical music, which I had heard little of before, and he taught me how to listen to it, a gift for which I can never thank him enough. Most of all, there was a mysterious intellectual isolation about him, an aloofness I wanted to break through at any cost.

Sam, whose last name doesn't really matter in this context, took my heart and never let it go. Half a century has passed, and he still has it, or that part of it which is the most vulnerable and most joyous, that part which beats so strongly during first love and which is never to ache that way again. Happily, he was as much in love with me as I was with him. But he sensed that my curiosity and energy would never match his stillness and introspection, and he was wise enough never to let our relationship go into its final phase, which would have been marriage. If we'd married, we would have been miserable. For as much as I loved him, I knew I wanted a different life.

That September, I entered my senior year at the Dominican convent. Sam and I wrote to one another and we saw each other as often as possible. But first love didn't relieve my restlessness to experience the world beyond the Monterey Peninsula. I began to put my mind seriously to the big escape. It wasn't that I knew so much or was so well educated, it was simply that I felt the convent couldn't teach me what I wanted to know. Its diploma was irrelevant to me.

By the end of the first term I had, after much pleading and nagging, convinced my mother to take me out of school. But what would she tell the nuns? All we had to work with was my physique—I was so skinny everybody called me String Bean or Beanpole—and my endless series of colds. For years, people would gawk at me and say, "Fatten her up and she'll be fine." Now, we decided, it was time to do just that.

A compliant doctor wrote a note to the effect that I might possibly have a spot on my lung. It seemed to follow that I should go to a dry, warm climate where I could exercise a lot and be in the sun, thereby restoring myself to perfect health—which I already possessed. Later, when I felt better, I would, of course, return to school.

I left the Dominican convent at Christmas time. My "Magic Mountain" was, of all places, Death Valley—the contradiction always amused me. My destination was the popular winter resort at the time, a charming hotel called Furnace Creek Inn.

My mother was a real sport about this. I think she had resigned herself to my flying away eventually—perhaps she had decided it was better that I do it with her blessing. Just before I left she somehow managed, without the help of my father, to buy me a gorgeous yellow Packard roadster, which I named the Flying Omelette.

I set off across the Mojave Desert in my Omelette, wearing a powder blue wool suit with a matching felt hat that had a jaunty

Sam.

flower on the side. With the convertible top down, the wind hitting my face, I thought to myself, "My God! I'm the prettiest thing that ever was!" It was unusually fancy attire for a road trip, but that was the point. I wanted to look grown-up. And I was looking forward to checking in at a motel along the way, opening my suitcase and choosing an outfit more appropriate for a desert climate. That, to my mind, was a smart silk dress. Preposterous, I know, but exhilarating—inside those clothes was a girl reveling in a sense of freedom she'd never known before.

This self-confidence quickly eroded as I crossed the desert. I became filled with absolute terror, worried that I might get a flat tire or that the engine would boil over, and my bleached dry bones would be found years later. But the thing that scared me most was the thought of running out of gas. Crossing the desert, there was nothing as far as the eye could see, so every time I spotted a sort of *Petrified Forest* gas station, I stopped. The attendant would say, "You're full." And I'd say, "Well, put more in."

When I finally reached Furnace Creek Inn, I caused quite a stir. The other guests were staid, middle-aged, and dignified. Now into their midst pulled a yellow convertible, top down, from which a slim, wind-blown, golden-tanned girl walked in and registered with the practiced aplomb of one who had been twice around the world.

That was what they saw. Their world traveler was, in fact, bitterly crestfallen. Furnace Creek Inn was a straightforward resort hotel. Very well run, very pleasant, and not too big. There were no other restaurants, no nightclubs, nothing but a big stone hotel on the side of the desert. However much that pleased an older crowd, to me it seemed back-of-the-moon dreary, not at all what I'd had in mind.

It took days before I opened my eyes and saw how beautiful the barren and threatening landscape really was. Hills surrounded the inn, and the light changed constantly as the day turned them beige, then pink, then purple, and finally blue-black at night. This experience awakened my eye. I began to see past myself.

I stayed at the inn unchaperoned for about two months. The staff and a changing cast of guests seemed to take a proprietary interest in this happy, good-looking kid who had blown up out of the desert and landed on the doorstep. I'm sure my mother wrote to them and said, "I'm trusting you with my daughter, whom I cherish and love. She's young, she's just out of school. Please take care of her as I can't be with her." If I didn't show up for a meal, someone came to find out why.

Furnace Creek Inn was far enough away from Los Angeles and at the same time close enough to be a resort that was visited often by people from the motion picture business. And, as it happened, during my stay two Hollywood men appeared to spend a week or so resting and restoring in the sun. They were the movie actors William Powell and Warner Baxter, both of whom were popular, romantic leading men of the day.

Warner Baxter (seated left) and William Powell (seated right) surrounded by fans at Furnace Creek Inn.

I dimly knew who they were. I had seen them in films, but as I wasn't a film buff they didn't mean much to me, and I wasn't star-struck when I met them sitting by the swimming pool. They had been around enough to know that I was no hooker; nor was I the femme-fatale spy I was pretending to be. To my surprise, they asked, "Why are you here and not in school?" I explained to them that I had been sent by my mother to get healthier. Then I added, "And by the way, why are you here and not working?" They loved that, and invited me to have dinner with them that night. I accepted, but warned them that I wasn't allowed in the bar as I was under eighteen; drinks would have to be sent to the table.

They decided to be my surrogate godfathers. And they were. They lunched with me, dined with me, wouldn't let me have a drink, and had an opinion on any plan I came up with. They didn't approve

SLIM

Taking the waters at Furnace Creek Inn.

of moonlight rides or moonlight picnics with some of the young male
staff I'd met while I was there. They
would say, "Call us when you get
back." Upon my return, I'd dutifully
ring them and say, "I'm home. Good
night."

Bill Powell, especially, thought I
needed to be protected. He dubbed
me his "Slim Princess." The "Princess" part dropped by the wayside
early on. "Slim" stayed with me forever, although I'm anything but the
sylphlike creature of my youth.

At the end of my stay in the desert
I was to join my mother in Los Angeles and then we would go home together to Carmel. Bill Powell very
sweetly asked us both to lunch with
him at his home in Beverly Hills. That
really was big-time Hollywood, and it
gave me a tiny taste of what wonders
the world held. Powell was debonair
and glamorous—very much like his
movie characters. He had a fast wit,
was well educated and remarkably
well read. His home was every bit
what I'd imagined a movie star's
house to be. There was an enormous
circular driveway leading to Geor-
gian-style pillars and an imposing
front door. The interior was all white, with fur carpets everywhere.

Later, I would come to see that Bill Powell had ghastly taste. But
in 1935, when I'd seen nothing of real style, his home looked absolutely marvelous to me. It's what opened my eyes—to a degree—to
the fact that such luxuries existed. And people could have them.

38

They were attainable. I instantly figured that that was the life for me.

Now, I'm the first to say that I was an impressionable youngster. My circumstances were far from awful. I had a good mother, a nice place to live, and a lot of friends in Monterey. But I just knew there

William Powell in his My Man Godfrey *get-up.*

was more—and it took only the sight of Powell's house to prove it to me.

After I returned to Carmel, Bill Powell would telephone me every now and then. I always hoped the local operators were listening. They wouldn't know that he regarded me as a daughter. For a California girl—hell, for any girl at that time—a movie star as hot as Powell on the phone was a good piece of work.

I don't doubt that people wondered why someone like Bill Powell would take the time to call young, unknown Nancy Gross. In retrospect, I think he was a bit jaded by Hollywood; he found my wide-eyed behavior refreshing, my reactions spontaneous and ingenuous. I was fresh and alive and graced with an acerbic wit. He looked on me as an extraordinary child, but I was simply a young woman responding to the give and take of smart, worldly people. The higher the quality of mind, the faster and better my motor runs.

And Sam? Once I was back home, our relationship continued, but what he found wasn't the same person who had left Carmel months before. I was now a bubbly, lively young woman who enjoyed everything he loathed with a zest and energy that he found neither comfortable nor familiar. The realization that I would never be satisfied by a totally introspective life was never more evident.

For my part, I was still under the spell of my sojourn in L.A.— and the Great Beyond in general. There was a lot out there, and I was determined to see as much of it as I possibly could. I just had to figure out a way to get at it.

WITH
WILLIAM
RANDOLPH
HEARST

Fate did not take its course too quickly after I returned from Lotus-land. I still had my mother, my one strong family tie, to consider, and she had the responsibility of my grandmother, who still lived with us. And so from 1935 to 1938 I stayed in Carmel with them, enjoying myself, taking advantage of every opportunity that was available, and waiting for the right moment to spring. Every month I would drive to Los Angeles for a few days and stay at the Beverly Wilshire. I craved not only the glamour of Los Angeles—the parties and movie premieres—but the vitality a city provides.

At home in Carmel, I kept myself busy with my first and last career aspiration. While at the convent, I had discovered I possessed a pleasant singing voice. I was very serious about it and took voice lessons four times a week from a former opera singer. But the closest I ever came to professional status was to sing—once—on Monterey radio. Finally, after a year of intensive training, I realized the rigid and disciplined life of an opera singer wasn't for me. That

At the Del Monte Hotel swimming pool, otherwise known as the "Roman Plunge."

ambition was, for me, about as realistic as wanting to be a nun. All was not lost, though. I managed to walk away with a wide repertoire of arias and lieder and a better understanding of classical music.

Sam was still in my life, but I dated other men. We both knew he wasn't a social animal. He didn't like dancing and going to night-clubs, and as I did, he couldn't see any reason why I should stay home.

I spent a great deal of time on the dance floor at the Del Monte Hotel being whirled around by the likes of Winston Frost, an attractive and well-bred young Virginian, who fifty-four years later is still in my life. When I met Winston, he had originally taken a sabbatical from Harvard to learn the real estate business at the Del Monte Properties Company. By this time, the magic of Hollywood had gotten under his skin too, and he was eager to get down south and learn the movie business. Winston and I cut a fine swath on the dance floor and he began to squire me around, introducing me to interesting people and opening up new doors.

The most fascinating door he opened for me led into a circus party at William Randolph Hearst's gigantic "Tara by the Sea" in Santa Monica. By this time, Hearst was long estranged from his wife Millicent. He was living openly with his mistress, Marion Davies. When we arrived, acres of big top were in place; the entertainment area covered two tennis courts, lawns, parking lots—everything that wasn't under a roof was under canvas. This party was my first taste of the miracle that was the Hearst operation. I have traveled the world a lot since then, through some very lush and rarefied terrain, but that life was the most pervasively rich I've ever seen.

Evidently I made a good impression at this bash, because after that Mr. Hearst and Marion invited me for a weekend at San Simeon. This invitation was conveyed by a gentleman called Colonel Joe Willicomb, a friendly man in charge of each guest's every move. How you got to San Simeon, what you did there—every arrangement and request was handled by Joe Willicomb.

It was sort of eerie. From the moment you stepped into the car Colonel Joe had dispatched until you were returned to your own front door, you were the guest of Mr. Hearst. You didn't have to bring your wallet; there was nothing to spend money on. If you weren't driven to San Simeon, you made the journey either in Mr.

With Phil Kellogg at the circus party for W. R. Hearst's birthday at "Tara by the Sea."

Hearst's plane—very dashing in those days—or in a private railroad car. Either way, you were finally driven up the hillside into another world and another time.

The first time I saw the "castle," it seemed unreal, strangely forbidding and frightening at the crown of the yellow foothills. The road up the hill to the castle went through a series of giant corrals, each fenced and gated and each containing all manner of wild animals. A private jungle-cum-zoo. No stopping or getting out. As each gate closed behind you, you felt more and more as though you were being swallowed up, that time was running backwards and you might never be seen again.

Climbing steadily up the summit to the last gate, hearing it clank behind me, sent a shiver down my spine. The car stopped at the base of the great stairs leading to the castle's huge double doors. The proportion of everything was vast: fireplaces you could walk into, tapestries disappearing into vaulted ceilings, banners hanging in limp rows from the lofty dusk of the dining room. The notion of being a guest amid this opulence was quite terrifying for me, as my total houseguest exposure had been a weekend or two with school-girl chums.

I was paired off with a young, good-looking blond fellow named Phil Kellogg, who had some connection with either the Hearst Motion Picture Company or the publishing empire. He had been asked for the weekend and had been told that he could bring someone he liked. Apparently he had no candidate, so it was suggested that he escort me.

The household was run on Spanish hours. You could come down to breakfast from 9:00 a.m. until 12:00. Lunch was at 2:30 and dinner at 10:30 (or 10:00 p.m. really, with half an hour for cocktails). Mr. Hearst or "the Chief," as he was known, frowned on drinking. The guests would gather before dinner in a giant hall, a really noble room with a huge burning fire and great works of art all about—not a cozy place for a drink with a few friends. There was a grog tray, which held a decanter of sherry and a silver shaker of sickly sweet Bacardi rum and fruit juice cocktails. You weren't offered anything, however, until the host and hostess made their appearance. And then the limit was one drink.

At about ten minutes before 10:00 p.m., an invisible door in the paneling would open and Mr. Hearst and Marion would appear as if

The front entrance of San Simeon.

47

by magic. They had descended in an elevator from their private apartment, which neither I nor, I think, anyone else ever saw. He seemed to me a very old man, but at age nineteen everyone seemed old to me. His head, on a long thin neck, was lowered between his stooped shoulders, giving him the appearance of an aged gray eagle studying his prey. He had pale eyes which drilled into you as he spoke in a high thin voice.

Marion, who was around forty then, was a jolly, raucous clown without style or beauty. Her clothes looked borrowed. She never went into a store to shop or snoop, as most women do. She never went anywhere. She was, in the truest sense, a captive. She stayed where he wanted her, which was as near him as possible.

After they materialized out of nowhere, the two walked about, saying, "Good evening," to their guests in a detached and regal way. There might be as few as ten people or as many as thirty. You never knew what sort of crowd they were going to draw.

Mr. Hearst would sometimes speak into the phone for a moment or two—a brief reminder that he was running a huge press empire from the top of his mountain. Beside each telephone he used, there was an atomizer of disinfectant, which was sprayed on the phone and wiped off before it was handed to him. He and Marion didn't drink with the guests. I think he hoped to discourage her, because she had a real drinking problem.

When dinner was announced, we would file into the long, high-ceilinged dining room, with its narrow refectory table that was almost the length of the room itself. On one wall was a massive sideboard that held a marvelous collection of silver, all rubbed to shining perfection. There was a rarebit dish of silver that I coveted because it had mice darting about its base, one or two disappearing under the lid and into the cheese inside. On the long wall opposite there stood a row of carved monks' stalls, raised up a step from the stone floor.

I was so dazzled by the grandeur of the set-up that I wouldn't have been at all surprised to have been seated next to an armored knight or two, or to have had a conversation with Cardinal Wolsey across that venerable table. We would, however, have been forced to converse over tomato ketchup bottles, A-1 sauce, and glass containers of paper napkins, which were placed at intervals down the

With Cary Grant at San Simeon.

A traffic altercation with David Niven at San Simeon.

length of the table and were the permanent and incongruous center-piece of that noble board.

Mr. Hearst always sat at the center of the table with Marion directly opposite. Each had a small dachshund on a chair behind them. Your proximity to the host and hostess depended on rank and importance. Obviously, I was well below the salt, but no matter—I was there.

The quality and size of the Hearst art collection is legendary. San Simeon gave you the feeling you have in a museum; you know it would take weeks to explore. On one stay, I reached my beautiful art-encrusted suite after a long walk through halls and passages and rooms still under construction. I saw concrete walls, steel beams jutting through cement floors, acres and acres of unopened but numbered crates. Crates that would in fact never be opened for a castle that would never be completed.

Outside, life seemed calmer. The castle rose out of a glistening white marble terrace. Below were the guest villas, grown over with bougainvillea and roses and filled with seventeenth- and eighteenth-century Spanish and Italian furniture. Beautiful old velvets and brocades covered the furniture and cascaded around the windows.

Below the villas was a black and white marble swimming pool filled with crystal-clear turquoise water. Its special attraction was a small but ravishing authentic Greek temple, sent piece by piece from Greece and laid out so you could laze and take the sun there —fun, if you didn't mind sitting on the hard marble with nothing but a damp towel. There was no pool furniture, no mats, no creature comforts.

The splendor of the surroundings was suitably complemented by the glamour of the cast: Cary Grant, beautiful and bright; David Niven, twinkling, witty, and outrageous; Charles Lederer, Marion Davies's nephew and a screenwriter by trade, funny, charming, and the darling of the movie community. At the time they didn't seem superstar glamorous, and most of them weren't yet. Niven was just beginning. Cary Grant was more established, but he hadn't gradu-ated to the Barbara Hutton stratum and the girl with him on my first trip there was Phyllis Brooks—a starlet, I suppose you would call her. She was very nice, and hanging for dear life to Cary.

My description of the weekends and trips with Mr. Hearst and Marion Davies may sound as though I wasn't having a good time. It

With Marion Davies (left) and W. R. Hearst en route to Ensenada.

was far from dreary, and yet you couldn't really enjoy yourself until the hosts were out of sight. When Mr. Hearst and Marion were present, we were children behaving well for stern parents.

I always thought Marion yearned to be in on the laughs and the jokes, but she knew she couldn't. W.R.'s intense surveillance meant she could never be free to be herself. It seemed to me that if Marion was laughing, she was drunk, and if she wasn't laughing, she was sober. Either way, she was a touching figure. She used to sit up in the tower—where their rooms were—making bed quilts by the hour. But she was better than that; when Mr. Hearst came upon rocky financial times, she gave him back much of the property he'd given her during their years together. After he died, she lived on in the most tragic way. She married someone called Captain Horace Brown, a merchant marine officer who bore a strong resemblance to W.R., and she died finally of cancer of the tongue. A horrible end to a very, very sad life.

At an early point in my friendship with this strange couple, they invited me to Ensenada, Mexico. Mr. Hearst had to be out of the country a certain number of days for tax reasons. They also took me with them to Wyntoon, W.R.'s 86,000-acre ranch in Northern California. Wyntoon was another remarkable establishment—in

Halloween at Wyntoon, the Hearst retreat in Northern California.

With Marion Davies (right).

53

this case a series of houses, built as if they were Swiss chalets, along the McCloud River in Northern California. There was a large main building where we dined and could play canasta or bridge or any game at all, or simply meet, as you would in a rec room. There were several separate three-story chalets where guests were billeted. And there was, of course, a very grand separate house for Marion and W.R. The most curious thing about Wyntoon was that no house had a view of another. You could never tell how far you were from anything, which meant a driver had to take you wherever you wanted to go. If you wanted to go swimming or to the stables or to dinner, you went by car—although it took all of fifteen seconds to get from one place to the next. The paths between the buildings weren't lighted and I suppose they didn't want you lost in the woods or eaten by wolves.

At age nineteen, I don't think I realized how peculiar these Hearst retreats really were. It wouldn't have mattered. I was so eager to explore and *learn*, I barely noticed the rigidity and joylessness in the Hearst environment.

My introduction into the world of the Hearsts, needless to say, only heightened my itch to move to Los Angeles. By the end of 1937, I was doing more than spending a few days down south. I began a commute between Carmel and Los Angeles that would have sent a whirling dervish out of control. To give you some idea of what my movements were like, here is an entry from my datebook in January 1938: January 7, drive to L.A.; January 14, drive to San Simeon for a week with the Hearsts. January 18, drive to Carmel from San Simeon to have lunch with Sam and tea with Mother and return to San Simeon in time for dinner. January 20, drive back to Carmel to see Cary Grant and Phyllis Brooks and, again, Sam. Later that night—to San Simeon. The next day, to L.A.

Fortunately for health's sake, this frenzied commuting came to a halt that spring. My grandmother died, and since the only family ties my mother and I had left were to each other, I asked her to leave Carmel with me. There was no real reason for us to stay. Ever the good sport, she packed herself up, leaving friends and a life she understood to move to Los Angeles with me.

ESTABLISHING THE CAST:

Howard Hawks
and
Ernest Hemingway

Somewhere else there was a Depression going on. In Hollywood, I was having the time of my life. Which can only happen to a girl in Hollywood when she's not obsessed by a screen career. Of that one thing, I was clear: I didn't want to be an actress. In fact, I had no career aspirations at all. I had a mother who supported me, doted on me, and spoiled me. For me, it was enough to be in Hollywood —it was where any girl who was operating on a mixture of instinct, charm, and good looks would have chosen to be in 1938.

So Mother and I settled into a darling house on Sunset Boulevard across from the UCLA playing fields. I promptly discovered that Los Angeles, a city I thought I knew, was different when one lived there. It wasn't the "Hollywood" I'd read about in the movie magazines I'd smuggled into the convent. In those magazines, ladies in white fox capes jumped into pools filled with champagne. Inevitably, the ladies bubbled up to the surface in dry furs with orchids pinned the wrong way on their bias-cut white satin gowns. They were pulled to safety by John Gilbert, who rescued them without having to rearrange his hair or straighten his mustache, then they all would drive off in Duesenberg touring cars.

SLIM

Reality was more interesting.

There was a hierarchy in Hollywood, and it was important to know who was in it and where. It was equally important to know who the good people were, and why it might be better to go out with a good person in the middle of the hierarchy than a bad person at the top. This was, remember, a town in which pretty girls were a dime a dozen and the booths of coffee shops were littered with young hopefuls whose dreams had been derailed because they'd made the "wrong" associations.

The person who really educated me in the inner game of Hollywood was the legendary restaurateur Mike Romanoff, who was my undying admirer and beloved friend from the day we met in Carmel until the day he died. He would say, "I'd love to take you to dinner, but it wouldn't be good for your image. You shouldn't be seen with me. You've got such promise and you've so far to go, don't mess it up at the beginning."

"I don't give a damn about that," I said. "I like you and I think you're fun and you're sweet and you're good."

"Well, the world doesn't think that. And it's not good for your name to be coupled with mine."

I knew what he was talking about. Mike Romanoff was a wonderful man, but as a Russian prince, he was a fraud. His real name was Harry Gerguson, and he was born in Brooklyn. Somehow, he had made it across the water to Europe, and when he returned, he had no passport. He ended up on Ellis Island, from which he escaped. Shortly thereafter, he turned up at the Stork Club and El Morocco as Prince Michael Romanoff, Oxford graduate. He was completely credible in the part—he was erudite, had marvelous manners, and a very quick wit. He was just sensational. And it tickled me that he could get away with it. In his consummate dishonesty, he was the most honest man I've ever known.

Mike Romanoff was right. The town was filled with drop-dead gorgeous suitors and soon enough so was my dance card. But Sam remained the focus of my life. I would still go to Carmel for a week with him, or he would come for a day or two to L.A. to see me. We knew we would eventually give each other up, but we just couldn't bring ourselves to do it; the attraction was too powerful. It was going to take something pretty big for me to break off my relationship with Sam. And that's just what came along.

ESTABLISHING THE CAST

August 30, 1938: I had a date to go to the boxing matches with Bruce Cabot, a social devil, eternal extra man, and B-movie actor whose most memorable role was as the hero who saved Fay Wray from the clutches of King Kong. It amused me no end that after the war he was an intelligence officer in Europe and Africa—Bruce was seriously dumb. Fortunately, Cubby Broccoli, our truly intelligent mutual friend, tagged along. He grew up to be Albert W. Broccoli, the producer of the James Bond film series, but he was then working as an assistant director at Twentieth Century–Fox and winning praise for his prowess as a spaghetti cook.

After the fight, my two escorts and I went for a nightcap to the Clover Club, a small but exclusive gambling house on what is now the Strip in Hollywood. It also had a nightclub with a dance floor and live band. The Regine's of its day, the Clover Club was *the* place to go at the end of the evening.

Cubby and I were having a twirl on the dance floor when Howard Hawks came in from the gambling room—a place, I was to discover later on, where he spent much of his time. He got himself a drink at the bar. After our dance, Mr. Hawks discreetly asked Cubby, "Who's the girl you're with? I'd like to meet her." That's how I met Howard. Of course I knew who he was; in 1938, Howard Hawks was one of the most successful directors in Hollywood. But he was also tall, good-looking, and extremely well mannered, and it was to all those things that I responded. We danced a couple of times, and then he asked the standard Hollywood question of the day, "Do you want to be in movies?"

"No," I said.

Howard Hawks was not a man who was easily shocked, but the look on his face was one of disbelief.

"You don't?" he said.

"No," I repeated, more calmly and matter-of-factly than the first time.

A successful director like Hawks simply took for granted that all the attractive girls in Los Angeles were there because they wanted to be in the movies. His "little black book" was filled with the names of pretty girls, each of whom thought that a quick once-around would set her off on a brilliant career. Howard was no fool. In those few minutes, he realized that his glamorous profession alone was not going to score a date with me, and he wasn't sure what to do next. So he very sweetly said, "Well, then, would you like to come to my house tomorrow for a swim?"

Why did I accept? Because I was intrigued by the *idea* of Howard Hawks. First there was the career. In the last few years he'd directed *Dawn Patrol, Scarface,* and *Twentieth Century;* and he'd just released *Bringing Up Baby,* the film that *New York Times* critic Vincent Canby would later call the greatest sound comedy ever made. And then there was the aura. I had heard that he was nicknamed "the Silver Fox," because, although he was only forty-two, his hair was fully gray, almost white. Howard's distinguished locks were not his only asset. He had a long, lean face and candid blue eyes. His lanky body moved with a kind of awkward, loose grace in perfectly tailored tweed jackets, beautiful flannel trousers, and shoes that were shined within an inch of their lives. He had a style in his looks and manners that was very un-Hollywood. In those days, important men assumed—correctly—that they could have any woman they wanted. To his credit, Howard recognized that I wasn't a casting-couch kid. He never pounced on me or put me in a compromising position. Very simply, he was a gentleman.

Hawks's home was a beautiful, proper house—rare in those days in Hollywood. Most houses in Los Angeles looked as though they had been rented for the summer season. It was a city of Moorish palaces and Spanish haciendas, each garishly out of place and hideous. This house, in contrast, was a lovely fieldstone building. The interior was English country house at its best, with tasteful chintz fabrics, real furniture, an excellent staff, and good food.

We had our swim, and afterward the butler brought tea and sandwiches down to the pool. I thought the whole ambience just great. He asked me all sorts of questions: Why wasn't I interested in being in the movies? Where had I been educated? How long did I plan to live in Los Angeles? What had brought me to Southern California? Not tough questions, but difficult for me as I had no real design on anything.

Howard showed more than a passing interest in my existence. He called me the next day and invited me back for lunch. This time, he revealed three small children—a lovely little eight-year-old girl, Barbie; a handsome, twelve-year-old son, David; and a very good-looking fourteen-year-old stepson named Peter, to whose mother he was, he said, presently married.

Howard Hawks as a yachtsman.

Aboard The Sea Hawk *with Albert "Cubby" Broccoli (center) and Mrs. Charles Wrightsman (right), then a.k.a. Jayne Larkin.*

"You're *married?*" I asked, trying to contain my surprise. It seemed so strange to me as there was no evidence of a wife and he possessed what I thought were all the qualities of a loner.

"Yes, I am," he said, "but my wife is not here, she's ill a great part of the time."

I innocently asked what was wrong with her. He said she was emotionally disturbed. Howard's wife Athole, he explained, was the sister of the actress Norma Shearer. Although much more beautiful than her famous sister, Athole had been sacrificed to Norma's career by an overly ambitious stage mother. The attitude of the mother and the competition between the two sisters had a lot to do with establishing the instability that eventually was the undoing of poor Athole.

That should have been the tip-off for me to say, "See ya around," because, in theory, the relationship was destined to go nowhere— in those days in California, you couldn't divorce a crazy. And crazy she apparently was.

But at that time in my life, the word "practical" wasn't in my vocabulary. I was crazy too. Crazy in love with Howard. In that condition, the problem of Howard's wife didn't discourage me for one minute. By this time I knew he was not only handsome, charming, and successful, he was exactly the package I wanted. The

Braced on the boom of Howard's sailboat, The Sea Hawk.

career, the house, the four cars, the yacht—this was the life for me. That he was twenty-two years my senior bothered me not at all. Of course, I said to myself, "Really, Slim, this man is old enough to be your father." But in my complete and awesome naiveté, I thought I was so sophisticated and mature that the difference in our ages was no factor at all. And it never was.

From then on everything moved quickly. After only two dates, Howard was as smitten as I was. He proved this on our third date, the Bendix Air Races at Burbank Airport—a solo flight made against time from Los Angeles to New York in one gulp. The race started at four o'clock in the morning, and although I was a twenty-one-year-old adult, I was still under my mother's wing and had to talk her into letting me stay out with Howard all night.

I remember the highly charged atmosphere of the event so clearly. It was night, and I was sitting on top of a station wagon in order to have a better view of the departing planes. I said something that made Howard laugh. He was standing below me, holding on to the luggage rack. He looked up at me and said, "You're the most remarkable thing I've ever seen. You're going to marry me."

"Well, we'll see," I said. "But thanks anyway." Meanwhile I was thinking, "My God! It's little Nancy Gross from Pacific Grove. How have I done this?"

I am certain that what impressed him the most about me then and always was the fact that I didn't want to be in the movies. Had I wanted to act, he would have made dead sure that he was going to help me, then get me. As it happens, I was what he wanted, but he wasn't sure he was going to land me.

Howard's marriage was at an end in every way except legally. Although it was not possible to divorce a mentally deranged person

Cary Grant and Charlie Lederer at the backgammon table in Palm Springs. I'm in the background.

A sleeping idol.

if he or she had been committed or declared mentally incompetent,
Athole hadn't been declared legally insane. So there was a very
good chance that, by pulling a few strings, Howard could divorce
her. At least that's what I wanted to believe, because by now I was
determined to marry him.

I was told by many that he'd never be able to get a divorce, that
I was wasting my time, throwing away my "best years." When I'm
challenged in that way, I'll kill myself in order to prove myself right.
So I hung in there for dear life. A lot of it was tedious and discour-
aging, and in many ways undignified—as any woman who's been
the girlfriend of a married man will understand.

I never saw myself as a fluffy Hollywood dolly-bird out to be kept
by somebody well placed in showbiz. I've never been kept, ever.
Unfortunately. I was determined to ride it out, and Howard was
determined to make the plans we talked of become a reality. And
in that way we went on.

It took three years for Howard to get his divorce. Aside from the
frustration of waiting, there was a lot of life lived during that time
—in a very contemporary "I don't give a damn" fashion. If Howard
took a house in Palm Springs for the winter, I went with him. If he
went on a fishing trip, I would go. If he was making a movie, I would

On the set with my childhood friend Howard Lackey (left), and Dick Rossen (right), Howard's second unit director.

On location for Sergeant York. Gary Cooper is riding the horse that got the job, and I'm on my palomino.

With my help, a stunt horse auditions for Howard's film Sergeant York.

spend as much time as he would allow me on the set.

Considering the movies Howard made during those years—*Only Angels Have Wings, His Girl Friday, Sergeant York,* and *Ball of Fire*—I particularly liked being on the set. I found moviemaking on this exalted level absolutely fascinating. I was spellbound by the

65

way it all came together: how it evolved, how it was made, and how it finally reached the public. And for the first time, I met show business people who became close friends: Rosalind Russell, Billy Wilder, Gary Cooper and his wife Rocky.

As open as we were about our relationship, I continued to live with my mother. And although I had become the de facto mother of Howard's three children, I still had a convent view of correct behavior. My mother must have known that I was intimately involved with Howard. But we never discussed it, and I took great pains to shield her from any behavior she might have thought tawdry.

Every place we visited was new to me, so my enthusiasm was boundless. We went to Mexico, driving in a car and getting so lost I thought we would never be seen again. We went to Sun Valley. He took me to New York, which I thought was the most exciting place I'd ever been. It still is.

It was on this trip, in December of 1939, that we decided to take an additional junket to Key West, Florida, so Howard could buy the film rights of *To Have and Have Not* from Ernest Hemingway. His entrée to Hemingway was the retired professional football player John Sims "Shipwreck" Kelly, a man of great wit and gaiety, terrific fun to be with, and a friend of Ernest's. So we took off from New York, the three of us, and we drove down the eastern seaboard from New York to Key West, stopping along the way. There I met Ernest Hemingway, who was to remain in my life until he died.

Hemingway had a charming house in Key West. Bumby, his oldest son, was away at school, but his other two sons, Gregory and Patrick, were with him. Their mother, Pauline Pfeiffer, was quite absent, as Ernest was in the process of dumping her for Martha Gellhorn. He had just finished *For Whom the Bell Tolls*, and was giving himself a breather. Along with that, he was doing some fishing and a good bit of drinking and enjoying a little bit of jollity in which he included Howard, Shipwreck, and me.

There was an immediate and instant attraction between us, unstated but very, very strong. When I first saw him, he seemed to take up more space, more air, than anyone I'd ever met. I was absolutely bowled over, and—for the first time in my life—starstruck.

The attraction was in no way physical for me; it was simply that

L. to r.: Ernest Hemingway, me, Gary Cooper, Howard, and Taylor Williams with the day's bag. In Sun Valley. (Photo by Robert Capa)

I had never known anyone so intelligent. His mind was like a light shining on everything, illuminating corners in your own head that you didn't even know were there. He had a tremendous influence on my thinking, my literary taste, my enjoyment of things simple and open, my recognition of and distaste for pomposity. That meeting was the beginning of a thirty-year friendship.

Shooting clay targets thrown by Howard. In Sun Valley. (Photo by Robert Capa)

Ernest's house had a small swimming pool in the back garden where I would swim. He would say, "I'm afraid for you when you go in the swimming pool, Miss Slimsky." I asked why. He said,

"Because you're so skinny, if you dive, you're going right down the drain and end up out in the ocean. So I have to stay and watch you 'cause I don't want anything to happen to you. I've only just found you."

In any case, the deal was made, and Howard began the four-year process of turning *To Have and Have Not* into a picture. I think Ernest was delighted to sell it and make a little money, of which he never seemed to have enough. And it was a very happy Howard who drove me all the way across the country, back to Los Angeles.

I didn't see Hemingway for another two years. In October of 1941, at Ernest's suggestion, Howard and I, along with Howard's son David, went to Sun Valley to join him for two weeks of partridge and pheasant shooting. But even in the upper echelons of Hollywood, there's no such thing as simple, straightforward, uncomplicated pleasure. This wasn't just a vacation, I discovered when we arrived in Sun Valley. It was a business trip.

By this time, the film rights to Ernest's novel *For Whom the Bell Tolls* had been sold to Paramount. Gary Cooper was contracted to play the part of Robert Jordan, but a director hadn't been chosen. Both Gary and Ernest wanted Howard to direct it. The studio did not. The idea behind the trip was for the three men to get together, discuss the project, and perhaps be able to have a clearer view of a film interpretation so that they could go back to the studio and convince them to hire Howard. (As it happened, the movie was made in 1943 starring Gary Cooper and Ingrid Bergman—but di rected by Sam Wood. Howard got nowhere in his efforts to convince the studio to let him direct it.)

As I wasn't involved in the business, I had a terrific time. Howard, David, and I stayed in a suite at the very grand Sun Valley Lodge. The rest of the cast consisted of Robert Capa, the great photo-journalist, Gary and Rocky Cooper, and Ernest and Martha Gellhorn, whom he'd married a year earlier. Martha in my view was just terrific. She was tender to Ernest's younger sons Patrick and Gregory, who were there with us. And she could do all the things Ernest thought important—hunt, fish, and shoot. She was strong, intelligent, and it was blatantly clear she would never be trampled by him.

While I was there, Ernest told me a story I found very touching. When he'd announced to his boys that he'd fallen in love with

Waiting for lunch with Gary Cooper. In Sun Valley. (Photo by Robert Capa)

Martha and was going to marry her, they asked him what falling in love is. "Well," Ernest said, "do you remember when you first met Slim?" Gregory piped up, "Boy, I sure do." And then Ernest said, "Well, what did it feel like?" "Like being kicked in the stomach by a horse," Gregory said. Papa laughed. "That's just what falling in love is like."

By coincidence, Leland Hayward, Hollywood's top agent, and his wife, the actress Margaret Sullavan, were there with the producer Bill Goetz and his wife Edie, the daughter of Louis B. Mayer. We weren't close friends, but we knew one another, and every party, picnic, or adventure proposed we all did together.

Looking back at the photographs of this trip, I find it ironic that three of the five men who were there—Howard Hawks, Leland Hayward, and Ernest Hemingway—were the very ones who would be most influential in my life. But on that trip I mostly noticed Ernest. This wasn't an attraction that was obvious to everyone present. I was, of course, stuck on Howard Hawks, and Ernest was stuck on and married to Martha Gellhorn. To those eyes, we only looked like two people who by some quirk of nature absolutely hit it off one hundred percent.

Was there a sexual pull? Yes—mostly on Ernest's side. I admired him, but I didn't covet him. I think it was his physical appearance

With Papa in the field. In Sun Valley. (Photo by Robert Capa)

—so exciting in photographs, so offputting in person. Ernest never seemed clean or bathed to me. His beard was scraggly. He'd wear the same clothes for five days.

For Ernest, my visit was a rediscovery of a fantasy object. Despite his teasing me about my thinness, I personified for him the outdoorsy, healthy, tanned California woman. And from Ernest's point of view, I wasn't just decorative—I could kill a bird if I had to. In the end, however, men really aren't attracted to a woman because she's a good shot.

Late one afternoon at the end of a day's shooting, I went back to the lodge to take a shower and wash my hair. In a dressing gown, I strolled into our sitting room to dry my hair in front of the fire. As it happened, Ernest and Robert Capa were there, waiting to see Howard. I knelt in front of the fire, head bent over, and began to brush my hair. Ernest walked over to me. "Can I do that?" he asked. "Sure," I said, and handed him the brush. He brushed and brushed until my hair was dry. When he was finished, he dropped the brush on the floor in front of me and said, "You don't know what that was like. It was very, very difficult. Both for Capa and me. You're a very provocative woman. I can't be around you too much."

Suddenly I twigged. Here I was, alone with two of the most attractive men in Western civilization, acting out a ritual charged with erotic possibility. The one thing a girl knows, in a moment like that, is if you're not planning to go through with it, make light of it. Any other way, and you're setting yourself up for a scene that's bigger and harder to wriggle out of. So, in a lighthearted and chummy way, I said, "Of course you can be around me. Howard's going to make your movie, and it's going to be wonderful, and you're going to write another book and Howard's going to make that too, and we're all going to know one another for a very long time." And with that, you could feel the room return to something like normal.

L. to r.: Leland Hayward, Margaret Sullavan, Taylor Williams, Jack Hemingway, Gary Cooper, and me. I'm attempting to pick up a dollar bill with my teeth while standing on one foot with my hands behind my back. In Sun Valley.

LEARNING
THE HARD
WAY

There was one other memorable event in 1941 aside from Pearl Harbor: Howard got his divorce. We decided to marry at the end of the year. In the meantime, we began to build a house for our new life together—or rather, I announced that we were building a new house. For reasons I'll never understand, I didn't want to live in Howard's marvelous home in Benedict Canyon. It was, I guess, on the order of "I don't want to live in another woman's house." So I made the poor bastard build me another one, which in the end he absolutely loved. As well he might have—I had come across the plans of the set that were used in Howard's film *Bringing Up Baby*. We had the architect Myron Hunt, who'd designed the Pasadena Rose Bowl among other less heroic structures, flesh them out to make the fantasy house into a real building, then we set it on a lovely stretch of land in Bel Air.

While designing and decorating the house, I discovered that with all my madcap qualities I was also a domestic animal. I loved building this home. I was there from the day the first shovel went into the ground and I tended it lovingly as it grew. I furnished it from top to bottom without a decorator. I created and planted the entire garden. I was very good at it and took a great deal of pride in it.

Wedding Day, December 11, 1941.

SLIM

Our wedding took place on December 11 in Pasadena, at the home of Howard's parents. As it turned out, we couldn't have picked a worse date. Four days earlier, the Japanese had bombed Pearl Harbor. The world was in shock, but my thoughts were only on the wedding and the chance that an invasion might screw up my honeymoon.

Nothing did get in our way. It was a proper and beautiful wedding. My bridesmaid was Dixie Cavalier, an old school friend. Howard's brother Bill was best man. The biggest problem of planning the wedding was to figure out who was going to give me away. Although I hadn't spoken to my father since our grim meeting at the convent, I was enough of a traditionalist to want him to take me down the aisle. But I didn't have the heart to put my mother through this ordeal, and in the end, I probably couldn't have gone through it myself, so Howard and I decided to ask Gary Cooper to do the honors.

I stood with Gary and my mother at the top of the stairs of Grandmother Hawks's house. Mother, with tears in her eyes, started down the stairs ahead of me, followed by Dixie. To my utter surprise, I suddenly had the coldest feet since the abominable snowman. I've come to know this feeling well—it has struck each time I've been married. I come up against a terrible moment of realization, almost like seeing into the future, and the fear of taking such a gigantic and seemingly irreversible step overwhelms me.

I turned to Gary and said, "I really don't want to do this." And he said, "Well, you have to do it now. The music is playing, the people are waiting, and the train has left the station. So let's go." Down we walked, through the hall, into the drawing room, and we didn't stop until I was in front of the minister.

Howard and I went immediately to Miami, where we took a house with another pair of newlyweds—Shipwreck Kelly and Brenda Frazier, the socialite who had been Debutante of the Year in 1938 and had never really grown out of it. We traveled by train, and it took ages to get there because by this time Army troops were being mobilized from across the country. Constantly, we'd be shunted off onto a siding every time a troop train roared through.

We finally got to Miami and did what honeymooners do when they're traveling together. We'd look at some scenic spot with Ship and Brenda, or go to the Jai Alai at night, or swim all day. It was

Our honeymoon in Florida with Shipwreck Kelly and his bride Brenda Frazier.

Christmas, and Ship and Howard went out and got a tree and decorated it. Brenda and I each got a dog for Christmas. But it was not a memorable honeymoon and this kind of trip wasn't my scene. In fact, it didn't seem like a honeymoon at all. Howard had fun because he and Shipwreck got along famously. They went off every day to golf or fish, and left me in the company of Brenda, with whom I had absolutely nothing in common. I think she would have preferred to be in Nassau where the Duke and Duchess of Windsor were now exiled. As it was, Brenda spent her days concentrating on how she looked, what she wore, and if her hair was right. The highlight of Brenda's day was her afternoon nap. And when she wasn't sleeping she was devouring movie magazines like a starstruck teenager. We made every effort to enjoy one another's company, but I don't think Brenda was any more at home in this situation than I was.

After a few days of this, I was eager to return to Los Angeles. I wanted to get back to the new house and begin to build a nest. And I wanted to learn everything about Howard's work so I could be a proper wife to him.

There have been hundreds of books that purport to tell a woman how to get and keep a man. My record in keeping one is spotty, but I've never doubted my ability to excite a man's interest. My method is simple—and genuine. I love good writing, good film making, good theater, good music, good art. And when I meet a man who's accomplished in any of these fields, I respond to the work. I'm not flattering him, I'm just interested. And because his work is often the best part of a man, he responds.

Learning about Howard's work was probably the most rewarding part of being married to him. Howard sat me down with a pile of scripts, and after I'd read them, we'd talk about their merits. I learned why a plot works and why it doesn't—I learned what makes a movie. Pretty soon, I read everything that was sent to Howard: I read them first and Howard trusted my judgment. On one particular occasion, he asked me to read a script called *Everybody Goes to Rick's*. I thought it was an absolute pig. Ungraceful and trite, and I didn't have any qualms about giving my opinion to Howard. He took my word on this one. That script, I'm ashamed to say, turned out to be *Casablanca*.

It was heady stuff to be the chief reader for one of Hollywood's princes. I was encouraged to believe that I could be Howard's partner in many ways—I had very high expectations for the marriage. It came as a surprise then to discover that Howard the man and Howard the director were different people. As a man, large chunks of Howard's life were not only closed off from me but were inimical to the very idea of marriage.

What I began to realize, a year or so into the marriage, was that the legend and aura of Howard Hawks had single-handedly been created by Howard. Everything that he did had a storybook quality to it. Every story or experience he related had him as the central character, committing great feats of derring-do or acts of heroic bravery. He added a dimension to everything he did. Each time I'd chance upon a new tale I'd say, "Oh, Howard's just searching for a plot, this is what creative people do." It took me a good while to understand that I was encountering disconcerting aspects of Howard's character, that the man I thought was a mesmerizing fantasist was really something less. And, over time, that realization was like standing on a piece of earth and having your husband, shovel by shovel, dig it out from under you.

There is nothing duller than being married to someone whose character is fixed and whose routine is unchanging. Give Howard credit: he was certainly full of surprises. Living with him was like watching a movie unspool.

If Howard went to the racetrack, for example, in his head he was suddenly a great owner-breeder from Kentucky. Then there was his sailing sloop, *The Sea Hawk*, which he more often than not didn't sail himself because he was usually hanging over the leeward side being seasick. But during the calm part of the trip—calm meant like glass—he would take command. And then he was the accomplished yachtsman.

It's true he made a trip to Honolulu, before I met him, but it is not true, as he often claimed, that he dove for and found hidden treasure in the caves and rocks around the island. I used to watch him in our swimming pool. Swimming up and down, he looked about as much at home as a horse in water.

As Howard's films prove, he had a great preoccupation with airplanes. Some of his best films, *Only Angels Have Wings*, *Dawn Patrol*, *Ceiling Zero*, and *Air Force*, are about flying. But he was not, as he led everyone to believe, an ace who flew in the Lafayette Escadrille until he was poisoned with mustard gas. In fact, he was almost always airsick when he was in the air, even on a commercial flight.

It was surprising, to say the least. I had been led to believe that he was a pilot of great skill and had been taught all sorts of wonderful flying acrobatics by Paul Manz, the famous movie stunt flyer. I think he might have been able to fly a double cockpit airplane if the pilot got sick or said, "Here, you take the stick." But that was his limit. His friends were flyers: Jimmy Stewart; Claudette Colbert's husband, Jack Pressman; Howard Hughes. But Howard Hawks was not. He may have been a liar, but not a flyer. I certainly wouldn't have flown anywhere with him.

Howard built such a fantasy life about himself that he came to believe it was true. He never thought I would square the fact with the fiction, but I did, simply by hearing him repeat the same stories to fresh audiences. Each time, the material was different—he would completely rewrite his script.

It's not that Howard was a liar because he wanted to best you or steal from you. He just had a terrible time with the truth. The lying was a psychopathic quirk. He dreamt when he was awake and he slept a totally dreamless sleep.

One of his ongoing dreams was to be a great breeder of horses from deep in the Bluegrass country, a crown prince in the sport of kings. When we would listen to the annual running of the Kentucky Derby on the radio, it was treated like an on-the-spot broadcast of the Resurrection. His eyes would tear up as the band in the infield of glorious Churchill Downs played "My Old Kentucky Home." He explained to me that the broadcast never gave the full wonder of this momentous event, and that one day he would take me to see the real thing.

He lived up to his promise and took me to the Derby. We flew— on a commercial airliner—as far as Kansas City. When the plane stopped to refuel there, we disembarked because Howard was air-sick, and drove the rest of the way. Of course, he claimed that the true reason for the switch to a car was that he wanted me to get a real feeling of the South and that the best way to do that was on land, but the only things southern I saw were headlights and road signs. Ignoring the latter, we proceeded on a pioneer route of our own, Louisville by way of Cleveland.

When we reached Louisville, it was early in the morning and everyone we saw was drunk. I soon found out that everyone was drunk all the time, day and night. No one ever seemed to have a hangover, because no one was ever sober long enough to get one. The town had the atmosphere of an American Legion convention. The streets, hotel lobbies, bars, restaurants, coffee shops were all filled with what newspapers call merrymakers. I was cross and tired and uncomfortable, but Howard said to hang on a little longer. He would call his friend General Miles and find out where he lived and how to get there, and all would be well. I held on.

At 9:30 a.m., we called the General, who gave Howard all the directions. It turned out that we were only ten minutes away as the crow flies. Unfortunately, Howard wasn't a crow, so we arrived at quarter of twelve. The stately southern mansion that I had waited for all these many hours was a square, red brick, eight-room house with the mortar still damp. It stuck up in the air with no trees around it, looking naked and embarrassed, like the only lady at the boss's dinner party who wasn't told to dress. I thought if it could only cross its knees, it would look better. There were no camellia bushes, no Spanish moss, and—oh God—no veranda. I fervently hoped there would at least be a mint julep.

We got out and rang the bell. There was no answer. I was really desperate by this time, so I opened the door and walked in. Howard was horrified at my display of boldness, but by now I was pretty desperate about Howard, too.

The front hall gave me quite a turn. It wasn't very large, and the walls were paneled from ceiling to floor with pictures of great animals who seemed to be suspended in what looked like a heavy sea. The remarkable thing was that all these scenes were made out of different colors and grains of plywood that had been varnished or stained. The animals turned out to be Derby winners of previous years, sawed out and glued to the walls and then surrounded by strips of wood whose grain had suggested to the artist, and only to the artist, grass leaning under a gentle breeze. The effect was astonishing. The entire house, I found later, was filled with cigarette boxes, photograph albums, humidors, and tabletops made from this unique product. It seems that the General, among many other enterprises, owned a plywood factory, of which I was sure he was the only customer.

After I got my breath, I called in my best southern accent, "Anybody home?" There was no answer, so I went to where I thought the kitchen should be, and there, at a very small table, sat two relaxed, comfortably attired blacks, drinking Coca-Cola and smoking. I asked them where General Miles could be found. One of them waved a vague direction out of the kitchen window and said, "He's down to the barn with his guests, showin' off the stock." Well, this sounded a little more like it, and Howard said in a rather smug way, "Let's walk down to the stable and see the foals and yearlings." I told him I wouldn't walk anywhere, with the possible exception of a bathroom, so we got back in the car and found our way down a winding little lane and eventually to the General and his guests.

They were all standing beside a fence gazing at, of all things, several fat and contented milk cows. This came as a terrible blow to Howard, who felt that if, by God, you were in Bluegrass, you ought to be in it with horses. He begrudged those cows every blade they ate. The General came as a bit of a shock to me. I had expected a man with a walrus mustache, or at least a Van Dyke beard like Colonel Sanders's. The only hair he had was very sparse and slightly pink, and it was located on the top of a face that had all the character and shape of a honeydew melon. He was a great, blustering greeter. He shook hands, slapped backs, and patted rumps all at the same time. One had a feeling that he was storming a beach-head when he said, "How do you do?"

Howard was a fellow whose most relaxed and carefree moments were fraught with a kind of Brooks Brothers button-down dignity. On meeting him, you had the curious feeling that both of you were under water. But with the General, he emerged. Now he too was full of hearty laughter and rib-punching joviality. Howard was suddenly a stranger to me. It was the most complete metamorphosis I have ever seen in a human being. And what threw me the hardest was that the General was calling him "Colonel Hawks" and introducing me to his guests as the "Colonel's lady."

"What's the matter with him?" I hissed at Howard.

"Nothing," he said. "He's just southern."

"Well," I said, "you're not, and stop acting so silly."

But the warning came too late. They were already talking about withers and fetlocks and "lean through the rump," and Howard sounded like a road-show Max Hirsch, the great trainer of the day. I don't think he ever knew what a fetlock really was. The Grand and Honorable Order of Kentucky Colonels, as it finally turned out, was a boys' club for old men. It was an invention, I think, of General Miles himself, otherwise he wouldn't have been the General.

They had a picnic, to which we went, where we ate something called burgoo. There was an awful lot of bourbon drinking, very little sitting down, and we had not had much sleep. The cumulative fatigue was so great that when we had finally pushed our way through the crowds at Churchill Downs, found a place to park the car, walked miles from the car to the wrong entrance gate, and at last found ourselves in General Miles's box, which was already overcrowded, it was all a bit anticlimactic. When the great moment for the playing of "My Old Kentucky Home" arrived, and the Run for the Roses was about to start, my eyes filled with tears. Real tears. Angry tears, tired tears, hungry tears, furious tears. I have never returned to Kentucky. And I don't think Howard did either.

This disastrous trip did not deter Howard. When we returned to Los Angeles he was horsier than ever. His one trip to the Derby had turned him into a lifelong Kentucky Colonel—he decided to buy some racehorses and run them. This struck me as an excuse to justify his excessive gambling habit, which was so out of control he would bet on his own horse. A true folly, I always thought.

Howard's fantasies also took the form of obsessions and hobbies. Like many creative people who immerse themselves in their projects, he found his relaxation in another kind of creation. He had curious, unrelated hobbies that would absorb him to the point of total concentration.

He had a great facility with his hands. He could make furniture, build rooms on houses; he even built a car from the bottom up once. This, of course, involved endless shopping tours to garages and junkheaps looking for spare parts. On most of these crazy projects, I was usually employed as an unpaid subcontractor.

He loved fast cars and motorcycles. He became fascinated by the latter to such a degree that a group of men dressed as Hell's Angels (long before their time) would gather every Sunday in our driveway, all leathered up. Each of them had a little gunk-soaked cloth with which he would polish his exhaust pipes for about an hour or so while discussing gaskets and cylinders. Then the Moraga Spit and Polish Club, as they were called, would all mount their machines, start their motors, and roar down the driveway making a decibel din up to then unknown. They would go off and ride around in a flock for about two hours or so, return, and be fed a hearty lunch which had been arranged by me. They had a marvelous, boyish time and they all loved it. The cast was noteworthy, to say the least. There was the director Victor Fleming, who was Howard's very good friend and our next-door neighbor. And William Wellman, equally talented and wildly attractive, who had a tiny delicious wife Dotty, who rode the biggest motorcycle and was better than any of them. There was Ward Bond, Keenan Wynn, and occasionally Van Johnson.

Howard's concentration and devotion to his hobby of the moment was as absolute, complete, and total as it was when he worked. He decided at one point that it would be marvelous to make a journey in his own very posh fully equipped trailer. So, he bought the biggest, strangest thing I ever saw. In the front, pulling it, was a sawed-off car painted two shades of green. The trailer itself—color-coordinated, of course—was large and roomy, with a Pullman kitchen and a bathroom. I think one uses nautical terms about such vehicles, so it had a head, a shower, a galley, a couple of double bunks that turned into sofas by day, and tables that appeared and disappeared into the floor as they do on some yachts. He never told me, nor did I think it sensible to ask, what he paid for it.

It was delivered and parked at the back of the property where there were garages and sheds that held equipment: horse trailers, extra cars, and so on. I was commissioned to outfit this land yacht. I spent a couple of dizzy days in Sears, Roebuck buying non-breakable plates and cups, tin flatware, sheets and towels, pots and pans —all the things that would be required for a trip, say, to Patagonia, though our destination was never decided.

Up to this point, he had never driven this monster, but the Sunday morning finally arrived when it was going to be launched. I was told to get into the trailer part, and he took his place at the wheel. There was an intercom system so that the poor boob in the galley department (me) could communicate with the driver. I can't remember now if I blew into a horn as in the old days when one communicated with one's chauffeur through a tube, thereby deafening him in one ear, or if I used a mike with a button to attract Howard's attention. Anyway, we set forth.

"Are you ready? Over," he said.

"I am ready," I said. "Over and out."

We started down the driveway and drove to the bottom of our street, about a quarter of a mile. The trailer part, where I was riding, swayed from side to side like a cork in a monsoon. I called a frantic SOS to the driver's compartment to please take me home, as I was going to be seriously carsick over the new upholstery if I wasn't returned to a standing-still position immediately.

At the bottom of Moraga Drive, where it was wide enough for this monster to make a U-turn, we did so. Travel time to here was about four minutes. But, God be praised, we were homeward bound. Back up the street, up the driveway, past the house, past the garages and sheds, past the horse paddocks to the stables. Could it be that he didn't know how to stop it? He then proceeded to negotiate a sharp right-hand turn that would bring the dreaded thing into a parallel parking position behind the stable and well out of sight of the curious. But he didn't reckon on the length of what he was pulling behind him. He made his part of the turn successfully, but back in the trailer I suddenly had the corner eave of the stable jutting through the ceiling, ripping a gash from one end to the other. It looked like a great sharp wooden knife, making an incision that went the full length of the "cabin." The entire trip and my entire

On the Warner Brothers studio lot with two new additions, a mastiff and a cocker spaniel puppy.

life in that machine consisted of that small seasick ride. I never got in it again, and neither did Howard.

This episode I think gives an accurate appraisal of the variety of mind Howard had. He was like a very, very rich child who could have anything he wanted, be it a boat, a land yacht, a fast car, silver-studded saddles for horses he didn't ride—and while he had it, it had him.

Everything Howard attempted or desired was done in a lavish and excessive way. He couldn't just bet a couple of dollars at the track and leave it at that. He had to also bet $6,000 with a bookie. Once, we decided to get a dog, but he didn't come home with one, he came home with eight. Another time he arrived and said, "I've bought you something," and it was not one but two mastiff puppies. Some present—it meant months and months of great mastiff mounds for me to pick up. Or clothes. Eddie Schmidt was a very grand tailor in Beverly Hills, and Howard would go to Eddie, but he wouldn't order just the standard blue suit or gray flannels and blazer that men have made every couple of years. It had to be twelve suits and seven pairs of gray flannels.

I never understood the origin of this behavior. Howard came from what I thought was nice, uncomplicated midwestern stock. He was born in Goshen, Indiana. His family went to live in Wisconsin, and then moved out west to Pasadena because of the poor health of one of his brothers. His parents were lovely people. He was well raised and well educated. But that he had talent always amazed me.

He had no interest in the arts; no reactions to things that would move me or other people, such as music and paintings. He did read voraciously, but almost entirely Erle Stanley Gardner. I suppose he was looking for material.

When I think of Howard Hawks as a movie maker and review in my head the body of his work, the list is indeed impressive. But I never felt that he made message movies. He didn't really have a message. He had a craft at which he was excellent. He was a marvelous storyteller in the most simple and generic sense.

So, while I respected his work, I don't think I ever admired it. Of all the pictures he made or that I saw him make, few moved me. They entertained me, they made me laugh, they engrossed me, but nothing ever made me cry or become angry. I felt I was just watching a skilled performance.

LEARNING THE HARD WAY

In his movies, there was only one scene that ever touched my heart. It was in *Sergeant York* when Gary Cooper, who played the title role, tells his mother, played by Margaret Wycherly, that he's been drafted into the war. And Mother York reacts to that. She says, "Well, I guess everybody will be in the war." York then asks, "What is war?" And she looks at him and says, "I don't rightly know, son. I don't rightly know." The first time I saw that scene, it nearly killed me, and still does, because both characters are absolutely locked with one another. It's a marvelously pregnant scene, simply played and beautifully photographed with silhouetted bodies and no background.

Howard wasn't complicated about what he did. If anything, he was slightly frightened of movie making and, I suspect, surprised that he was able to do it at all. He used to tell me that on the first day of shooting a new picture he would stop the car, get out, and throw up a couple of times on his way to the studio. That process would go on for about a week until he got into the rhythm of the work and the movie started rolling along. He once said, "You know, when you walk onto a set and there are three hundred extras and a crew of fifty people, and you're the one with the microphone in your hand and you haven't got a thought in your head—it's a terrifying experience."

That he was a master of the camera there is no doubt. He had control over his films, whoever the producer was. He knew how to shoot in such a way that the studio couldn't recut or fuss with it. And as he said, there were no tricks. He was not trying to impart any great piece of information that was political or psychological. He just made movies. Although his talent lay in being able to tell a story, it always seemed to me that he told the same one over and over and over. The characters never had any intellectual reactions, only emotional ones. This always puzzled me because as a person, Howard's emotional thermometer was stuck at about six degrees below 98.6. He was frozen there. He did not take emotion into any part of his existence; neither through his children, his wife, nor, I think, his work.

HOWARD
THE
DREAMER

It was, she later wrote, the most beautiful house she had ever seen, rich and comfortable and tasteful. The grounds were large. There were stables. There was a pool. But what she mostly recalled, on that first visit, was the gigantic bedroom, more like a bed-sitting-room, with a dressing room packed with enough shoes to open a store, hundreds of handbags on hooks, shelves filled with sweaters. Did kings live any better than this? she wondered.

It is easy to understand how impressed the nineteen-year-old Betty Bacall was by the life she saw twenty-six-year-old Slim Hawks leading in 1943. Betty had just come to Hollywood for her first screen test with Howard. To Betty—and probably to anyone on the outside looking in—ours was an existence defined by beauty, glamour, and famous, talented friends.

Not quite.

Although it wasn't uncommon for women to be married in their early twenties, most women didn't have the responsibilities I had taken on. By becoming Mrs. Hawks, I inherited three children who were—at seventeen, fifteen, and eleven—old enough to have passed for my younger siblings. Then there was the building of a

Hog Canyon Farm.

With Howard at Hog Canyon Farm.

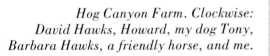

*Hog Canyon Farm. Clockwise:
David Hawks, Howard, my dog Tony,
Barbara Hawks, a friendly horse, and me.*

new house during wartime, when the materials needed for construction were scarce and rationed. And there were the special problems of maintaining a relationship with a film director who had, in addition to a Hollywood-size ego, some special twists all his own.

His first flaw—that is, the first I twigged to—was gambling. As I lived with my mother before we were married, I didn't know that the first call Howard made every morning was to his bookie. If he had put a little bet on the football matches or on a horse, I wouldn't have thought twice about it. But his gambling was a compulsion that turned the entire household upside down. He'd take everything out of the checking account, go to the races, and bet the entire amount. In a matter of minutes, all the money that had been earmarked to pay the monthly bills would be gone. Naturally I found out—while Howard was at work, the tradespeople would arrive at the house demanding to be paid. That was just sheer embarrassment. What was worse was when Howard couldn't pay back his enormous losses and the bookie would send his thugs over to the house demanding payment. That was sheer terror.

I don't know which was more unpleasant, Howard's gambling or his infidelity. Once married, he didn't waste a lot of time before indulging himself, though I don't believe his running around was due to an over-active libido. Seeing himself as the world's greatest Lothario was another form of his longing to be a bit more than what he was—in this case, he imagined himself a white-haired Clark Gable no woman could resist. The lady's-man image made him more macho, which seemed for him to be the most important thing in the world.

Beneath that jaunty exterior, I think there was a great deal of sexual confusion and insecurity within Howard. When I look at the role of sex in his films and compare it with his life, it's very interesting. The love scenes in the movies are invariably the same. There's a terrible fight, the woman insults the man, he insults her back, she insults him again, and then suddenly they're in each other's arms and slashing around in the hay. This scenario was, I think, a way for Howard to put sex on the screen that didn't make him want to gag. In his own life, he had a very tough time with tenderness or sentimentality. Even at the height of our courtship he was a tentative partner. Sex was simply a physical need that had no relation to the person he was with.

Jean and Dusty Negulesco's wedding in my garden at Hog Canyon Farm.

Because a relationship meant so little, there were a lot of girls. I used to keep a list of them in my head, but age has dissolved my memory for these things. I do remember Dolores Moran, the supporting actress in *To Have and Have Not*, whom I called Dollarass Moron. And there were others, whose names I won't mention, that I actively knew about. But in Hollywood legend, Howard was always slipping around somewhere.

I never caught him necking in the tack room, but there were many, many nights I often kept dinner warm, only to be rewarded with a telephone call saying, "He's in the projection room and is not to be disturbed—he's working with the cutter." Later, I came to realize that more often than not he wasn't with the cutter at all, he was probably in somebody's dressing room. I would read for a while, listen to the radio, do some needlework until eleven-thirty and think, "Well, I'd better go to bed, I don't know what he's doing." I'd try not to obsess about it.

When Howard came in at three-thirty or four in the morning, I'd say to myself, "Don't move. Pretend you're asleep. Just overlook it." But I knew very well that he'd been off snoozling around with somebody. If you run a house and you run it well, you know what the laundry situation is, and you understand how his shirts are supposed to be done and what it means when the laundress says, "I don't think I can get the lipstick off this shirt." You do the right thing and you say, "I must change it, I must wear another kind." Over time, I learned to save myself a lot of heartache by remembering that I was in Hollywood, where there were hundreds of young pretty starlets who wanted to be in the movies and would do anything for a man who held the keys to the kingdom.

Howard's third character flaw had nothing to do with Hollywood, and it was, in the end, why I left. Howard was, simply, cold and self-centered. You couldn't fight with him, he'd just clam up; you couldn't light a fire under him, he was just too remote. Eventually I lost a feeling of empathy for him, because I felt that what I got was unreal, that his fantasy life was so much stronger than what was actually going on. I never knew whether he truly loved me or his children or whether he even knew the feeling of love. The emotions that real love produces—that it hurts a lot sometimes, that it feels marvelous sometimes, that there's always a slight anxiety about it, that you're always kind of edgy and you're walking a very difficult line—never seemed to affect Howard.

What was he feeling? I told myself that he must have emotions, because you don't throw up on your way to work unless *something* is going on inside of you. This one little card held a lot of mileage for me. Any time he showed me anything like that, I took it as proof that we were of the same species after all. And that created a bond for me.

Like all naive wives everywhere, I thought I could build on that modest bond—I thought I could change Howard. In the beginning,

Croquet in Palm Springs. L. to r.: Cesar Romero, Tyrone Power, Howard Hawks, and Darryl Zanuck. (Photo by Jean Howard)

therefore, I excused him everything. Although I would eventually see that his character flaws made a healthy married life impossible, at that time I was always able to find a reason for his inattention, his absences, and his emotional indifference. And as I looked around at other Hollywood marriages, I didn't exactly see any that made mine look so awful.

Basically, I felt that certain problems in show business marriages were inevitable. Like other directors', Howard's film hours during the shooting of a film started early in the morning and ended very late. I accepted that, and many of my evenings were spent alone. Unlike many of the Hollywood wives of that era, I wasn't the sort of woman who had a group of card-playing girlfriends to help take the edge off the lonely nights. I preferred to do things that soothed and satisfied me—a lot of needlework got finished in those years. I'd work in my garden, or can fruit, or make hams out of my own pigs. I'd ride, or I'd go to the skeet range and shoot skeet. Or I'd go to

Santa Anita and visit my mother. Hardly intellectually satisfying activities, but it never occurred to me that I might have more to give someone or that there might be someone out there who could offer me real love and companionship and an intellectual foundation in which we were better matched.

When Howard wasn't working, our routine was pleasant enough. In the winter, we went to Palm Springs; in summer, we stayed in Los Angeles. We had a small group of friends we saw frequently: the Gary Coopers, the Victor Flemings, the William Wellmans. It has often been said that I entertained a lot and that it was a big feather to be invited to my house. On the contrary, I didn't have a salon, and I only gave two or three big parties during our marriage.

I think the legend of the Hawks party service evolved from the famous East-West Croquet Tournament that Howard and I hosted. I didn't court the publicity, but one tournament ended up as a photo spread in *Life*. Not because of us but because of the dazzling cast: Sam Goldwyn, Darryl Zanuck, Tyrone Power, Moss Hart, Douglas Fairbanks, Jr. At these matches we had huge lights scattered on the grounds so the men could play all day and on and on into the night. In the house, there was usually a cutthroat poker game going on between Robert Capa, Constance Bennett, and Lew Wasserman.

For all of Howard's coldness, he always wanted me with him. He appreciated my style, and the comfort I provided his guests and the little things I did to make our home special; but mostly, I think he liked the way I looked. For him, I was a fabulous armpiece, the ultimate decoration, the embodiment of the Hawks woman. It wasn't about the woman herself, it was about a look. Howard liked a no-nonsense femininity. His woman could be chic, she could be sexy, but you'd better believe she could also make a ham and hoe a row of beans.

That was pretty much how I looked when I met Howard. He took it a step further by supplying me with gear—sporty things, always in beige. He liked me in well-cut, man-tailored styles. If you can compare this look to anything today, it's the Ralph Lauren image of a woman.

In film history, this clean-cut, frank female has come to be known as the Hawksian woman. She's unusual in the Hollywood movies of the thirties and forties because, although she's quite direct about wanting to be with a man, she's not passive, clinging, or dependent. On the contrary, she's an equal. She can hold her own against any man in verbal Ping-Pong, as Katharine Hepburn did in *Bringing Up Baby*. She can work on the same professional level as a man, like Rosalind Russell in *His Girl Friday*. And although Carole Lombard regresses at the end of *Twentieth Century*, we remember her mostly for her strong-minded refusal to be duped after years of being strung along.

There were many flavors of this Hawks woman. Physically, though, I think there were only two: Lauren Bacall and me. The former was created by Howard Hawks to be a screen image of his wife. I'm not saying that I was the inspiration for the Hawks woman —Howard had been working out this formula woman for years in his films. Rather, it was that, until he met me, the woman of his dreams was only in his head. And until Howard got to Betty Bacall, there hadn't been an actress to make that dream come alive on screen.

I want to be clear here. In *To Have and Have Not*, Howard wasn't exploiting me, not in the least. I knew he was having trouble casting the role of Marie—the character Bogart always calls "Slim." And I knew that the "natural look," which is what Howard wanted, wasn't to be found in the actresses then popular in Hollywood. There were tough women, there were outdoorsy women, and there were sleek women; but you couldn't name one actress who, in one movie, could be all of those women. And *To Have and Have Not*, as Howard envisioned it, required an actress with a knack for sultry, insolent delivery but who could maintain a thoroughbred look.

Betty Bacall would have surfaced sooner or later. Thanks to Diana Vreeland, she was often on the cover of *Harper's Bazaar*. And she deserved to be; in those shots, Betty was just outstanding. So, when I saw her picture on the cover of *Bazaar*, I knew that she was the unknown Howard had been searching for. She was certainly my taste in beauty—scrubbed clean, healthy, shining, and golden. And there was definitely a bit of the panther about her.

I showed Howard the magazine. He immediately had Charlie Feldman, his agent and then partner, call to find out about this girl. They flew her out to Hollywood, gave her a screen test, then had her hang around for six months until the movie came together.

Though I'm often credited with "discovering" Betty, what was more significant was the way Howard used me as the model for her character in *To Have and Have Not*—he used my clothes, my name, and my speech. Once he hired Betty, he suddenly became very interested in everything I had to say. Now he listened to me as if I were speaking lines created by the screenwriters Jules Furthman and William Faulkner. In his eagerness, Howard would sometimes show his cards and directly ask me what I'd say in a certain situation. Dutifully, I'd answer the question. The next thing I knew, Furthman and Faulkner were running it through their typewriters.

At the end of this process, Jules Furthman told me, "You know, Slim, you should also get screen credit on this film, because so much of the material is yours. The character certainly is." All those memorable lines like, "You know how to whistle, don't you?—just put your lips together and blow," or, "No matter how bad it is, don't apologize for it; there it is, take it or leave it," were certainly not Hemingway's words. Nor were they Faulkner's or Furthman's.

Howard was no ingrate about my contribution. I didn't get a writing credit, but he did acknowledge me for discovering Lauren Bacall. When he signed her for the film, he put her under contract —and gave me half ownership. Later, we "sold" Bacall. This was my first—and last—lucrative business deal, similar to selling a very fine racehorse. It sounds crass and absurd to talk about contractual ownership of a person in this way. But that was how it was done then. The important thing is that Betty Bacall understood my interest in her extended far beyond a business deal. We were friends then. Forty years later, we still are.

Lauren Bacall. (Photo by John Engstead)

THE PLOT
THICKENS

By the time 1944 rolled around, I pretty much knew the score as far as my marriage was concerned. Or thought I did. Then my mother died. She'd had heart disease for some time, but she was only in her early sixties, and I thought as children so often do about their mothers that she was immortal. Now she was gone, and as I had no contact with my father or my sister, Howard was all the family I had. And Howard came through. It was the surprise of my life, but he came through. In the gentlest way, he came in one morning and woke me up to tell me my mother had died. He made all the funeral arrangements. And when that was over, he took me away to Palm Springs. That sort of kindness goes a long way with me, and it made me think that maybe I'd been too hard on Howard. I turned out to be wrong about that, but those few weeks of care and attention bought Howard another two years.

Which isn't to say I was happy. I knew I couldn't go on as Mrs. Howard Hawks, that ever-so-bored wife who spent her afternoons riding her horse around her vast acreage. And I knew that in a town like L.A., I'd better find something pretty absorbing soon or I'd get into the kind of trouble that would end my marriage but leave me alone and adrift.

THE PLOT THICKENS

I knew this was a real danger. World War II was eventually going to end, and the male stars who had gone off to fight would come dribbling back into town. I might have been tempted, but, in June of 1944, Clark Gable was discharged from the Air Force.

Before the war, I knew him only slightly. He had been married to Carole Lombard, until she was killed in a plane crash in 1942. To assuage his grief, Clark joined the Air Force. He was the biggest star in the world, but instead of deciding to sell bonds like Ronnie Reagan, he decided to do what every non-celebrity his age was doing: go to war. If you've ever seen pictures of Clark in the service, you'll never forget how he looked in the same terrible haircut as everyone else.

Clark returned from the war as Major Clark Gable, recipient of the Distinguished Flying Cross and Air Medal for his bombing missions over Germany. The war cannot have satisfied his itch for danger, for one Sunday afternoon—still in uniform because he was not yet detached from the Air Force—he came zooming up the driveway on his motorcycle. He'd heard about Howard's Moraga motorcycle club and wanted to be a part of it.

Maybe my own restlessness was in high gear that day. I know this: when Clark Gable appeared at my doorstep, I had never seen anything more breathtaking in my life. I couldn't believe he was true. Or that I'd see him again. But he began to show up every Sunday along with the other motorcycle riders. And a little flirt began.

Clark was a perfect gent. He'd invite me to his house in Encino for lunch, and, after lunch, we'd go horseback riding. Though the opportunity was right there and the attraction was obvious, nothing untoward occurred—which is how I knew we could get serious at any moment. And I knew I was crossing into the danger zone each time I went to see Clark. But I took a philosophical attitude about it: Here was the number one man in the world, and I'd be a fool not to have a look.

Even with our relationship undefined, we fulfilled one another's needs in some ways. I reminded him of Carole, and he was good for my ego, which by this time had become fragile as a result of Howard's infidelities. Clark understood that I had a great need for attention and company, but he didn't want to be involved with a married woman. So while we struggled to resolve the conflict between desire and duty, Clark and I became companions. This wasn't nearly so artificial as it may sound. We both enjoyed the outdoors. He was as passionate about his ranch as I was about my farm. And he had a deep sense of privacy, which was and is for me the only important thing money can buy.

In the end, alas, Clark wasn't very bright. Not that I really cared. Like every other woman who'd seen him in the movies, I was totally absorbed in his physical presence. And I wasn't immune to the egotistical thrill of having the "King of Hollywood" attracted to me.

To avoid getting sucked into an affair with Gable, I decided to make more constructive use of my time. I had no idea what I was going to do or how I was going to do it. Fortunately, I met Carmel Snow, then editor of *Harper's Bazaar*, who asked me to be photographed. From that understated offer came four magazine covers in one year. I was presented as Slim Hawks, or Mrs. Howard Hawks, always in an editorial sense. I never modeled for money nor did I want to—my ambition was simply to keep busy, although I did get a charge out of being photographed by people like Man Ray and Louise Dahl-Wolfe.

Because coverage breeds more coverage, other magazines were soon doing lifestyle pieces on me and the house Howard and I had built. Soon, I was quite busy. And I had a chance to become busier —I was offered the job as west coast editor of *Harper's Bazaar*. I never had to decide whether I was up to balancing an actual career with marriage for, in the late spring of 1945, I learned, to my utter surprise and delight, that Howard and I were going to have a baby.

This condition put a severe cramp both on my lifestyle and my budding career. I was not only sick from beginning to end, I had the worst case of insomnia imaginable. Early on, I retreated to my bed, where I spent my days—and nights—wondering how I was going to raise a child in a loveless home, for the prospect of fatherhood had not changed Howard in the least. When I saw him, which was rarely, he seemed completely uninvolved with me.

In Howard's defense, I must admit that I wasn't the most scintillating companion either—I was bleary with fatigue and duller than donuts. Still, I don't think my condition excused him for not coming home at night. After a few months of this shabby behavior, his own mother went to him and said, "You've got to behave in a more

(Photo by John Engstead)

*Wearing my own clothes,
these fashion photos were published
in various women's magazines.
(Photos by John Engstead)*

HARPER'S BAZAAR

In bed at Hog Canyon Farm with my new baby girl.
(Photo by John Engstead)

proper way. Slim's shivering and shaking and can't go to sleep. She's having a very hard time doing this." But the whole nesting business just didn't interest Howard. He already had three children.

Kitty Steven Hawks was born February 11, 1946. When I opened my eyes after the delivery, the first face I saw was my doctor's, not Kitty's father. Howard eventually made an appearance at the hospital, and I began to think, rather foolishly, that the worst was behind us, that if he only saw his beautiful daughter it would change everything.

I arrived home from the hospital with Kitty in an ambulance— Howard did not call for me—but I was hopeful of a new start. Grandmother Hawks was waiting to receive me with the news that Howard had just stepped out for a business appointment. She was as scandalized by his conduct as I was. Like me, she seemed very skeptical that Howard's "business" was about a film.

The realization that our daughter would have no effect on our marriage made me decide very early that Kitty was not to be Howard's baby. I would have the sole responsibility for her forever, and so she was mine. How right I was! Howard took no part in her life at all. It was almost as if she didn't exist. He never saw her until she was a young woman and old enough to react to him. In the end, the bitterness I still feel toward Howard has less to do with anything that happened between us than it does with his lack of interest in Kitty. Howard died in 1977; what a shame he never knew what Kitty could have meant to him.

Kitty with her mother and father. 1946.

SLIM

Once I was home from the hospital and took stock of the situation, I knew that as soon as the doctor gave me permission I'd go away by myself for a while. This wasn't such an unusual thing for me to do. Quite often during my marriage I'd retreat to a cottage in La Jolla for a few days and rest and read—sometimes, I'd just check into the Good Samaritan Hospital in L.A. for my retreat. Cottage or hospital, it made no difference; to me, being alone anywhere is like going to a spa.

This time, I wanted to travel a little further than La Jolla or Good Samaritan. And I wanted to be around people. I decided on New York—quite the daring choice, as I'd never been there on my own.

In early April, I left for New York on the Super Chief, feeling deeply unloved and unneeded and, in a sense, like a culprit leaving the scene of a crime. Although I knew Kitty would be well taken care of by a competent nanny, I still felt guilty to be leaving her behind—not because I felt she needed me, but because I knew I needed her. But the gloom that had descended over Hog Canyon Farm was such that getting out of town for a while was the only way I knew to deal with it.

I arrived in New York and went on a whirlwind of cocktail and dinner parties, and dancing at El Morocco. There was no dearth of people to see, and there were even a few escorts. This two-week trip, designed to rebuild my smashed ego, was going even better than I'd expected. So, although I was still feeling somewhat tender from the birth, I decided to add a week in Nassau.

This wasn't quite as successful as my visit to New York, and after a few days of dinners and lunches and lying on the beach with people I barely knew, I called Ernest in Cuba and explained that I was now the mother of a darling girl and the wife of a man I couldn't stand. When I finished, he simply said, "Get on a plane and come down to the Finca for a week. You need to be with people who love you."

By this time, Ernest and Martha Gellhorn were divorced, and he had married Mary Welsh. Ernest met me at the airport. He had an off-center smile I hadn't seen before. "Miss Slimsky," he said, as he engulfed me in a bear hug, "why don't we ever find each other *between* marriages?"

The Finca Vigía was an old estate located in the village of San Francisco de Paula, about fifteen miles outside of Havana. The

106

*Papa
at home.*

Finca had the charms of both a farm and a resort—there was a somewhat rundown villa with a guesthouse, an unused tennis court, and a serviceable pool, surrounded by thirteen acres of gardens and fruit trees. The living room was long and narrow. The dining room, which was actually part of the living room, was dominated by a Joan Miró painting that now hangs in the Museum of Modern Art. The decor was simple: a large sofa and two over-sized armchairs covered in white duck. One was Papa's throne. This was where he plowed through the infinite amount of reading material that was piled on all the tables in the room.

It was not a memorable house, but it didn't matter. The attraction was Hemingway.

His bride of just six weeks couldn't have liked my being there. But then, it was hard to know what she would have liked. This was no Martha Gellhorn, a woman with a genuinely commanding presence. This was a fidgety banty hen of a woman, always scurrying around, doing needless things that she thought made her indispensable. She had been a war correspondent in England, and perhaps she had learned a thing or two in the war, but she didn't have a clue how to run a house with Ernest Hemingway in it. She was tatty-looking. She adopted a deep, affected voice which wasn't hers at all. And she wasn't sophisticated enough to disguise her displeasure at my having been invited to Cuba because of her husband's great affection for me.

Mary made efforts, as I did, to be civil, which wasn't too hard, as I didn't stay in the main house. And, because of Ernest's work habits, I wouldn't see him all that much. Ernest worked standing up from first light until lunchtime. While he wrote, I'd sit by the pool and read, or have a swim, waiting for lunch before going up to the main house.

Then Ernest would appear, and the house would come to life. Sometimes, over the first drink, he'd say, "Good day today, fifteen hundred words." Some days, he wouldn't mention his writing at all. But no matter how his writing had gone, lunch was always gregarious, with far too much drink and bad food.

After lunch, Ernest would sit and read the newspapers. You sensed that he wanted to be alone, so you left him alone. As for Mary, I don't know what she did; sometimes, she fiddled in the garden. I'd take this opportunity to return to the little house and stay there and read all afternoon.

In the shank of the afternoon, Ernest would have a snooze. This totally revived him; when he got up he was roaring like an animal, ready to do anything. Now he was full of steam: "Let's go shoot," "Let's go swimming," "Let's go to the Floridita and have a Papa Doble."

I quickly realized that dinner at the Floridita bar was the easiest option—everybody was more relaxed. Mary wouldn't be agitated about the cook, there would be people for Ernest to talk to, and there would be round after round of Papa Dobles—double daiquiris made from Ernest's recipe, which consisted of no sugar and just double the rum and fresh-squeezed lime. This lethal brew was put into a blender and whizzed up, then poured into giant glasses that you'd dive into and do a backstroke around. It tasted like nothing except the best thing you ever tasted. So good in fact that you didn't realize they were knocking you out.

Ernest seemed very much at home in Cuba. And as a visitor, you quickly became an appendage to his scene. I could see how even first-time visitors came to feel that although they weren't spending

*With Papa in
the Floridita
bar in Havana.*

*At the Floridita, the world's greatest bar. Ernest with admiring Cuban
fans. Mary and I are in the background.*

all that much time with Papa, they had been admitted to the heart of his inner circle. It was a pleasant routine.

Then there was the fishing.

Now, I'd been on boats before. But I'd never been on the *Pilar*. And in all my time on the water, I never encountered a scene as odd as this. For starters, there was Mary. The bride would spend the whole day in a little boat—the *Tin Kid*—attached to the back of the *Pilar*. It was remarkable. The sun was broiling and her skin was already leathery, but she'd climb out there each morning and fish, alone, with no protection from the sun.

Then there were the sleeping arrangements. Papa and Mary— the honeymooners—slept in the area where we dined. It had a banquette with a removable table; they slept on the cushions. I was given the cabin with the bunk, which was nice but sort of pointless as I had insomnia.

The oddest thing of all, of course, was that I was even aboard. Here Ernest was, hugely complicated and newly married, taking great pains to entertain a woman whom he openly fancied. He made no effort to modify his adoration for Mary's benefit. For him, Slim came first. "Is Slim comfortable? Is she warm enough? Does she need another pillow?" He was very dear, which didn't make his wife any happier or make her love me any more, because she didn't love me at all. How could she? He would look at me, and in the look was the message.

On this trip, to my great discomfort, Ernest was sometimes even more overt. He had a great big cashmere shooting shirt that you wear under your other shirt. He'd wear it in the chill of the evening when the wind came off the water. One night, he said, "Put this on, it'll keep you warm." I put it on; it felt cozy and nice. The next day, when I gave it back to him, he said, "I'm never going to let this be washed as long as it lives." I asked why. He said, "Because it smells like you, it smells of Slim. I'm never going to let it be washed." If that isn't a pass, I don't know what you'd call it.

Why did Ernest act like this? After four days at sea on a cramped boat, with long uninterrupted hours in very close quarters, I began to form a theory that I've never abandoned. As has been documented in his novels and by his biographers, Ernest had physical

Papa at sea.

problems—sexual problems. And the way he dealt with them was
to create a conflict. No sooner would Ernest marry someone than
he'd get stuck on somebody else. He didn't have to consummate
the flirtation; in fact, it was key that he didn't. What he was looking
for was the feeling that he was making a great sacrifice for the
marriage. So, although he might be having a silent love affair in his
head, he was faithful to his wife.

I wasn't the only woman to have this relationship with Ernest. A
few years later, when he and Mary were on safari in Africa, he
wrote to tell me what I was missing. In the process, he went on
about a black girl, a native, who was madly in love with him. He
admitted that he had a sneaker for her. But he wasn't going to do
anything about it. "When I go with girls," he wrote to me, "I am
always empty in my arms and I'm empty in my heart too." Which
tells it all.

Whatever Ernest's troubles were, I could put up with them, for
when he shone his light on me, there was no more powerful medi-
cine. I wanted him to pay attention to me. I wanted him to talk to
me. I wanted him to say, "Slimsky hasn't got enough tomato juice.
Get Slimsky some more." Or, "Do this for Slimsky," or, "I want
the sun to be out so we have a good dove shoot, because it's Miss
Slimsky's last day of shooting," or whatever. Those were like presents—and they were better than gifts others might send from Cartier.

The best present Ernest gave, though, was his wisdom, which
was specific and useful and just what I needed to hear at that
moment. On this trip, for example, we were hunting for marlin but
catching mostly shark or barracuda. I hooked a shark. Ernest said,
"You kill it, it's your fish."

"I can't," I told him. "My arms will fall off."

Ernest turned to the captain. "Nobody touches the rod but Slim."
Then he kneeled next to me. "You have to kill it yourself. It's the
only thing that counts."

I tried and tried, and I think they cheated a little bit and helped
me by running the boat in the direction that would make the line
slacken. When I finally did kill the fish, Ernest was very proud.
"Miss Slimsky killed her fish and that makes all the difference," he
said, again and again. I understood what he meant: Slim needs a
big, positive thing to reestablish what's been crushed and broken.

And, for Ernest, catching the fish was the way to do that. A purposeful thought on his part, but it didn't work for me.

Once back on land, I looked forward to the peaceful routine at the Finca. This was soon shattered. A carload of unexpected visitors—movie producer David Selznick, actress Jennifer Jones, agent and producer Leland Hayward and his wife Maggie Sullavan, and William Paley, the founder of CBS—arrived at the gate to pay their respects to the great man. They'd been cruising around the Caribbean, stopping in all the noisy ports of call. At some point, they'd heard through the California grapevine that I was staying with Ernest. Still, it was pretty bold of them to appear at Hemingway's house unannounced.

Leland Hayward didn't make much of an impression on me. He had a kind of electricity that everyone was conscious of, but he didn't grab my attention. All I remember about the Haywards on this trip was Maggie's questioning of a natural blond, almost white streak I had in my light brown hair. She asked me point blank in a restaurant if I dyed it. I said, "No, I don't." And she said, "Well, it's just amazing. Two kinds of hair on one head like that." Leland later told me my streak really worried her, and she didn't believe it was natural.

David and Jennifer wanted me to leave Cuba with them and continue the boat trip. The last thing I wanted was that. Bill Paley, an unmarried man and a mighty attractive chap whom I'd never met until this trip, came to the Finca alone for dinner. He thought it would be fun if I joined them on the boat and it would make the numbers right. That would, I suppose, have made me his date.

Fortunately, I declined. Had I agreed to go, I might have muddied the beginnings of an immensely rewarding, lifelong friendship that I later formed with Bill and his future wife Barbara. Even at the time it seemed better to spend a few more days with Ernest and Mary, and then make my way to Miami. I was homesick for a little child I didn't even know. And I was feeling silly. What on earth was I doing, running to every port of call like a sailor on a spree? Despite Howard's lack of interest in his wife and child, it was my duty to go home and behave like a real parent.

I arrived back in L.A. feeling more sure of myself. There, awaiting me, was this wonderful three-month-old baby. I was absolutely fascinated by her. When Howard asked me to come to Palm Springs with him and leave Kitty behind, I had to fight the impulse to refuse. In the end, I went. I figured that I'd gone off and done what I'd wanted to do; I owed him one weekend.

And so Howard and I trudged along on a very insecure foundation. But it wasn't destroying me. I felt more confident now, and I took just enough time from the baby to make sure I had a life of my own. If I wanted to have lunch with Robert Capa, I would. If Howard and I went to a party and I wanted to stay longer than he did, I would. At one of David Selznick's famous Sunday night dinners, I did stay late—and that party became the turning point in my life.

On July 14, 1946, a Sunday that is forever ingrained in my head, Howard and I went—as we had many times before—to David's. On that one invitation we were in complete agreement; a Selznick invitation was a guarantee that you were going to have a marvelous time.

David was, in the true sense, a life enhancer. You simply had a better time with him than you did with anybody else. He brought gargantuan enthusiasm to anything he put his mind to, notwithstanding the fact that he could be so vexing and frustrating that you wanted to kill him. He was never on time, he was never ready, he hadn't shaved yet, he wasn't dressed, the food hadn't come from the market. No matter. One always had the best possible time. Joseph Cotten's first wife, Lenore, used to call him "Uncle Bim." For those of us old enough to remember Andy Gump of the funnies, Uncle Bim was the Daddy Warbucks of the Gump family: an expansive, improbable joy-giver.

On the Sunday night in question, the guest list was the usual. The Louis Jourdans, the Joseph Cottens, Anita Colby—and, among others, Leland Hayward, who was solo, as his wife, Margaret Sullavan, was away. Howard had to excuse himself because of an early call—or fatigue or boredom or a late date. He suggested I stay on, providing I could get a ride home. I assured him I could because the Cottens drove past our house.

After dinner, six or eight of us played "Derivations," a game about the origins of words, while lolling about on David's gigantic "playing fields of Eton" bed. I was given the word "Spoonerism." Leland said, "There's no such word. Someone made it up."

"It is a word," I said, with great confidence. "It's mixing up words of the same sound to give a different meaning, as in 'Red

114

*My dear friend
David Selznick. (Photo
by Leland Hayward)*

Door' as opposed to 'Dead Roar.' It's named after the old English scholar and clergyman, Reverend W. A. Spooner, who was prone to making that type of mistake."

For once, I lucked out. Leland was absolutely rocked. His eyes opened up and he said, "Well, I'll be damned. You look like that and you're a very smart woman as well."

I said, "Well, I try to be."

"How are you going to get home?" he asked.

"I guess you're going to take me home."

This was not a gloomy prospect. Now that I was concentrating, I realized that Leland Hayward was a difficult man to ignore. He had large china blue eyes that had a perpetual look of pleading in them, as if he were asking a favor of you and hoping you would grant it. He wasn't handsome, he was adorable: a college-boy crewcut, an enthusiastic smile, and a charm that rendered its recipient weak in the knees.

Leland later told me that my lucky answer riveted his attention in such a way that he never looked at anyone else for a long time.

115

"You really went a long way on that one line," he used to say to me. That's not quite true, if you look at the whole picture, but at the time maybe it was. He drove me home to the marvelous house and garden that I had built, furnished, landscaped, weeded, pruned, and loved. He stopped the car at the end of a long, oleander-lined driveway, making no move to get out or see me to the front door.

When I started to thank him for the lift, he said, "Just a minute. I want to ask you something."

"What?" I asked.

"Why don't you blow?" he said.

"What do you mean, 'Why don't I blow?'"

"Why don't you quit? Why don't you leave?"

"Leave what?"

"Leave Howard!"

"Because he's my husband. He's the father of my child, who isn't even a year old. What are you talking about?"

"Well, it's obvious that you don't get on. It's obvious you have nothing together. You have so much to offer. There's so much ahead for you. You can have a giant life if you get the hell out of here."

I was pretty jolted by his boldness and somewhat defensive. All I could say was, "Thanks again for the ride, and the cheap advice."

And I got out of the car alone, crossed the lawn to my front door, walked in, and closed the door behind me. I went to my bedroom window and looked out. Leland's car was still there. For the longest time, it didn't move. It wasn't until I turned off the lights that I saw the lights of his car move slowly down the drive.

The encounter had certainly shaken me. "I wonder what the hell he really means?" I thought, as I lay in bed. I went through the old questions for a long time, and then, just as I drifted off, I arrived at a satisfactory answer. Leland Hayward, I decided, was just plain crazy.

The next morning I received a delivery of every kind of white flower that God ever created—bigger, grander, more breathtaking than anything I'd ever seen or had ever received from anyone. Flowers always knock me over, and I've never gotten over the thrill that these gave me. I ripped open the envelope and pulled out the card. It simply said, "No Signature."

WHAT TO
DO TILL
THE
DOCTOR
COMES:

From Howard Hawks to Leland Hayward

It was only a matter of days after our "recognition scene," as Leland and I always called it, that he phoned and asked if I'd come to his office. I remember saying to him, "God, that sounds forbidding and businesslike."

Leland's response was a cavalier "Don't worry, I just want to ask you something."

Well, he could have asked me over the phone. But he was looking for an excuse to see me. And I certainly wanted one to see him. So I packed myself off to his office at MCA, where he was making another of his charmed career transitions. Leland had flunked out of Princeton at the end of his freshman year and started in show business as a press agent for United Artists. He married Lola Gibbs (a beautiful New York debutante whom he eventually divorced, remarried, and divorced again) and moved up the organization to become a talent scout. With the release of the first talkie in 1927, he sensed there was big money to be made from the studios, which suddenly wanted playwrights from Broadway and stage actors with trained voices. Leland convinced a literary agency called the American Play Company to set up a motion picture department that

117

would represent these writers and actors—in essence, Leland almost single-handedly invented the movie agency business.

A few years later, Leland went out on his own and built what was probably the most prestigious roster of clients in Hollywood. His stable of one hundred fifty actors, writers, and directors included the cream of Hollywood: Greta Garbo, Henry Fonda, Fred Astaire, James Stewart, and Leland's second wife Margaret Sullavan. Just before I met him, he'd sold the agency to MCA—retaining a third of the agent's fees his former clients earned as long as they stayed at MCA—and produced his first play, John Hersey's *A Bell for Adano*. He'd gone on to produce *State of the Union*, written by Howard Lindsay and Russel Crouse. It had been a great success on Broadway, and now Leland was preparing it for a national tour. When I entered the picture, this company was rehearsing in Los Angeles, with opening night not far away.

There were just a few loose ends for Leland to tie in the production. And this, he said, after he ushered me into his office and sat me down like a regular visitor, had prompted him to think about me. I had great fashion sense, I liked people—would I sign on as the costume overseer?

This was all very nice, I said. But there was a problem: I had never worked. Not a day in my life. I had never acquired the discipline a job demands and I didn't want to make promises only to run the risk of losing interest in the job.

Leland waved my objections aside. He explained that I wouldn't have time to get bored—opening night was only a month away. Moreover, he said, he knew I could do it. *State of the Union* is about a presidential election. It featured the usual stereotyped senators and campaign managers, as well as their very lumpy Helen Hokinson–type wives. All Leland wanted me to do was dress those wives.

To put it mildly, Leland was the most persuasive person I'd ever met. Did it matter that even this small job terrified me? Not when Leland laid out its many advantages, not least, of course, its proximity to him.

I had terrific fun fingering my way through racks of frumpy dresses and boxes of accessories. My criterion was elementary: I chose what I thought the women would have chosen themselves. When it all came together, I thought it looked damned authentic.

At last it was the day of the dress rehearsal, my big moment. I was sitting in the darkened theater along with the rest of the people involved in the production. Like them, I was looking for errors. Unlike them, I saw none.

There's a moment in the play when the two senators and their wives enter the candidate's hotel suite. This was my triumph—in this scene, every woman I dressed was onstage. I sat back and said to myself, "Well done, old girl."

It was exactly at this point that Howard Lindsay, the coauthor-cum-director and a most imposing man, rose from his seat in the eleventh row, marched down the aisle and right onto the stage. We watched, riveted and aghast, as he went over to one of my poor little women and ripped the tightly clutched evening bag from her hands.

I froze. The bag was made of silver sequins. It was, I knew, exactly what the character would have chosen. But here it was, being snatched away. Without a word, Lindsay walked offstage.

The only beat that was missed was my own heartbeat.

What he had seen was something I'd never considered—that the twinkling handbag became, under stage lights, a lighthouse beacon. It was all the audience saw.

I was embarrassed beyond measure and slunk quietly out of the theater, saying to the third stage manager sitting in the last row, "Tell Mr. Hayward I quit." I got into my car and left—fast. I promised myself I would never work again. It's one promise I've kept.

Still, my job had been a clever idea on Leland's part, allowing us time together. Day after day we saw one another, worked together, and had dinner together, without broadcasting the fact that by now we were besotted with each other.

By mid-August, the project was over and we had to devise other ways. There was no question that we truly wanted one another. Leland was wooing in earnest and I was absolutely delighted to be wooed. I was fascinated by him and by his pervasive vitality. It was like a perfume, an odor. It permeated the room and enveloped the person it was directed to. He wasn't attractive in a conventional way, but I used to adore looking at his craggy, worn face with its dazzling blue eyes, long eyelashes that didn't curl and his funny short hair.

What made Leland irresistible was his boyish attentiveness. He didn't play golf or tennis; he thought all that was a lot of crap. His

With Leland during our courtship.

sport was women, and I adored him for that. He wasn't into con-
quest, he wasn't at all macho—he just loved being with the opposite
sex. He always made me feel I was with a very close friend. I could
tell him things I might tell a woman. And yet the physical attraction
between us was undeniable.

When a man of that force comes into your life, you find yourself
endlessly twinkling and charming. I did all the things women do in
that condition: I ran to the hairdresser, dressed with my lover in
mind, started and finished every day at a dead run. And Leland
would do anything to see me. He flew his own plane and sometimes,
at lunch, he'd fly over Hog Canyon Farm and dip his wings, both
thrilling and scaring me. When he called me at home, he'd use a
series of ethnic disguises; his favorite was Chinese. "Meet me at
the corner of Rilshire and Ra Cienega at five-fifteen," he'd say.
Five-fifteen would come and go, and I'd still be at home—I had a
bright Kelly green car that everyone in town knew was mine, and I
didn't want to be caught sitting on the corner waiting for him.

Leland's most outrageous and aggressive move came when he
decided he had to see me at home, in Howard's presence. This

required, of course, a completely legitimate excuse. For Leland, that was no obstacle.

At this time, Howard was in pre-production for *Red River*. He had already cast John Wayne, but still needed to find a young actor for the second lead. Leland, not surprisingly, had a client he thought was absolutely right for the part—Montgomery Clift. Monty had already made a name for himself in the theater, and there was, around Hollywood, a sort of mystery about him and his ravishing good looks. Leland called me—this time in his own voice—and suggested that he bring Clift for lunch so Howard could meet him.

It was very clear from the minute Clift walked in that he wasn't at all interested in making an "oater." He was, it appeared, even less interested in Howard Hawks. What did catch his eye was me. Knowing as we now do the whole story of Monty Clift's inclinations,

Montgomery Clift.

his interest was ironic. Much to Monty's seeming dismay, I didn't stick around for their lunch. In jeans and a denim shirt, I went off to work in the garden.

After lunch, Leland and Howard began to negotiate a deal, on the offchance that Monty might agree to do the film. I had by then completed my chores and, for Leland's benefit, changed into a white floating robe-de-chambre—as I look back on it, an amazingly inappropriate get-up for three in the afternoon. I floated in, took Monty by the arm, and suggested we have a walk in the garden. Howard nodded, Leland grinned.

As soon as we were out of earshot, Monty asked me. "Should I do this?"

"Absolutely."

"But it's a *Western*."

"Howard can make a great Western."

"The thing is," Clift said, "I don't know how to ride a horse or shoot a gun or walk in funny boots."

"Well, that's the *easy* part. You learn all that very quickly. More importantly, what you will learn from Howard Hawks will be invaluable for the rest of your motion picture career, provided you intend to have one. You'll have two first-rate teachers—John Wayne, who understands his craft and is a generous, nice man, and Howard, who's as good as they get."

Those lovely questioning gray eyes looked into mine, and then he said, "Okay, I will."

Into the house we went. Howard and Leland looked up in surprise —we were back too soon. Monty announced, "I've decided to do it. She talked me into it."

Howard was amazed, I was amazed, and Leland was ecstatic. In that moment, I impressed Leland as much as I had that one night at Selznick's house when he learned that I knew the meaning of "Spoonerism."

The making of *Red River* provided a convenient vehicle for Leland and me to continue our affair. There was, of course, lots of pre-production preparation for a picture of that size and scope. *Red River* meant many location-scouting trips for Howard. It meant negotiations for cattle that could act, or at least all walk in the same direction—a more difficult challenge than you might imagine, for the cattle Howard was shown tended to be half-dead, too lean, or too fat. It meant hours of looking at stock footage of cows grazing, fording rivers, stampeding, marching across Texas to market. And it meant, because Howard was such a thorough craftsman about every aspect of film making, that he wasn't around very much.

With the opportunity at hand, Leland and I were able to spend more time together. Our romance deepened, and we found a very serious mutual commitment. Just a couple of months after Leland's prophetic advice in my darkened driveway, he asked me to marry him. When he did, there was not one second of doubt in my mind that he and I would have a life together, and that it would be wonderful. We were, as is often the case, too much in love even to weigh the difficulties of extricating ourselves from our present commitments.

Although Leland's marriage to Margaret Sullavan was a continuing storm, he had done nothing to end it. Maggie was one of the most stunning actresses—on stage and screen—of the thirties and forties. Having been discovered on Broadway in *Dinner at Eight* in 1932, her electric personality and her versatility made her an instant film star in 1933, when she appeared in *Only Yesterday*. Cast as a romantic lead in such tearful melodramas as *Three Comrades*, *The Shop Around the Corner*, and *Back Street*, she was best known for her bravura performance on Broadway, in John Van Druten's three-character drama *The Voice of the Turtle*.

Though Leland had been Maggie's agent for several years, their romantic relationship didn't happen until 1936. At that time, Leland was having a big romance with Katharine Hepburn on the west coast, and so he began conducting a "captain's paradise" kind of life with Kate in Hollywood and Maggie in New York, who was performing on Broadway in Edna Ferber's *Stage Door*. Maggie eventually got pregnant and had to leave the play—something she could only do, according to her contract, if it were prompted by an act of God. (That led Edna Ferber to say some very rude things about God.) Leland married her in Newport at Clarendon Court, the home of his father and stepmother, and later the unlucky home of Sunny and Klaus Von Bülow. When Leland was courting me, he told me all about this, and admitted he'd awakened the next morning and cried—knowing even then that the marriage was all wrong. As for Kate, she was having dinner with George Cukor one night and heard, along with everyone else, the news of the wedding as Walter Winchell broadcast it on his Sunday night radio show. Perhaps I should have learned something from that anecdote.

As accomplished as Maggie was, she was also an unsure woman given to depressions and self-doubt. Moreover, she hated Hollywood—and for Leland, Hollywood was his life. So he stayed on in Los Angeles, mostly alone, while Maggie took the children to their house in Connecticut, where she struggled to abandon her career and fulfill her fantasy of being a full-time mother.

Maggie's absence couldn't have been more destructive for their marriage. As I was later to discover, Leland was not a man who was very good on his own. What he lacked—and clearly wanted—was a woman who could have an identity and still be his constant companion.

Fortunately, he came into my life at a time when I was emerging as a personality in my own right and, like him, wanted a partner who was my equal. "Slim Hawks"—that woman who was invariably described as all-American, long, lean, and tawny—was about to be dubbed the first "California Girl." This was the culmination of a few years of the coverage launched by Carmel Snow, the editor of *Harper's Bazaar*. I'd found the "Slim Hawks look" funny and fun. And I'd been nothing but amused when, in 1946, I was named the number one "Best Dressed Woman in the World," a title about as empty as "Miss Butterfat Week" in Wisconsin. But if it was clear I had any talent at all, it was my talent for individuality. That was getting considerable attention.

I was approached by Stanley Marcus to be the first "consumer" to receive the Neiman-Marcus award, an annual accolade usually given to two or three designers, American or otherwise, who Stanley felt had made a lasting contribution to fashion and merchandising. Stanley presented a very alluring picture of the experience. I would be wined and dined, and all that would be asked of me was a short acceptance speech on the night of the awards ceremony. It all sounded fine—except for the speech. I told Leland I would be too terrified to stand up in front of all those people and say anything.

A great confidence builder, Leland said, "Don't be silly, go and do it. I'll get Lindsay and Crouse to write a speech for you. All you have to do is read it." With two of the country's most gifted writers behind me, I decided to give it a whirl.

Lindsay and Crouse wrote a graceful, charming, funny little speech. I thanked them profusely, folded it up, stuck it in my bag, and flew off to Texas to enjoy all the promised attention and activity. The night of the awards, Stanley Marcus spoke, others spoke—I was being saved for the last, the *pièce de résistance*. I listened in awe as the other honorees confidently bounded onstage to receive their silver plaques and make their eloquent remarks. Then it was my turn.

Stanley made a charming introduction. He spoke of a marvelous woman whose touch was *so* sure, whose taste was *so* impeccable, and who epitomized the *best* of American looks. And then, just as I was thinking that this was all too ridiculous for words, he held up a large, engraved slab of silver and turned toward me. I do remember taking it from him. And I'll never forget staring across the blur of faces. Beyond that, I don't know—I simply froze, suffering the worst case of stage fright imaginable. After what seemed like a considerable silence, all I could do was look deep into Stanley's eyes and say, "Thank you very much." Needless to say, sure, impeccable, ever-so-Slim Hawks did not bring down the house.

When I returned to Los Angeles, Lindsay and Crouse questioned me thoroughly about the reception of their work. I told them we would probably get an Oscar. As it happened, a few months later, my illustrious speechwriters found themselves traveling on the 20th Century Limited to New York with Stanley Marcus. They chatted for a while, then Lindsay asked, "Tell us, how did you like Slim's speech?"

"What speech?" Stanley intoned. "All she said was 'Thank you.' "

"She said, 'Thank you,' that's *all?*" Crouse asked. "We wrote her a very good speech and she told us it was a great success."

"I don't know what to tell you," said Stanley. "All she got out was 'Thank you.' "

This was reported back to Leland. He never again suggested that I speak in public.

By the autumn of 1946, Howard had returned to Los Angeles and the domestic routine of the Hawks establishment started up again. For Leland and me, this was tough going. We'd gotten used to seeing one another daily, and now that we couldn't, we became love-starved creatures.

With Stanley Marcus in Dallas, waiting to receive the Neiman-Marcus Consumer Award and to deliver the brilliant speech created for me by Lindsay and Crouse. It is clear that I'm tongue-tied.

Leland's solution was to drive an hour or so down the coast to a small house he had rented in La Jolla, which was then a sleepy little seaside village where no one we knew ever went. The first time, I found this romantic, with the required amount of danger. But we never went back; it was too far and I was too scared. Leland's variation on this idea was to rent a house in Palm Springs.

Leland's recklessness excited me and challenged me. Hell, I was only twenty-nine, much too young to settle into any unhappy rut. But if I was completely aware that my marriage to Howard was, at

126

its core, small and diminishing and unimportant, I did not feel so young and reckless that I could tell him it was over.

The closest I came was in September, when I went to visit Howard on location in Tucson. In that confrontation, we agreed we were wasting each other's time, acting out the motions of a marriage. Leland wasn't mentioned in this conversation, but our romance was common gossip in Hollywood; Howard had to know. By the end of the month the press was calling me. I'd ducked the calls, but Hedda Hopper printed just enough about an unnamed director's wife and an unnamed agent/producer to titillate her readers.

The inquiring press has always frightened me. I duck it whenever I can. My brain and judgment seem to stop functioning when those questions about uncertain terrain come up, and instead of the safe "no comment" ploy, I tend to say something, anything, usually the wrong thing.

So when Hedda Hopper printed her item, I felt the heat was really on, and I decided to get out of town for a few days. To the most remote and private place I knew. That meant Idaho—and Ernest. As always, he had a few words of wisdom for me. When I told him about my media problems, he simply said, "You don't have to answer a question that a person has no right to ask. Just ignore the press." Considering what almost happened on this trip, I was lucky I didn't have more to worry about than a squib in Hedda's column.

I'd come to Ketchum at partridge season and every day Ernest and Mary and his two sons and I went out to shoot. One afternoon, after I'd been there a few days, we were returning home almost empty-handed. Six guns, and we'd taken down ten Hungarian partridge at best. Our feet were sore, we were tired and dirty and hungry. As we drove home, Papa shouted, "Huns! Huns! Huns!" The car came to a sudden halt and everybody got out, loaded up, and tippy-toed around, waiting for this poor bird that had made it through the day without being killed. But it was a false alarm; he didn't turn up.

In those days I shot with a Browning 16-gauge automatic gun, a very unsportsmanlike weapon more suited to shooting skeet than live birds. The gun normally had a plug in it so that it would only hold two shells. I'd had the plug taken out so I could load it with more shells. This modification complicated the unloading process;

you had to put your finger on a ring, pull it down, open the magazine, and then the shell would drop out of the chamber. My habit was to empty the gun and then pull the trigger so it was locked closed.

But after this mad scurry for the partridge, I wasn't paying close attention. I sat on the fender of the car and unloaded the gun. Then I put it in my lap, fired the trigger, and pushed the safety. Unbeknownst to me, there still was a shell in it. The gun fired. The stray shell flew right in Ernest's direction, grazing his head and singeing the hair off the back of his neck.

A very long second followed. I threw the gun to the ground and started to cry, shrieking, "I almost killed my friend, my best friend."

He said, "It's all right."

I said, "It's not all right. I could just die!"

He said, "Well, we're going home now, we'll have a drink and it won't look so bad to you. Besides, think of how famous you would have been! The woman who killed Hemingway!"

"Well, I don't want this gun. I'm going to leave it right here on the ground."

He said, "You can't throw away an expensive gun like that."

"Oh yes I can," I told him. "I never want to see it again."

Ernest picked it up, took it home, and eventually took it to Abercrombie & Fitch, where he kept a lot of his weapons. Having made the weapon disappear, it was, for him, as if the incident had never happened. All the same, it was a terrible, terrible moment for me.

I returned to Los Angeles still unsure of how I would get out of my marriage. The end came several months later. One morning, I received a telephone call from Miss Barker, Leland's secretary. "Mr. Hayward was taken to the Cedars of Lebanon Hospital last night," she said. "He's hemorrhaging very badly and they don't seem to know the cause. He wanted me to tell you that he would be in touch with you as soon as it was possible for him to do so."

I paced the floor for two days. Leland was not only sick, perhaps dying, but he was inaccessible to me. In all that had happened, I'd forgotten that he still belonged to someone else, and that, as the life ran out of him, she would unquestionably be there.

There was nothing I could do but wait near the phone. Maybe, just maybe, he would be alone and strong enough to call. Four days later, he did. His voice was fuzzy, drowsy, weak, but all the same, it was Leland.

"I don't know what the hell is the matter with me," he said. "I'm bleeding like a stuck pig, and they're pumping blood into me as fast as I pump it out. I want desperately to see you. Could you come?"

"Of course, whenever you want me to."

Leland had made a confidante of the head nurse. He handed the phone to her, and she arranged to smuggle me into the hospital and keep me out of sight, more or less, until the coast was clear. But our reunion wasn't at all romantic or reassuring. Leland was shockingly gaunt and gray. His great blue eyes had sunk back into his head. Still, he was smiling, which was all the encouragement I needed as I wove my way through bottles and tubes and needles and held him for a long moment.

"We *will* have a life, we *will* have each other," he whispered. "I'm not going to check out now that I've found what I've wanted for so long."

I was less confident. Leland had had an identical attack in 1943. The profusion of the bleeding seemed to indicate more than an ulcer. As far as I could see, Leland's doctors were satisfied that the problem was an ulcer. But their treatment wasn't working.

I took the situation into my own hands and called my physician, Dr. Lawrence Chaffin, who explained that medical ethics prevented him from intervening in a case where the patient was already under a doctor's care in a hospital other than his own. I pressed him at least to visit Leland in the role of a consultant. And, to make it all ethically correct, I got Leland to call him and request the consultation.

When he examined Leland, Dr. Chaffin felt as I did that the bleeding was not the result of an ulcer but came from some other source which could only be located by an exploratory operation—at his own hospital, of course. He suggested that Leland leave Cedars of Lebanon, convalesce somewhere healthy and peaceful, and return to Good Samaritan Hospital, where the operation was to be done.

Leland took this advice. First, however, he went to Palm Springs to rest and heal in the sun and desert air. Maggie did not accompany him; I did. We sat quietly together in the sun—reading, talking, and thinking too.

It was no longer necessary to invent reasons to go out of town with Leland. Though we didn't discuss the situation, Howard knew everything, and it was clear that there was no way to take things back to where they once had been.

Howard behaved like the gentleman he had been brought up to be. He knew I was suffering and he went out of his way to be sympathetic and supportive. One can forgive much—whatever indignities, hurt, and loneliness one has passed through—in the face of such conduct.

Leland's operation was scheduled for a Wednesday morning. I woke with the dawn and paced around my bedroom, looking out windows, staring at book spines, tidying dresser drawers, passing time any way I could. About noon, the phone rang. It was Dr. Chaffin.

"We found nothing," he reported. "We made a thorough double search of every inch of the intestine and bowel and found nothing. Whatever caused the bleeding has to do with tension; it's like a bloodshot eye which hemorrhages after too much use. But there's no cancer, no polyps, no ulcer. The bleeding may never happen again, or it may happen tomorrow. I'm afraid this uncertainty is part of the package."

I put down the phone and burst into tears.

Unknown to me, Howard had entered the room during this call. When I looked up, he was standing at the foot of my bed, watching my face.

"Is he going to be all right?" he asked, as though we were talking about an old friend of ours.

"Yes. I think so."

"Good," he said softly. "I know how much you care for him. I'm glad he's going to be all right."

With that, Howard was gone. And I sat there for a long time, in total disbelief that my marriage had just ended with the most impeccable ease and grace.

EMERALD
OVERSHOES
AND A
DIAMOND
WRAP

The next twelve years—the twelve years that Leland and I were together—were the happiest of my life. He was my lover, custodian, partner, and friend. In him were all the qualities I love in a man. He was exotic, eccentric, and charming. Most of all, he had spontaneity and imagination. Even when we were alone together—and there were blessed weeks when life was just the two of us—I never tired of him. No one did; there was an air of excitement when he was around.

Even after we were married, when the courting ceases for most women, Leland would, for example, call from his New York office on a Tuesday morning in November and ask, "How would you like to go to Paris for the weekend?"

"Which weekend?" I'd say.

"This weekend."

"Don't you have to work?"

"No, I've got nothing to do."

And we'd get on an airplane Wednesday afternoon or Wednesday night, and spend Thursday, Friday, and Saturday in Paris, come home on Sunday, and he'd be in his office on Monday. It was just

With Leland.

like going to Connecticut for the weekend, there seemed to be so little effort to it. We'd go to a restaurant or two we loved, discover a new one; go to the Jeu de Paume, look at some beautiful paintings, and come home. Wonderful!

Leland's extravagance was always tied to his taste, which was very refined. He knew a lot about good things and grand things, and he knew the difference between good and grand. He loved fine art, he loved beautiful jewels, he loved sable coats—he loved all the kinds of things I loved, and that made him a constantly delicious companion. Sometimes I'd say, "Let's *not* go to Paris. I'd rather have new curtains for the dining room." Leland would reply, "Oh, screw the curtains. We'll get the curtains. But we're also going to Paris."

This expansive way of life was all ahead of me in 1947, when Leland recovered from his illness and operation and I moved out of Hog Canyon Farm with Kitty and rented a house in Brentwood. The prospect of so much joy minimized all the pangs and regrets. We admitted that neither of our marriages had been happy, that it was better for our children to be children of divorce than to grow up in

With Kitty and Meatball in California.

unhappy homes, that life is too short to be spent in recrimination.

What seemed so simple, it soon became clear, was only simple on my side. Howard had been a gent about the break-up; he wasn't going to be a monster about the divorce. There was only one child to consider, and Howard and I both assumed that Kitty would be with me.

On Leland's side, though, there was a more painful process. Though he was sure he wanted us to be together, it wasn't as easy for him to extricate himself from his marriage. Maggie had money, the promise of a generous settlement from Leland, and she was certainly capable of earning more. But Leland was distraught about his children. They were old enough to be devastated by their parents' decision to separate, and that gave Leland enormous guilt.

Ending a marriage in California wasn't easy in those days. Before you filed for a first decree, behavior had to be immaculate. Any transgressions could be held against you, so our contact was sparse during those months.

Leland began his enforced solitary spell in New York, where he was then doing most of his business. I settled into the rented house in Brentwood, where life took on—even at the time—the quality of a blurred movie, with the sound distant and out of sync.

What I remember most about this time was a lot of going on about Clark Gable. It began getting around Hollywood that I'd left Howard. For Clark, this was the signal to thrust his beautiful face onto the scene once again. It was all very basic for Clark: if I wasn't going to be married to Howard, I might as well be seeing him. Clark knew about Leland, but it didn't deter him. And while Leland was in New York, Clark proceeded to wine and dine me. My evenings with Clark were innocent enough, but they kept Leland on edge. The more he suspected something, the more frequently he'd call, and, if I was out, he'd grill the housekeeper.

One evening Leland's jealousy reached maniacal proportions. Clark and I had been out for dinner and afterwards I asked him in for a drink. Leland kept telephoning every fifteen minutes saying, "Where have you been? What are you doing? Who's there?" He was firing the questions so rapidly I wouldn't consider answering him, and he was calling so often Clark and I couldn't have much of a conversation.

When it seemed that Leland would continue this barrage of phone calls forever, Clark finally said, "This is just crazy. Are you sure you're in love with this man?"

"Yes, I am," I said.

"Well, good luck. Great. I'm delighted. I hope you're getting it right," Clark said, and he got up and left.

With that, Leland called again. "You were not alone. I *know* you were not alone."

"I might as well have been, with all those telephone calls. You've got to calm down."

Leland said he would, and he did, but Clark stayed in my life a bit longer all the same. I knew I was very much in love with Leland, and I felt about Clark the way I had in 1945—I was in love with the idea of Clark Gable, with the attention he was lavishing on me, but never with Clark himself. In the end, I was merely fond of him and wanted to keep him in my life as a friend. I always think you can do that with a man, but you really can't.

I didn't know that then, not nearly. In fact, since I'd been completely honest with both Leland and Clark, I saw no reason why we *all* couldn't be friends. After Kitty and I moved to New York to be with Leland, Clark came through town on his way to Europe. I decided to introduce him to Leland. I thought they'd get on famously, and I'd have two wonderful escorts for an evening out, although I'd had ample warning that this was not my best idea. In private, Leland called Clark "the Kewpie doll." And Clark referred to Leland as the "Rah-rah boy" because he wore his hair in what was then a college haircut. But I had a ridiculous fantasy; the little girl from nowhere, squired around New York, taken around the world, escorted to the most marvelous places by two incredible men! So I made them take me to dinner at the Colony Restaurant, the Le Cirque of its day.

We were given the premiere table. I sat back to listen, dead sure they were going to hit it off and talk about shooting and hunting and everything masculine and terrific. Well, they never said a word to each other. And to salvage this unforgettable disaster, I had to chatter on like a magpie.

In those days, you didn't go home unless you went to El Morocco first—so, although there was no help for this evening, we went on to El Morocco. The three of us sat down at a table, and naturally the cameras that followed Clark wherever he went started snapping away. The next day, there we were in the paper, Clark Gable and me, and by my other side, a bent hand—Leland's. Leland was furious, but I have to admit, I thought it was funny. Trying to make it better, I said to Leland, "I don't understand why you don't like Clark. He's so nice."

His only reply was, "Silly bastard. I hate all actors."

In this, he was seconded by the well-known actor hater Alfred Hitchcock, who saw the photograph and wired Leland: "Did you send for me?"

Clark, still determined to hook me, asked if I would go to Europe with him. I said, "I can't. Don't you remember that I've got a fella I'm very stuck on?"

"Well, the least you can do is come down to the boat and say goodbye," Clark said.

I had never been on an ocean liner, so I was all for that. In the morning, Clark picked me up and we went to the boat together. And then Slim, the supposedly sophisticated woman of the world, did a truly dumb thing: I walked up the gangplank of the *Queen Mary* with Clark. The press went absolutely ape.

Clark had taken a suite of staterooms. They were filled with friends and service people from MGM. Eventually the others gradually cleared away and just the two of us were left in his sitting room. "You know, you really ought to come with me," Clark said, smiling.

"I just can't," I said. "I don't function like that."

We chatted away about what the future would bring and what it held. It seemed the time to be absolutely definitive. "I think I should tell you exactly what I feel, Clark, which is not only what you know—that I'm in love with Leland Hayward—but that as soon as he's divorced I'm going to marry him."

Clark didn't seem surprised. He didn't carry on. All he said was, "I'm against it, I just think it's all wrong for you."

It was a grown-up scene and not at all mushy, except that the bell that tells you when to get off the boat had long since rung and we hadn't heard it. There was finally a knock at his door, and someone screamed, "All ashore that's going ashore." I tore out of the room, off the boat, down the gangplank, and into the arms of a mass of reporters, who said, "Well? What's going on? What did *he* say? What did *you* say? Are you going to marry Mr. Gable?"

With Clark Gable at El Morocco. The hand at my left elbow belongs to an irate Leland Hayward.

When I caught my breath, I said, "I'm not going to marry anyone, and neither is he, as far as I can make out. We've been friends for a long time, and we simply said goodbye and didn't hear the bell."

I jumped into a waiting car and breathed a sigh of relief, muttering to myself, "Well, at least it's over, he's gone." Later that night, Leland and I returned to our hotel and got into the elevator. In those days the St. Regis evening elevator operators would keep a stack of the next day's *Daily News* on the floor of their elevators. I looked down and there was my face splashed across the front page with the headline: MARY WAITS WHILE SLIM AND CLARK SAY FAREWELL.

Leland was livid. I don't blame him, I would have been, too. I said, "It wasn't like that. It really wasn't like that." And he believed me—I guess—until some weeks later. Just when everything had settled down, Clark sent me a postcard from Europe. This is all he wrote: "You were wonderful."

"Wonderful doing *what?*" Leland demanded.

"I was just wonderful being wonderful."

"Come on, what did you do?"

And once again I said, "I didn't do anything!"

SLIM

Leland said he believed me, but I don't think he really did until Clark returned from Europe and married Lady Sylvia Ashley.

At the end of 1947, Leland and I were able to file for our first decrees. All we had between us and marriage was the obligatory year's wait for the final decree.

Now that we could be together, Leland set us up at 13 Sutton Place in New York, in an adorable house where we waited out the time with Kitty. The place belonged to Miriam Hopkins, and had last been occupied by James Mason, his wife Pam, and five cats. It was right on the river, and on a damp day when the mist rose up off the water, the cat pee would rise up off the carpet.

It was from this house that our life together began to take form. Shortly after we moved in, Leland was scheduled to spend Christmas in Miami with Josh and Nedda Logan. He and Josh were producing *Mister Roberts*, which Josh and Tom Heggen, the author of the novel, had adapted for the stage. The play was finally finished, and—although it was our first Christmas together—Leland was going to Florida to have a working holiday with Josh.

I was desperate to go too, so I deluded my little Kitty into thinking that Christmas was three days ahead of when it really was. Santa Claus came down the chimney on December 22, and we opened the presents and had Christmas dinner. As she wasn't quite two, Kitty didn't know she was being duped. Still, I left New York with a guilty conscience.

My guilt vanished in Florida; this was a Christmas never to be forgotten. Josh went out and bought a little, stringy, balding tree, then sat down at a table with a box of watercolors and scissors and paper and made all the ornaments for the tree—charming little cherubs, Santas, and colored chains. But even as the art proceeded, he and Leland were on the telephone, working on the production. Nedda kept them going with buttermilk borscht and what she called cheap advice, though any advice Nedda ever gave was shrewd and to the point.

There was one ritual that hadn't been observed, and Josh performed it on the night before Christmas. In a terrible place called the Gulf Stream Hotel, he read *Mister Roberts* to us in its entirety. He played all the parts, set the stage in our minds, and permeated the room with tropical ocean heat, oppression, the boredom and tension of life on that beleaguered boat "sailing from tedium to apathy and back again." For me, this was the best performance the play ever had; when it ended, we were all shattered. And we all knew that Leland and Josh had a huge hit.

On this same holiday I saw Josh and Leland each reading a book called *Tales of the South Pacific*. Although they hadn't yet started rehearsals for *Mister Roberts*, they decided to buy the rights to James Michener's book. It felt good to see them with two projects, because they worked so well together and they'd been friends ever since Josh had been a part of the University Players with Maggie Sullavan and Hank Fonda. They were back together in the little clique of their youth. Everyone was so witty and Leland was so loving and success was so much in the air that I enjoyed every minute of it.

We returned to New York after the New Year. It was 1948. We were terribly happy, and we knew that we could go on being happy for a very long time—we were on a big, big roll. New York and the theater unfolded their wonders before me as I was dropped, running at full speed, into Leland's heavily populated playground. He was the best possible guide, and even when the bad times finally came, I still thought of 1948 through 1950 as the golden years, the best, most vibrant years of my life.

Upon our return from Miami, *Mister Roberts* went into rehearsal, with Henry Fonda cast in the title role. And it was a wonderful experience for me simply because it was my introduction to the living stage, which is a love affair I've carried on, without interruption, ever since. I would sit in the theater all day long and watch rehearsals of *Mister Roberts*. I traveled with Leland when the show went to New Haven, Boston, and Philadelphia before the Broadway opening. Wherever it went, it was warmly received, and everyone involved knew this was a big hit.

It was fascinating to watch all those egos operating on twelve cylinders. I always imagined keeping a diary of a single play, any play, beginning with the day it's sealed. Everybody signs the contract, and everybody loves everybody so much! Then you go to everybody's house for dinner, and they all come to your house for dinner, and you're just the best of friends. The rehearsals start, and you're still just the best of friends. But then you get to New Haven, and you're not such good friends. You start hearing things like, "That little sonofabitch upstaged me," or, "He doesn't like his costume, the stupid bastard!" The little hatreds and the little jealousies and the little competitions among the participants multiply. You watch an actor who doesn't like a director begin to carve away at him, and then the wives take the sides of their husbands, and the wives get so they're not talking to each other much, and it becomes a great maelstrom of jealousy and fatigue—until it comes into New York. There's a thick lull of silence between the time you get off the train from New Haven or from Boston until the opening night. If the play is a dud, everyone goes home with their private hates and furies. If it's a hit, everybody loves everyone else again. In the fifteen or so shows that I watched from start to finish, it was always a version of this.

With *Mister Roberts*, there was one pleasure that never changed, and that was watching Henry Fonda work. He was the ultimate professional. He never didn't know his lines, he never fumbled a piece of business, he never forgot a stage direction. And he had range—he could hit every emotion—and, most of all, he made you feel you were watching a man who knew what he was doing and had the confidence to do it right.

For all his poise onstage, Fonda was a loner, with a deep sadness somewhere in him. He was definitely not the sort of man you'd want to go to lunch with if you were expecting good fun and to laugh all the way through. His was a black humor. I remember one of his star turns was a pantomime of seven painless ways to kill a baby.

My most revealing memory of Henry Fonda dates from deep in the run of *Mister Roberts*. His wife Frances Brokaw, from whom he was separated, had had a long history of stops at various places for people who are mentally disturbed; late one night, she killed herself. When we heard about this, at nine in the morning, I asked Leland if there would be a performance that night. "I would think not," he said. "The press will know this, and it's perfectly reasonable if Hank doesn't play." But Hank did. He arrived at the theater on time, walked into his dressing room, put on his makeup and costume, walked onto the stage, and played the performance perfectly. You never could tell what was happening inside of him.

Despite all his travails and marriages, Hank always had a climate of youth. He was lean like a young man, and he moved like one— awkward and graceful at the same time. It was extraordinary to

140

Leland with Henry Fonda at Frankie and Johnny's Steakhouse.

watch him move across the stage within the confines of direction but with total spontaneity, as if he were doing it for the first time.

There was something romantic about him, something still, quiet, old-fashioned—almost Victorian. He treated his profession with such respect that he was treated with equal respect; he really didn't think he was just doing some dumb thing to make a buck. Hank didn't talk about his craft a lot, but he was deadly serious about it. There was no guile in his work, he just came out and did what he was supposed to. A modest genius is the most endearing; of all the actors of that era, I've always thought that Hank was the best.

After the birthing and stunningly successful launch of *Mister Roberts* in February 1948, Leland and Josh began working on *South Pacific*. Again I observed firsthand the evolution of a classic—and again, some of my best memories don't come from the theater itself.

One day after Richard Rodgers and Oscar Hammerstein II had finished most of the score and lyrics, Leland, Mary Martin, her husband and manager Richard Halliday, Josh and Nedda Logan and I went to Connecticut to Dick Rodgers's country house to hear their work-in-progress. Dick played and Oscar sang, and that beautiful score unfolded itself before us. Right then and there, Mary Martin did every song that had been written. It was heartbreaking to hear her sing "Some Enchanted Evening"—and to watch the disappointment on her face when Dick told her it was for her co-star, Ezio Pinza.

This project was unique in that, throughout pre-production and rehearsal, it ran as smooth as glass. The only problem they ever had with the show that I can remember was in the scene where Mary Martin really and truly washes that man right out of her hair. When she finishes it, she comes downstage, right down onto the footlights, and sits on a tin can and sings "I'm in Love with a Wonderful Guy." By now the audience cared so deeply about Mary that people worried about her catching cold in her wet costume; no one could concentrate on what she was doing. Somebody very practical said, "Have you ever heard of Scotch Guard? If you squirt this stuff on upholstery, the water runs off it like a duck's back." They found some, used it, and thereafter she sat in what looked like a dry costume.

From the beginning, it was clear *South Pacific* would be a big moneymaker. As Moss Hart once said, "The show is doing so well, they're shipping the money in by barge from Boston down the East River." The only person who was uneasy about it in the New Haven days was the show's notorious ass-pincher, Ezio Pinza. He didn't seem to understand that a new musical was inherently different from an old opera—it had never been performed before, and there were bound to be kinks that had to be ironed out. I always thought he was miffed because the audience didn't stop the show after each of his songs and stand up and scream as you do after an aria at the opera.

For Leland, the toughest part of *South Pacific* took place long before the show went on the road. That was negotiating with Dick Halliday, Mary Martin's husband, agent, and career maker. If Mary Martin wanted something, Dick Halliday made sure she got it.

For *South Pacific*, Mary wanted her nurse's uniforms and her khaki uniforms made by Mainbocher, New York's number one designer. They were. They could have been purchased at the PX and

With Mainbocher at the New Haven rehearsal for Call Me Madam.

The curtain comes down on Mary's final performance of South Pacific *in New York.*

The composers, the director, and the producer of South Pacific *presenting a diamond bracelet to Mary Martin on the occasion of her last New York performance as Nellie Forbush.*

altered and would have looked the same, but Dick insisted: "She only feels comfortable in Mainbocher clothes." Mary knew what she wanted, but hated to get it for herself. So she made the snowballs and Dick threw them.

Mary Martin is the only star I've ever known whose sweetness, purity, and naivete are totally genuine. Leland's constant use of profanity used to drive her crazy. She'd tell him, "You've got to straighten up, I just can't listen to this." It was only talk—they adored each other.

I remember once when Mary was doing a play called *Kind Sir*. In that show, she walks on stage to tumultuous applause, sits in a chair, picks up a basket of needlework, takes it out, and starts to stitch. I had taught Mary how to do needlepoint and she was mad for it. She'd sit in her dressing room and do it by the hour. One night I had gotten some canvas and made some needlework of my own that said, "Fuck you!" on it, well aware that Mary's dirtiest word was "plop."

Leland and I stood in the back of the theater that night. When Mary came on, she picked up my needlework, looked at it, made a stitch or two, then folded it up and went on with the scene, steady as a rock. I was so disappointed. She laughed a lot afterwards, and then she lectured me, "Oh, Nan, why do you say those terrible things?"

"So you'll get used to me, dear Mary. I intend to be in your life for a long time." I have been. A long, reassuring time.

With Leland and Mary after the show.

UNLIMITED
PARTNERSHIP

Early in June of 1949 our divorces were final, and without missing a beat, Leland and I got married. The wedding took place on June 10, in Bill and Babe Paley's garden at Kiluna, their estate in Manhasset, Long Island. My stepson, David Hawks, then at Princeton, gave me away. The bride cried. The groom was also seen to mist over.

From our wedding lunch, we hurried to the airport for the plane to Paris and a stay at the Ritz. It was actually my first of many, many trips to Paris I took with Leland—it was also the first time I'd ever been to Europe—and I adored the whole thing. We ate, we drank, we shopped, and I developed my only enduring addiction, to French shoes.

From Paris, we went to Antibes in the South of France for a few days at the Hôtel du Cap with Nedda and Josh Logan and a visit with Marion and Irwin Shaw. Then, with Quique and Louis Jourdan, we moved on to become the impresarios in charge of getting David Selznick married to Jennifer Jones. We were all to board David's chartered English yacht in Antibes, sail to Portofino, then drive to Genoa for the marriage. To this first-time traveler, it prom-

Wedding #2. June 10, 1949. L. to r.: The bride, the groom, David Hawks, who gave me away, the Justice of the Peace, Barbara Paley, Leonora Hornblow, John Menari, and Jeanne Vanderbilt.

Wedding lunch.

In France. Self-explanatory. (Photo by Leland Hayward)

ised to be a glamorous, languorous trip, with nothing to do but bask
in luxury.

Having been put in charge of the food for the boat trip, I'd gone
to a marvelous restaurant called Felix au Port in Antibes and bought
every regional delicacy. Unfortunately, the chef on the yacht turned
out to be English—and so untalented he couldn't sling hash in a
diner. I wasn't aware of that when he asked what we'd like for
the first night out. Innocently, I suggested the standing rib roast,
which we could then finish off for lunch the following day. The look
on his face read, "What's this dreadful American talking about?"
Ignoring me, he proceeded to boil the beef until it was dark gray
and inedible. I told David, "This is never going to do. As much
as I know how to run a kitchen, I can't run this man. He's just
awful."

But the cook's intransigence was a metaphor for the behavior of
the bride-to-be. Despite the ghastly meal, we all sat out on the stern
after dinner in the romance of moonlight, light-years from the world
of movies and theater. Jennifer, at the peak of one of those magical
moments, suddenly asked, "David, why are we doing this?"

UNLIMITED PARTNERSHIP

I said, "What are you saying?"

She said, "Well, we're perfectly happy the way we are. I don't know why we're getting married."

I said, "You're getting married because you've gotten four friends to come out on this rotten boat and sail to Genoa, and by God you're getting married! We're not going to let you out of it!"

Jennifer held her ground, and the air was soon rent with the sound of four people shrieking, "You cannot do this!" David said nothing. He only sat there, looking puzzled.

We arrived at Portofino in the wee hours of the morning, and the boat was too big to bring into the port itself, so it was anchored outside the harbor. The next morning, when we awoke and looked out the porthole, we were totally surrounded by little putt-putt boats, all filled with pink oleanders and cameramen. This was no encouragement to Jennifer, who decided her safety lay in spending the rest of her life in her stateroom. To get her off that boat and onto dry land was not easy. We had to sneak her down the other side of the boat, put her in a speedboat that was faster than any of

Honeymoon in Antibes with Irwin and Marion Shaw.

the press boats, and skim off to the hotel in Rapallo where David had taken six rooms.

During the night, as we traveled by sea, Jennifer's maid, chauffeur, and all her dresses traveled by land. By the time we arrived in Portofino, they were hung up all around her room—so many dresses that I had to ask, "What are they for?"

Jennifer, who'd been standing on her head doing her yoga, eased herself to the floor. "I'm going to get married in one of them," she said.

"One would have been enough."

"Well, I can't make up my mind which one I want to wear, so I brought them all. What are *you* going to wear?"

"It doesn't matter what I wear, it's your wedding," I said. "Whatever you wear, I'll wear something that looks dull and dim beside it."

"I think I'll wear that one."

She put her favorite on. It looked just wrong for the occasion.

There are moments to keep your mouth shut. This wasn't one of them.

"No, I don't like it," I told her. "Take it off. Give it to the maid." When her choice was finally made and she was dressed, she looked so young and damp and beautiful. One forgave her everything.

Like all brides, Jennifer had to have something old, something new, something borrowed, and something blue. Leland had given me, for a wedding present, a marvelous sapphire. I was crazy about it. It was new to me, old to God, blue and ripe for borrowing; it filled all the requirements. So I said, "Wear my ring, Jenny. It will bring both of our marriages good luck."

Jennifer put my ring on, and we started a hair-raising, white knuckle journey by car to Genoa, a trip so terrifying that Edmund Hillary wouldn't have attempted it. We arrived at the City Hall in Genoa and were met by wonderful little Italian officials—all played by Henry Armetta—who were about waist-high and wearing ribbons with a bow on the side. The service was translated, with a lot of help and a lot of laughs. There's a phrase in the Italian service that calls for the bride to support her husband if he comes upon hard times. I kept saying, "Don't agree to that!" We were all having hysterics, behaving very poorly. David, on the other hand, took it most seriously. After the ceremony, he did the most amazing thing.

Leland. (Photo by Richard Avedon)

He sent a cablegram to the ex-Mrs. Selznick, which just said: "Mrs. Irene Selznick, Pierre Hotel, New York. David."

Irene later described receiving that cable. She called the telegraph company and said, "I've got a cable here, but all it says is David. Where's the rest of the message?" "Why, that's all there is, madam," they told her. The cable didn't turn out to be all that unusual given David's friendship with Irene: his regard for her never diminished throughout his life.

After David and Jenny's marriage, Leland and I traveled throughout Europe, then returned to New York so Leland could begin work on the production of Garson Kanin's play *Rat Race*. It turned out to be a flop. Unfortunately, it was the first of four back-to-back failures. It wasn't until 1950 that Leland regained his stride with *Call*

SLIM

Me Madam, leading off a decade that included such hits as *Gypsy,*
Peter Pan, and, finally, *The Sound of Music,* which is where I made
my exit. After that—coincidentally, I'm sure—Leland never had a
hit again.

I've always thought the key to his run of success was a result of
three things. First was Leland's marvelous taste in material. Second
was his love of every aspect of show business. Then there was his
personality, the glue for the other two. And, of course, there was
the advantage of vast experience in show business.

Leland's talent as an agent—his genius in the control and handling of some very idiosyncratic people—was enormously helpful
when he decided to become a producer. He had a knack for putting
the right people together and for using them to get his projects off
the ground. That kind of talent makes everyone in the room feel
safe and essential and enthusiastic. It was as if Leland came in with
a squirt gun of confidence and sprayed it around the room.

In the end, though, what we're talking about is personality. If he
couldn't get what he wanted by his wits, he made damn sure he got
it by his charm. He was by no means devious, unless you weren't
smart enough to know that he was conning you. But then, a lot of
people are pretty dumb. And Leland was a fairly subtle man.

A prime example of his technique was when he'd bought the
rights to *The Old Man and the Sea.* He wanted Spencer Tracy to do
the film, but Spence thought it was the most ridiculous idea to make
a movie about a fish—and judging by the way that film turned out,
Spence was right. But Leland managed to convince Spence to mistrust his own instincts and sign on.

When he was turning the charm on, Leland was blasphemous,
direct, and relentless—but always amusing and stylish. His meth-
ods never evoked the toughness or coldness that is often associated
with other people in the same business. Those people he could
generally beat. What challenged him were men of his own kind,
actors and agents as dogged and clever as he was. They'd say,
"Leland, I'm not going to buy this. I don't care what you say." In
his most arrogant tone, Leland would shoot back, "What do you
mean, you're not going to buy it? Who's *selling* you anything?
What's happening is that you're walking out on six million dollars,
you fool."

Underneath that bravura and expertise, though, was enormous

anxiety about his serious, life-shaking problems—two very, very disturbed children, and his own medical troubles. I always agreed with Dr. Chaffin that his undiagnosable bleeding came from strain: a compilation of handling other people's lives, maintaining his own, earning a living, supporting his children, and all the time, underneath that fizz and bombast, longing to be an artist. If the word "tragic" can be applied to a man as successful as Leland Hayward, it was that he had the desire but not the vehicle or the voice to do creative work.

He did vicariously, I suppose, feel a sense of creation when he brought a script or an idea to fruition. But he wanted to be a stage director, and said that to very few people. He never got his wish. I used to give him long, elaborate lectures: "What you do, you do better than anybody else. And you must (a) take satisfaction from that, and (b) regard it as a valid artistic contribution."

Leland heard me, but he couldn't put his dream away. Once, when he was doing an adaptation of John Marquand's book *Point of No Return*, he had to fire the director, Henry Potter. He hired Elia Kazan to come in and doctor the production, but Gadge couldn't get there for a couple of days—and so Leland finally had his chance to direct. I'd like to tell you that he was wonderful, that he blossomed and became the man he so badly wanted to be, but all he really was was *active*. He was on that stage, he was running back and forth, he was sitting in the back of the house, in the front of the house, he was directing the bejesus out of it. I don't think he hurt it, but he did not improve it.

Among other impediments to Leland's directing hopes was the way he talked, which was at eighty miles an hour and with all the subjects dropped out of his sentences. He clipped his adjectives, and replaced them with blasphemy. If Leland had an appointment at a church, it came out like this: "Have to go to that goddamned church!" Every second word was "goddamn" or "sonofabitch." He'd talk about the most benign, pleasant thing and manage to swear. It was almost a speech defect.

For all his charm and smarts and profanity, Leland was no bully. The Henry Potter firing, for example. It took him about three days to get up the guts to do it. I said, "When are you going to tell him?" Leland said, "After lunch." He paused. "Or maybe we'll have a drink before dinner."

He would have been happier to fire the poor man on the telephone. Leland loved phones, and was never better than when he was on one. He'd say, "I know that's a good part, but it's not as good as the other part and that's what I want you to do. You will be so sen-sa-tional you'll break their goddamn hearts." He had calls planned out long before he made them. He knew how to convince his victims that the part they hadn't wanted was really the part they'd wanted all along.

Mary Martin once made a needlepoint portrait of Leland and me. We're each sitting on a stool, and I'm sewing, and there's a long thread that comes from my sewing that turns into a telephone cord which is connected to a telephone held by Leland. She got it exactly right. Though he was better in person, he had a compulsion to talk on the phone. If we were making a trip somewhere and the airplane would stop to refuel, he'd run into the airport and make four phone calls.

Leland's other need was for sleep. He'd hibernate, like an animal, for days. We'd go to the country for a weekend, and he'd go to bed on Friday night and get up on Monday morning. He would sleep for six hours, get up and drink a quart of milk and go back to sleep for eight hours, drink some more milk and go back to sleep again. He always said he was "banking" the sleep: "That's sleep I have forever, and when I can't have sleep, I'll use that." This point of view worked for him, because he had a lot of stamina when working.

Even when he produced a dog—like *Remains to Be Seen*, *The Prescott Proposals*, and *Daphne Laureola*—his enthusiasm and staying power never flagged. Curiously, he was more badly affected by his hits. With a hit, he was terribly happy on the way to it, during the birthing, but he was always very, very depressed after it was open and acclaimed and solid and there. It was like postpartum depression.

Another eccentricity: he was a fanatic about his food. In the thousand times he went to the Colony for lunch, he ordered an omelette every single day. And every day he'd say to the waiter, "Not too soft, not too soft," waving a finger that had been broken so it pointed out. Of equal importance was having the same table every day, set for him with a bottle of Wild Turkey so he could pour his own.

Photograph by Cecil Beaton that was published in Vogue.

A man whose days are this high-powered and nervous-making generally carries around some exotic quirks as well. Leland did, anyway. When he left his office at 655 Madison, the first thing he'd do was look up and down the sidewalk pavement, checking for rattlesnakes. He wouldn't swim in the sea: "Think of the things that might be in there!" And then there was his method of getting to sleep.

Invariably, it began with a long debriefing, the news of the day in review. And not just the business news—Leland could do forty-five minutes on how beautiful Mona Williams looked at lunch in her sable coat. Then there was the information so hot he'd say, "I can't tell you who told me this." I'd say, "What if I guess?" "Well, then, maybe I can." "How many guesses do I get?" And we'd carry on like two children.

Or, if Leland read a book that he thought was good, he'd want to share it. I remember him bringing *Catcher in the Rye* home when it was first published. He read a bit, laughed, and said, "Here, read this." And we began to read back and forth to one another. Those were memorable moments.

Did we ever fight? Yes. Our differences were about other people; our biggest disagreement during our happy years was that I always felt Leland was watching me to see if I was going to make a move toward someone else. He was very jealous. And he had some reason to be. I am by nature very open and outgoing and flirtatious. I flirt with dogs, I flirt with plants, I flirt with anything that has life in it. And a lot of things that don't—like pearls. And that flirting used to drive him crazy.

On my side, I was jealous of women from his past. I cared so much about Leland that once, in "21," he only mentioned Katharine Hepburn's name and I threw a cup of *marron glacé* in his face. On our honeymoon, he brought up Greta Garbo—who was one of the girls on his scalp bracelet—and was rewarded with a glass of champagne in the puss. I could never bring myself to watch Fay Wray in *King Kong*.

Every evening we would talk or read for about an hour and a half. We never ran out of subjects for conversation; we never came to that grinding halt where you sit and look at each other and say nothing.

Along with the gossip was the bedtime snack. We had a table set up in the bedroom with all kinds of cereal and a Thermos filled with ice-cold milk so that we could have a bowlful before we went to sleep. Or rather, before Leland played mental baseball, which was his substitute for counting sheep. In these games, Leland starred at every position, excelling at both offense and defense. In the morning, I'd ask, "Who won?" And he'd say, "I did, I had a home run." When you're in charge of things, you can do that, can't you? But there were bad nights, too, when he couldn't strike anybody out or he'd get hit by a wild pitch.

These games worked for Leland. Nothing worked for me, but he was always there to help me with my insomnia. If I was jumpy, he would get up and distract me by baking bread. That would take all night. Naturally, I would then become sleepy—and there he'd be waiting for the bread to rise for the third time as I slipped into dreamland. Leland was never angry about it. For him, the focus was on me. It was as if I was his best client. Certainly, I was his most grateful one.

Leland understood me. His analysis was sound, accurate, and very helpful. He once said, "I can't call you 'Slim' because you really aren't. That's an invention. It's a brilliant one. You've made it up, you make it work, you've *become* that in a way, but you're really Nan. You're quite a different person than you appear to be in public. It's true of most of us, but much more so of you because you're such a successful invention."

Who was Nan? She was the lady who cared about what he ate, who saw that his bed was properly turned down, who snuggled with him and loved him. She was perishable, sometimes illogical, and she could be a pain in the ass a lot of the time—but she was, first and last, his wife.

LIFE WITH
LELAND

Sometimes you get such a long run of good fortune that you think luck has your home number. In the brightness of 1951, Leland and I bought a house from Eddy Duchin's widow, in Manhasset, Long Island. Here, I felt, I would create a home where Kitty and Leland, who had become her father figure and who adored her, could flourish. Here, we would entertain the brightest, most interesting people. We would have a house from which we'd travel to exotic places. And, because Leland's work was so relentless, we'd make a retreat where he could recharge.

As it turned out, a retreat was very much what we needed. In the first three years of our marriage I'd had several miscarriages. The problem was my Rh negative blood—every time I conceived, the chance that I'd carry the child to full term decreased. Still, Leland and I were desperate to have our own child and for Kitty to have a sibling. I especially wanted a son; I'd adored my male stepchildren, and, going way back, I'd never got over missing my brother.

The last of these pregnancies was the most traumatic. My doctor had told me it was a ninety-nine to one chance that the child would be born. I decided to take the chance. Seven months later, the baby

Gardening with Kitty in Manhasset. (Photo by Leland Hayward)

died in my womb; the doctors had to deliver it by cesarean section. The day after the operation, a nurse came into my room and said, "You have to sign the death certificate for your male child." She might as well have thrust a knife in my heart and twisted it. It took me a long time to level off after this pregnancy. Once I'd recuperated, I went back to the doctor for a check-up. He did a Pap smear, it came up positive—back I went to the hospital for a biopsy. To this day I don't know whether they found cancer or not, but they gave me a hysterectomy to be on the safe side.

I was a mess. It took me a long time to recover to the point where I didn't cry if I saw a baby in a pram. It would have made more sense to simply be thankful for the miracle of my healthy, enormously bright, beautiful daughter.

My unhappiness with my inability to give Leland a child reached maniacal proportions when Jimmy Stewart's wife Gloria gave birth to twins. She had been medically mishandled and became gravely ill after the birth. There was a point when we thought Gloria was going to die, and as Leland was an old and dear friend of Jimmy's, I began to think that if she did, Leland and I could have the babies. It didn't occur to me that Jimmy would naturally keep the twins himself, so cuckoo was I at the time.

What brought me out of this crisis was the vast network of good and caring friends Leland and I made together. This cast couldn't

Louis Jourdan cooking in my kitchen in Manhasset. (Photo by Leland Hayward)

Me advising
Bernard
Baruch at home
in Manhasset.
(Photo by
Leland Hayward)

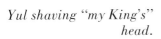

Yul shaving "my King's"
head.

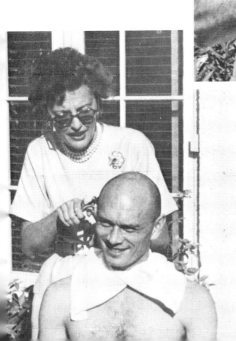

My turn.

have been more lively. During the week, we lived in our New York apartment and had Leland's showbiz life. We saw a lot of Nedda and Josh Logan—a manic depressive, Josh was marvelous when crazy, not so marvelous when he wasn't; at those times, Nedda should have been sainted for putting up with him. And Garson Kanin and Ruth Gordon, a set piece—they did their act long after the curtain dropped. And Mary Martin and Dick Halliday—she was as sweet offstage as on, and he had dedicated his life to preserving that. Richard and Dorothy Rodgers—we called her "El Perfecto" because of her preoccupation with tidiness. And Oscar and Dorothy Hammerstein, one of the world's most enduringly romantic couples.

On weekends, we went to Manhasset, where we led a totally different life with a different cast of people—Betsy and Jock Whitney, Jeanne and Alfred Vanderbilt, Tex McCrary and Jinx Falkenberg, and always, city or country, Bill and Babe Paley.

Bill Paley and Leland had been close friends long before Bill had married Babe and I'd met Leland. I first met Babe shortly before Leland and I were married; Bill had called Leland to invite us out to the country for lunch because he wanted me to meet Barbara. This first meeting proved to be quite a shock. In those days I was very sure of myself. But when we arrived at Kiluna Farm, I took one look at Barbara Paley and thought, "Well, Slim, you're not number one, she is."

I'm not by nature a competitive person. Even if I were, I couldn't help but like Barbara, she was just so marvelous. We eventually became the Paleys' neighbors in Manhasset; from there, Babe became the best woman friend I've ever had. She possessed all the qualities that one looks for in a female friend—totally trustworthy, kind, thoughtful, and funny. I admired her more than any woman I've known, on every level. And I learned a tremendous amount from her about character, goodness, kindness, manners—hers were the best of anyone's—and taste. Babe wasn't as smart as my friend Irene Selznick, few people are, and she wasn't as provocative as some other women I've known, but all round Babe Paley was the *best* woman I've known.

It's a little hard to describe Babe and her astounding beauty without sounding silly. She had an aura around her. It was as if she were inside a bubble and everything in that bubble was perfect. But that was just the impression she gave, it wasn't the woman she

In the Adriatic on board Alexander Korda's yacht Elsewhere. *Alexander Korda, Bill Paley, and Graham Greene. (Photo by Leland Hayward)*

really was. Babe was in fact very perishable, shy, and unsure of herself. Like truly remarkable women, she didn't believe who she was or what she was for one minute.

I remember taking a five-week trip along the Dalmatian coast on Alexander Korda's yacht with Babe and Bill. I watched her on this trip in total awe. In my experience, no matter how attractive people may be, they usually look pretty rotten on boats. Babe was the exception. She looked more beautiful each day. Her makeup was always perfect, her hair was unaffected by wind and salt, and her clothes were never wrinkled. How she did it I'll never know. But that was Babe.

Babe died in 1978, leaving a circle of friends to watch over Bill. And watch over him we do. I look at this darling eighty-odd-year-old man I've known almost all of my adult life, and he'll say, "Ohhh, Slim-girl, I have backaches. I'm an old fart." And I'll say, "Not to me you're not. You're my beautiful Paley and you'll always be and I love you and where does it hurt? Should we get the doctor?"

The Paley I know has many new friends and thinks totally in future terms. At age eighty-eight, he tells me with great energy that he's about to start a new garden. And he does. He involves himself in long-range planning for the Museum of Broadcasting, and then he merrily goes about implementing those plans.

The Paley I know is not, apparently, the same man who ran CBS. There he could be ice-cold, even ruthless. I'm told that when he was at the top of his stride professionally, to follow a negotiation between him and Lew Wasserman was like going to the most dangerous bullfight ever seen. Two bloodless killers trying to outnegotiate one another. And, of course, there are the endless stories about the hell he put his underlings through.

Once, I told him I'd made up a joke. "A man comes home from the office. And he's silent, moody, depressed. His wife says, 'What the hell is the matter with you?' He says, 'I don't want to discuss it.' She says, 'Well, you can't go through the evening like this, you have to tell me what it is.' And he says, 'Well, all right, I will. I've just been made president of CBS.'" Which means he has the job for a month, because Bill kept changing presidents; every year there was somebody new. Paley did not laugh. He said, "Don't you ever tell that to anybody again as long as you live!" As you can see, I haven't.

Barbara and me pretending to play chess at my house in Manhasset.
(Photo by Leland Hayward)

With Bill and Babe
in Honolulu. (Photo
by Leland Hayward)

That's about the only time I ever saw him angry. To me, he's been kind, he's been a friend, he's made me laugh, we've had fun together. He's a man of impeccable manners, without being condescending or precious. And he has something that very few people I've ever known have—a zest, a real enthusiasm for everything. For everything he eats, everything he sees, every girl who walks into the room.

In those heady days of the fifties, Bill and Babe were a golden couple who loved to entertain. So did Leland and I. Babe and I worked it out: Saturday night was her night, Sunday night was mine. Her evenings were rather grand, while mine were much schleppier, more relaxed—a long table with a row of bottles of wine running down the middle, and everybody screaming and laughing. The cast of characters on those Sunday nights was a delightful mixture of our different lives. There would be our Long Island neighbors, and then there would be Kitty and Moss Hart, or Harry Kurnitz, the screenwriter and playwright, or Rex Harrison and his then wife, the English actress and skyrocket of a girl, Kay Kendall.

Kay always supported my theory of entertaining. That is, the greatest compliment you can give your guests is to serve them what you like the most yourself. If you love brisket of beef or corn beef hash, that's what it should be. You shouldn't have a standing rib roast with carved radishes just because there are guests for dinner. Your friends should be treated as though they're part of your family.

Kay Kendall and Rex Harrison on their wedding day in my garden in Manhasset. (Photo by Leland Hayward)

OPPOSITE:
Babe, perfect on the Elsewhere. (Photo by Leland Hayward)

In Kay's case, I always served the same thing whenever she came for dinner: smoked salmon with hot boiled potatoes served in their skins with hickory salt, and two small dishes on either side, one of sour cream and the other marinated raw onions. Kay would eat this dish for the first course, the main course, and for dessert.

The 1950s also brought me some other rewarding friendships, some enduring, some not. Irving "Swifty" Lazar, that all-purpose agent to stars in every category, was one of the fixtures. I've entertained him, I've traveled with him, he's looked after me during troubled times. He'd been around since the days of my marriage to Howard Hawks and the East-West Croquet Tournaments.

Swifty was there for the laughs, but he stayed around for the dark times as well. What I remember, though, are our trips together—particularly the trip to the Feria of San Ysidro in Madrid with Truman Capote, the writer Peter Viertel and his girlfriend Bettina Graziani, and Marion and Irwin Shaw. The best part of that trip was going for the weekend to the finca of Luis Domínguin, the great bullfighter hero of the day. His wife Lucia had arranged the sleeping quarters, and Swifty's bedroom was to be across the hall from Leland and me.

Swifty Lazar is the biggest germ freak who ever lived. Whenever he travels, he always covers the floor of his hotel rooms with bath towels. So when we arrived at the Domínguins' finca, Swifty's first task was the ritual sterilization of his quarters. He called the maid and gave her a great many pesetas to bring him ten towels, which he laid in a tidy path from his bed to his bathroom. He then cleaned the entire room with Lysol, which he always carries with him. Then he joined us at dinner, which began at one o'clock in the morning and went on for what seemed like six years. There were flamenco dancers at 3:00 a.m., we were all dancing at four, by five I'd had it. I announced that I was going to bed. This reminded Sra. Domínguin of something. "Oh, Truman, I've switched you to the room that Irving was in," she said. "I've put him in your room." At that, Swifty realized he had to do another entire scrubdown. A terrible blow as the sun was rising.

Time has not made Irving less fastidious. A few years ago we were driving out to Southampton, Long Island, together. We were about twenty miles outside of Manhattan with a good two hours to go when I looked over at him. He was the color of putty. I said,

*Peter Viertel (left) and
Luis Miguel Dominguín
at the Finca Dominguín.*

Swifty Lazar in Mexico.

*At the Feria in Madrid with
the cuff links, Truman
and Swifty. (Photo
by Leland Hayward)*

"Are you all right?"

"Yes, yes, yes," he said, "but is there a hospital nearby?"

As it happened, we were near Manhasset, so I knew there was. I told the chauffeur how to get there. I didn't know what the hell was going on, whether he was having a heart attack or what. I kept holding his hand, repeating, "Are you all right?"

"Yes, I'm *fine*."

"Well, why are we going to the hospital?"

"I want to go to the *bathroom*."

"What about a gas station?"

"I won't go in a gas station."

"That's what everybody else does."

"Well, that's why I won't," he said.

As it turned out we got hopelessly lost and couldn't find the goddamned hospital. I told the driver to get back on the highway and head for the nearest gas station. When we stopped, Irving got out, went in, and came right back.

"There was water right up to my ankles! I couldn't stay in there. I'm going across the street."

Now, to cross the highway was to take your life totally in your hands. He went into a Szechuan restaurant across the highway and didn't come out for a long time. I finally said to the chauffeur, "You know, I'm worried about him. If he doesn't come in five minutes, I want you to go over there and find him."

Just then, Irving came sauntering out and crossed the road as though God had parted the way.

I said, "What the hell were you doing?"

"Well, I didn't think it was right to just go in and pee. So I had a whiskey with the owner first."

But of all the people I met in those years, only one became indispensable to me—and still is, forty years after we met; he is my closest friend in the world. The first time I ever saw Jerome Robbins, I was sitting in the darkened cavern of the Shubert Theater in New Haven at a rehearsal for *Call Me Madam*. That day the company was working on one of the dance numbers Jerry had choreographed. It had to do with a beribboned band of mad, headstrong Gypsies coming down out of the mountains of Graustarkia to perform at a fête that Madam Ambassador—played by Ethel Merman—was giving for the visiting senators who had come to look over her post.

LIFE WITH LELAND

Jerome Robbins.
(Photo by Leland Hayward)

The number involved a sort of wild folk dance, the stage seething with yards of colorful skirts and lace petticoats, wimples, babushkas, garlands of fake flowers, and tambourines. On cue, they all came scurrying in and whirled about like dervishes. The finale required a young man in tights, a full-sleeved blouse, and a jerkin to swing a great bird-like construction on a string around the circle of dancers. The whirling animal looked like an out-of-work bat with a glandular problem. As the dancer twirled the string around his head like a lariat, the bird flew at great speed over the heads of all the dancers and, by some miracle, eventually came to earth without decapitating any of them. The whole scene made for a confusion on stage as though someone had just yelled, "Fire!"

The number was a dog. Jerry knew it, everyone watching the rehearsal knew it, and it was mercifully cut from the show. But if the dance number died, the bird lived on.

I acquired the dreaded fowl through a circuitous route and a bit of skulduggery. The thing was made of wire and silk and paint and streamers. It weighed about ten pounds and had a five-foot wingspan—an unwieldy creature indeed. I arranged to have it bedecked in flowers and delivered to Jerry as his opening-night present.

But Jerry felt it was too good for him; he soon gave it back to me. I was unworthy of it; I presented it to him once again. In this way,

171

Absorbed in our own thoughts. (Photo by Leland Hayward)

it was exchanged back and forth for a long time. I got it for my birthday. He got it back for Christmas. When *Peter Pan* opened, I took a bit from the play in which Peter confuses kisses with buttons. With my own hands, I sewed a thousand buttons all over that bird and it went back to him. He sent it back to me covered in pearls.

Finally, I got a letter from Jerry saying, "The bird must die. I'm sick of it, and you must be sick of it." I agreed. The poor thing was retired to the cellar and eventually lost. I believe our friendship was in some way cemented by this silly bird. It was the recognition of similar humor, which for me is always a prerequisite for any friendship.

We saw a lot of one another when Leland was producing *Call Me Madam*, and as time went on we became good friends and then close friends. To this day, he is closer to me than any man or woman in my life. Trusting people has always been hard for me; deep down I'm wary of others. I've spent a lot of time in my life with professionals, trying to overcome this problem or to at least figure out why it exists. Once my dear friend, the eminent psychiatrist Shervert Frazier, asked if there was anyone in the world I trusted. I replied without a pause, "Yes, Jerome Robbins. I would trust him to the end of the earth."

Perhaps it is Jerry's obsessive need for privacy that makes me feel so secure. Or his ability to sit quietly and listen to one's troubles and fears and terrors without overreacting or preaching. He's able to hear every word you say, he equates the truth with the condition, and then he comes back with short little bits of advice, without shooting you into a pulp. And his advice is almost always right. He makes astonishingly accurate observations of situations and people. He sees truth, but always with a sort of twinkle which puts pretension right out of business. But better than the advice is the sense of

The rudiments of ballet with the master, Jerome Robbins. (Photo by Leland Hayward)

love that he gives, whether you're right or wrong. He loves you for how you are.

For all the wonderful friends I saw, and the good times, and the trips, I never measured my life during these years by what I was doing. I told time by the projects Leland was working on. To his first love, which was the theater, he was, in the early 1950s, adding the movies. Here again he started at the top. His film properties included *Mister Roberts, The Spirit of St. Louis,* and *The Old Man and the Sea.*

The genesis of this last film, as it so often is, was a personal

Hemingway's original "Old Man" (center).

An evening at the Stork Club. Clockwise: James Stewart, Gloria Stewart, Leland, Frank Sinatra, Lew Wasserman, Ginger Rogers, Dennis O'Keefe, and reflected in the mirror is Carol Saroyan Matthau.

relationship—in this case, my friendship with Ernest Hemingway. And it all started innocently enough. In 1952, Leland and I went to Cuba for a vacation, and while we were there, Ernest very shyly asked me to read the manuscript of his latest novel.

The Old Man and the Sea was originally meant to be the coda to what Ernest called "the Big Book." The coda had been in typescript for a year, but he wasn't at all sure what should be done with it—it was short, and different—and so he hadn't shown it to Scribner's, his publishers. He hadn't, he said, shown it to a lot of people either, but he wanted me to take a look at it.

Once I had gotten over the initial flattery, I sat down to read it. And was undone. So, in a different way, was Leland. He didn't know Hemingway very well, and was a little astonished that I'd been given the privilege of reading this unpublished manuscript. As I sat in the corner of our room at the National Hotel in Havana, he gradually moved closer. Soon he was leaning over my shoulder. We read in silence, non-stop, and when we were finished, we looked at one another and shivered—I mean, there was no doubt that we had just read a masterpiece.

"He's crazy to sit on this," I said.

"Yes, but I understand his worry," Leland said. "You don't just throw this into the stores. You want to . . . *present* it."

This gave me an idea. "It should be published—in its entirety—in one issue of *The New Yorker* like John Hersey's *Hiroshima*."

"No," Leland said, with a look of excitement that told me, before he could say anything, that he was going to top me. "*Life* should publish it in one issue—with illustrations."

I knew that Leland, through his connections, was capable of making this happen. So did Ernest, who loved the idea from another angle: it meant money, which he always needed, and it meant that approximately five million people would be reading him at one time. So he gave Leland the go-ahead.

But Leland wasn't finished with *The Old Man and the Sea* once he'd arranged the sale to *Life*, and seen its unusual publication assure its enormous success. He wanted more of it—he wanted the movie rights. By this time, Ernest so respected Leland that he was more than happy to sell him the property. In the early stages of Leland's negotiations with Ernest, the movie wasn't to happen immediately. The original plan, which was mine, was for Spencer Tracy to do a reading of the book from a bare stage. He would play in a series of one-night stands across the country in much the same way that Charles Laughton was doing Shaw's *Don Juan in Hell*. Leland thought this would generate enthusiasm for the film that followed. But the stage reading never came about—Spencer was frightened to death of acting in that arena.

As he was putting together the film of *The Old Man and the Sea*, Leland had the wheels going for a movie version of *Mister Roberts*. He was also trying to secure the movie rights, with Billy Wilder, to Charles Lindbergh's autobiography, *The Spirit of St. Louis*. The big stumbling block that confronted this venture was Lindbergh, who, for reasons we all know, was a man who avoided publicity at any cost and was impossible to reach.

At this point in my life my doctor was Dana Atchley, the number one internist at Columbia Presbyterian Hospital in New York, if not in all of America. A marvelous, sensitive, and reassuring man, Dana had in time become a close friend as well. As it happened, he was also a close friend of Anne Morrow Lindbergh. I suggested to Leland that if he appealed to Dana to put the idea to Mrs. Lindbergh, she might be able to persuade her husband to see Leland. The prescription worked. Lindbergh agreed to meet Leland in New

*With
my doctor,
Dana Atchley.*

Haven in, of all places, a little Italian restaurant. He wanted the
meeting to be as inconspicuous as possible.

The only people who knew about the meeting were Leland and
me. We went to the restaurant at the appointed time and in walked
Charles Lindbergh. He was quiet, alert, and older than I thought
he would be. Although he didn't seem enthusiastic about a film
being made from his book, he didn't flinch when Leland suggested
that he come to California and meet with Billy Wilder.

Those who know the curiosities of Los Angeles know that public
transportation is generally to be avoided. Lindbergh didn't know
Los Angeles, but he wasn't fazed by a little inconvenience. He took
the streetcar from Pasadena, where he was staying, to meet with
Billy Wilder in Beverly Hills. The streetcar deposited him at the
bottom of Beverly Drive on Santa Monica Boulevard; from there, he
walked the six blocks to Billy's house. But Lindbergh's approach to
everything public was conducted like that. He became so anony-
mous he was almost invisible.

In any case, a deal was struck. As 60 percent of Lindbergh's book
takes place in the confinement of his plane's cockpit, it was essential for Billy Wilder to see the aircraft, which was in the Smithson-
ian Institution, hanging like a dead bird from the ceiling.

For the purposes of Billy's research, a scaffolding had been built,

177

along with a stairway and platform leading to the aircraft itself. I went with Billy and Leland on the day that Charles Lindbergh was showing them the plane. Billy walked up to take the first look. Leland followed. Then Lindbergh turned to me and said, "Would you like to see it?" I nodded enthusiastically and was escorted up to the platform by the aviation hero himself.

The door of the aircraft was open. You could look in and see the instrument panel, which was about as complicated as the dashboard of a Model T Ford. The seat in which Lindbergh had sat for those long hours across the Atlantic was a sort of wicker beach chair with the legs sawed off so that he was, in effect, sitting on the base of the fuselage itself. There were controls, a joy stick in front of the seat, and a safety belt—the most minimal sort of equipment, which brought home even more vividly the size of this man's accomplishment. He'd flown across the ocean astride the wind as though he was a bird. No radar. No radio.

After a few moments, Lindbergh stepped inside the plane and sat down in the wicker chair. He reached for the two sides of the seat belt which, when he attempted to lock them, did not meet. He'd obviously become a bigger man, although he was, like me, still called "Slim." Lindbergh looked at the panel in front of him, reached out, and took hold of the button marked "primer." Then he said, entirely to himself, "This is not supposed to be in this position, it should be thrust in." And he very quietly pushed the primer into its proper position.

I could only imagine what he must have been feeling, what memories were going through his mind when he made that almost tender caress of a gesture. I looked away. He got out of the plane, turned his back on it, and we walked down the stairs. It's a moment I think of often.

After Leland had finished negotiating with Lindbergh, he began producing *Peter Pan*. By the summer of 1954, *Peter Pan* was in rehearsal in Los Angeles in preparation for its opening in San Francisco, and so we found ourselves summering at the Bel-Air Hotel. This suited Leland, who was simultaneously making plans to go to Hawaii to film *Mister Roberts*. His workload worried me, but Leland was happy. The important thing, he said, was that so many of his loved ones were under one roof—in addition to Kitty, we had two of Leland's children, Brooke and Billy, spending the summer with us.

On the Normandie *with Kitty. Though she's holding my hand, it is under duress. When we ascended the gangplank Kitty said, "Mother, my little heart is so happy." That was the last sentence she addressed to me for the entire crossing. All communication was made through her governess. (Photo by Leland Hayward)*

Bridget, his other daughter, was in Switzerland in school.

The Hayward children were, on appearance, like storybook children: golden, bright, and alert. Brooke, the eldest, was and still is the most like her father—very sure of herself and capable of charming anything and anyone. She was enormously talented. She could paint, she could draw, and she could write extremely well—as we found out when her autobiography, *Haywire*, was published in 1977 and showed us, in vivid and moving prose, what it was like to grow up as the daughter of two of Hollywood's magnetic people.

Bridget was Brooke's antithesis: quiet, shy, and ethereal. It was as if she'd drawn a circle around herself which you felt you wouldn't dare invade. Like Brooke, Bridget drew beautifully; she once wrote

Kitty, my little wood sprite. (Photo by Leland Hayward)

Amid my duties at home, there were always the social obligations. Here is the "I like Ike" rally at Madison Square Garden with Ethel Merman. In the background are Noël Coward, Skitch Henderson, and the balding head of composer Richard Rodgers.

and illustrated a little book for us entitled *Bridget's Book of Rules,* a humorous account of all the things she was and wasn't allowed to do at home.

Billy, the youngest, was so adorable you could eat him with a spoon. He was terrifically funny, with a real knack for pranks and enough charm to make you overlook them. He too had dark places you didn't want to touch; there was a lot of the daydreamer about him, and when you broke into those fantasies he always cringed, as if he were afraid of being hit.

Fortunately for me, Leland's children made an easy transition between Maggie and myself, and we enjoyed a warm relationship right from the start. In the years between 1947 and 1954, they were bouncing, healthy, happy, and typically competitive with one another. But for all the sibling rivalry, they were also very close to each other; as a result of their parents' divorce, they stuck by each other. When you were with all three of them, you had the feeling

181

they were involved in some sort of conspiracy.

In that summer of 1954, I wasn't so confident of all this domestic happiness that Leland thought we'd share at the Bel-Air Hotel. Brooke was seventeen that year, and quite a handful. Beautiful and coming into her womanhood, she was flirting with everything that walked. Meanwhile, Billy was thirteen and aimless, skulking around the hotel with nothing to do. To solve the problem, Leland gave the manager a hundred bucks and got Billy a job as a pool boy. For a few weeks, Billy was quite purposeful. Then he found out Leland had bought him the job. He confronted his father and said, "Is it true?" And Leland, making it worse, replied, "Does it make any difference?"

In the middle of this summer, I got a call that my father was gravely ill in Carmel. Fortunately, several years earlier Leland had encouraged me to make peace with my father. To his eternal credit, he convinced me that I was of an age and ability to do that, even though my father couldn't. As usual, Leland was right. Though the reconciliation was far from total, I was able to fly to my father's final sickbed as his daughter, not as a guilt-stricken stranger.

My father had remarried. His wife met me at the airport and drove me to the hospital. By the time we arrived, he was dead. I walked into the room where his corpse was lying and on the table beside him was the watch and ring he'd always worn. I picked them up and held them. My stepmother—a nice enough woman—suddenly showed a different side of her character. "They're not yours," she snapped. "They're mine. He gave them to me." I wasn't going to tangle with her. So I calmly turned to her and said, "I don't want them, I just wanted to touch them. Of course they're yours, everything is yours. I'm not here for that. I'm here to pay my respects to my father." It was nothing more than that. I didn't react strongly to his death. I didn't cry. There was nothing to cry about. Though my father and I had been reunited, I still didn't feel love for him. The funeral was a lightly attended affair. There was none of the traditional going back to the house for lunch and receiving visitors. My sister had come, but we didn't even exchange words. I left immediately after the burial service, wishing I could feel more but knowing there was nothing more to feel.

Rather than return to Los Angeles, I stayed on another day so I could have dinner with my stepson Peter Hawks, who was now

married and living in Carmel. In the middle of dinner, Peter was
called away to the telephone. When he returned, he didn't sit down.
"I've got to tell you something that's kind of rough," he said. "Leland is in Good Samaritan Hospital, he's bleeding."

And I said, "I have to get to him. How can I do it?"

It was late. There were no more planes until morning and none
that could be chartered on short notice. I was getting frantic when
Peter volunteered to fly me to Los Angeles in a borrowed plane. I
said he didn't know how to do that. He insisted he did. Against all
reason, I agreed to let this kid, who acted as if he was just driving
me to the market, take me into the sky at nine o'clock at night and
fly down the coast. Peter turned out to be a very good pilot. I didn't
notice. All I wanted was the news, which was, as I expected, all
bad.

Leland had collapsed—in a pool of blood—in the lobby of the Bel-
Air Hotel. From his point of view, the embarrassment of this third
bleeding attack was the worst of it. Privately, the doctors told me
how wrong Leland was. They'd been pumping blood back into him
as fast as they could—by the time I arrived they'd replaced his
entire blood volume—but they still didn't know what was wrong.

I moved into the hospital to be with Leland. He was in that bed
for a month. The bleeding would stop, then start again, and each
time it did, the nurses and doctors went in and replaced his blood.
By the end of his stay, Leland had received massive transfusions
several times over.

As a matter of routine in those days, the blood bank asked its
recipients to arrange for donations of twice the amount of blood we
used. Leland had taken so much from the blood bank that his
friends couldn't give enough—I made an appeal to MCA for donors.
Lew Wasserman and his entire organization gave blood. I believe
Swifty Lazar even donated some, which, for him, was like jumping
off the Brooklyn Bridge.

Leland, never the best patient, was kept heavily sedated so he
didn't know what was going on around him. They took the phone
out of his room, and we shielded him from all business. And, gradually, the bleeding lessened and whatever had caused the problem
mended itself, never to trouble him again.

Once Leland was sufficiently recovered, Kitty, Leland, and I flew
to Honolulu, where we took a house that was Leland's headquarters

during the time *Mister Roberts* was being shot. From there, Leland commuted back and forth to the remote island of Midway, where filming took place. How Leland ever managed to get up the courage to set his foot on this island, I'll never know. He had always been highly concerned with creature comforts not found on Pacific atolls. On a vacation, he couldn't bear to even put his foot in the sea. Clearly his confinement in the hospital had so unnerved him that any film set was preferable.

In another circumstance he wouldn't have been on the set as much as he was, but the director was John Ford, who was eccentric in many ways. And difficult in every way. It was hard for Leland to control Ford because—among other things—he had a penchant for hootch. And Leland felt he should keep his eye as close on the production as possible.

While Leland scurried off to Midway every few days, Kitty and I had a real mother/daughter, buckets and spades holiday. We would sit for hours playing on the beach and in the sea, drinking up the pleasures of Honolulu, which in those days was not a tropical board-walk but a lovely island with beautiful empty beaches. Kitty, at age eight, had become a real companion for me; she was curious and precocious. What I'd discovered about being a parent was that it gives you a legitimate excuse to be a child again. We'd play all those ridiculous card games I used to love as a kid—casino, spit, and war. Only this time I had to learn every possible way to cheat so I could lose. Because, just like her mother, Kitty would sulk and slam her cards down on the table if she didn't win.

When *Mister Roberts* was finished, we returned to New York and resumed our daily life. My hope was in vain—the summer of 1954 was a prelude to the dire events of the following summer. And those troubles, in turn, led to five difficult, painful years, with agony for Leland's children, crisis for Leland, and, for me, the undoing of a marriage that I'd foolishly imagined would last to the end of my days.

With Kitty in Honolulu. (Photo by Leland Hayward)

ALL-
AMERICAN
STEPMOTHER

Before the summer of 1954, I had very little contact with Leland's children. They lived with their mother in Greenwich, Connecticut, coming to Manhasset only for an occasional weekend or to New York for a day. I'd spent two weeks with them once, but that was in Bermuda, where Leland and I took them for a holiday, and on that trip they were off at the beach all day.

We would happily have seen more of the children, but the red tape that Leland had to go through to arrange even the shortest visit was beyond ridiculous. Not with Maggie—direct communication was verboten. Instead, his lawyer made the arrangements with her lawyer. There was always some snag about dates or places, so the lawyers had to make a great many phone calls back and forth. This put Leland off so much that he didn't take the initiative to see his children as much as he wanted to. And this was sad, for they loved being with their father and had accepted me with amazing ease.

I could certainly understand their zest for time spent with Leland, who couldn't help spoiling them. He wasn't buying their love, he was just so irritated when they'd show up in ragged clothes that he'd immediately take them out on a shopping spree. Even when they were spruced up he didn't sit around with them. Ever curious about what was going on, he'd take them to movies, circuses, or performances of whatever play he was producing at the moment. He wasn't trying to avoid being with them, he didn't concoct ploys to distract them; he was giving them his presence at the same activity level he brought to relationships with his peers.

Leland was no outdoorsman. When Billy was having his aimless period at the Bel-Air Hotel, I suggested to Leland that he take him fishing—that tried and tested father-son diversion. Well, he did. But Leland's idea of a fishing trip was to take Billy to the Sportsmen's Lodge, a restaurant that featured a tank of captive trout. Armed with the short pole they provided, you dropped your line into the tank. Within seconds, the hook would be taken by one of those poor overcrowded fish who must have thought they were already dead and tinned, so densely were they crammed into that tank. I mean, it was instant strike time; the whole operation took three minutes, from "stream" to skillet. But the outing was a success, even if it wasn't quite what I meant.

For all his eccentricities, Leland had a difficult time relating to his own children. Like many parents, he became impatient when he saw even the slightest bit of himself showing. At the end of a day with Brooke and Bridget and Billy, he'd say, "I don't know why I'm more tolerant of Kitty than I am of my own children." I always reassured him that this was normal. "Other people's children can sometimes be much more lovable than your own," I'd tell him, "because you see so much of yourself in yours, and you're not crazy about what you see."

Though I deeply resented Howard for relinquishing his parental duties after we were divorced, it was in some respects easier for me and, I thought, easier for Kitty. Now I know that she would have benefited from a real relationship with her father; at the time, as I considered what Leland was going through with Maggie and how much he adored Kitty, I was grateful that Kitty had been spared all those problems.

This was a blessing, for the pains of the Hayward children were on a much larger scale than I ever imagined. They were also more deeply rooted than any of us suspected, and were not the product of Leland and Maggie's divorce. All we knew at the time, however, was that the children had suffered from the break-up of the marriage and were dealing with a difficult mother.

Distress wasn't what you first noticed in Leland's children. They were bright, eccentric, and bordering on the neurotic—a combination that produces a lot of irresistible surface charm. What I didn't know until the dramatic summer of 1955 was that two of them, Bridget and Billy, were deeply disturbed.

That year started out as another stellar one in the photo-perfect life of Mr. and Mrs. Leland Hayward. Leland had recuperated so well from his bleeding attack of the previous summer that, for him at least, it was mere history. I lived on pins and needles that the slightest bit of stress, strain, or fatigue would trigger another attack. And there was stress galore—Leland had two movie projects going on at once. He was in pre-production for *The Spirit of St. Louis*, which was to begin filming in June, and he was deeply involved with *The Old Man and the Sea*. At this point, he was in negotiations with Spencer Tracy for the title role and in deep conference with Peter Viertel, who had been chosen by Ernest to write the screenplay. The filming was slated to begin after Leland was finished with *The Spirit of St. Louis*.

Rather than spend the summer in Manhasset, Leland thought it would be much more enjoyable for Kitty and me to go to Biarritz for the month of August. The early parts of the picture would be shot in Newfoundland and other awful places like that, and then the production would make its way to France for the filming of Lindbergh's landing. Once there, Leland said, he'd come and spend some time with us in Biarritz.

This seemed like a shrewd and glamorous idea, so I packed up my whole caravan—Kitty, her French nanny Zellie, and a maid—and settled into a suite of rooms in the Hôtel de Palais. But no sooner had I arrived in Biarritz than I got a call from Leland, who was still in New York. Maggie had thrown Bridget and Billy out of the house, then called Leland. "I don't want them," Maggie said. "Just take them. I can't deal with them anymore."

Leland was at a total loss. He was trapped between his work and his duty to his children. "I'm in the middle of a movie," he said. "What should I do?"

I said, "Well, I don't think there's any question or decision as to what to do. They're your children, you're half of them, you take them and send them here to stay with me. There's nothing else to be done."

Kitty and her dearly beloved "Pop," Leland.

He said, "How do you feel about it?"

"I'd rather be in front of a ten-ton truck, but I'm your wife and they're your children and I'll take them. I don't know if I can do it or not, because I think they're slightly crazy, but God knows I'll try."

*Kitty atop the Hayward children. L. to r.: Brooke, Bridget, and Billy.
(Photo by Leland Hayward)*

He said all the things anyone would at that moment: "You're the greatest living woman, what would I do without you?"

The reason I was even slightly nervous about my offer was that we'd received some unsettling reports the previous winter from the boarding school that Bridget attended in Switzerland. Apparently she would go on hunger strikes, and she had the curious habit of covering her room with photographs of her mother one day, only to take them down a couple of days later and then repeat the entire process all over again. Leland and I had taken her from boarding school to Paris, Rome, and Sicily at Christmas and Easter. Although I couldn't pinpoint anything specific when she was with us, I sensed an unusually neurotic strain in so young a person. As for Billy, I suspected he was nutty in a wild, glamorous, swashbuckling kind of way.

But what had triggered Maggie's rage wasn't anything the chil-

In Rome, with Bridget assisting me at the morning toilette. (Photo by Leland Hayward)

dren had done. It was something small and completely neurotic on her part: she'd found and read Bridget's diary. In it, Bridget had written all the things that any girl of sixteen might think about her mother: "I loathe spending the summer here. She doesn't understand me, and I hate her."

We've all said these things. They're perfectly normal, completely natural sentiments in the mother-daughter relationship; but Maggie, who desperately longed to be the perfect mother, was stunned by Bridget's private confession. She confronted Bridget with her findings and said, "If you feel that way about me, then perhaps you should live with your father."

With Bridget Hayward in Gstaad. (Photo by Leland Hayward)

Much to Maggie's surprise, Bridget agreed. Poor Billy, then four-teen, was drawn into the whole affair because Maggie asked him if he would like to leave with Bridget. That summer, Brooke was in Europe with her stepfather, Kenneth Wagg, and apparently the thought of being alone in Greenwich with his mother wasn't a cheery prospect for Billy. So he also elected to leave.

When I went to fetch Bridget and Billy at the Biarritz train station in La Negresse, I was greeted by two waiflike creatures. Little Bridget was so beautiful in a totally original way. She had striking, albino-like looks, with white eyebrows, white eyelashes, almost white hair, and transparent skin. On this day, however, she was like a little mass of ectoplasm. You could almost see through her. Billy had somehow gotten a Maurice Chevalier straw boater and cane, and was playing the part as he swaggered toward me on the platform. And I want to tell you, I fell in love like I've never fallen in love in my life.

Seeing these two wonderful creatures on the platform, I forgot that I wasn't just taking two healthy kids and packing them off to the beach. They were quick to remind me how grim reality was. No sooner had I settled them into their rooms than Bridget turned to me and said, "Can I call you Mother?"

I said, "Well, let's get a name that isn't quite like that. Because you have a mother who, no matter how you feel about her this minute, does love you very much. Mothers *always* love their children, no matter how bad their children are to them, and no matter how bad they think their children are. So Maggie will always love you and she'll always be your mother, and we can't change that. But you can call me Nan, or Mama, or anything you want." In the end she decided that Nan was okay.

I believed all that. I was certain that Maggie was devastated by her children's ready acceptance of her rejection, and I think she knew from the moment she set it up for them to leave she'd made a huge mistake. But there was no turning back, so I planned to stay in Biarritz with the three children until September and then head back to America, where I would get them ready for school.

It didn't take long for me to see that these were two very mixed-up kids. Early in their stay, I called Leland and said, "I can't do this by myself. This is for a pro. I will do anything the pro tells me to do, but I cannot take responsibility for children as sick as these.

I simply don't know enough. And you're going to have to get me a lot of help."

Leland didn't seem to have a clue. "I don't know what you're talking about," he said. "I don't know what you mean."

And it was indeed very hard to explain. Bridget had an exaggerated sense of privacy that seemed to border on the psychotic. She'd brought some letters with her that she kept in locked boxes with little things on them so that if they were touched, she'd know it. They were letters from schoolgirl friends, and I doubt if there was anything of interest in them to anyone. I was immaculate with her about her privacy and she grew to trust me because of it.

Still, what we had to go through to let the maids come in and clean her room was unbelievable. I would say to her, "Listen, the maids have to do what's called the thorough cleaning, so there will be somebody in your room today. If there's anything you want me to keep for you until that's over, we can put it in a special hiding place. I just don't want you to come in and think anyone's been looking through your things."

Billy, on the other hand, seemed vague and disoriented; his non-specific behavior only revealed itself as sickness when he threatened to jump out the window of the hotel. Although he and his sister were initially partners in crime, they began to quarrel so bitterly that I had to keep them in separate parts of the hotel or Billy would have threatened to jump again.

Then there were the freeze-outs. They'd go for days without speaking to anyone—especially each other. And Bridget would go on hunger strikes, or have days when she would eat only pablum. It was stressful on all of us—particularly for Kitty, who, at age nine, thought it all had something to do with her. And in a way, it did. For Kitty, who'd always been the center of my attention, now had to share me with two needy adolescents. I wasn't surprised that Kitty was bewildered by these new arrivals. Subconsciously, she suffered from her own father's rejection; when my attention had to be divided, she felt short-changed.

When Leland finally arrived in Paris for the Lindbergh landing sequences, I was so tired of dealing with everybody's problems that I decided to leave all the children in the care of Zellie and join him for a week or so. My junket was interrupted by a call from Zellie telling me I'd better come back, there were very strange goings-on

—more suicide threats, more days of silence, renewed refusals to eat. And, in a roundabout way, Zellie told me that she shared my point of view, that these were serious situations requiring professional handling. So I hurried back to Biarritz.

Leland followed as soon as he could, but he didn't quite get the seriousness of the situation. He thought he could simply cheer the children up by taking them to a bullfight. I quickly vetoed that idea. I said, "I don't think this is the right time for a bullfight. It's just too disturbing. I'm a grown-up, and it's a very emotional experience for me when I see one. Children shouldn't go unless they're Spanish, and these kids aren't Spanish. They're crazy, but they're not Spanish."

The summer finally ended, and we all got on the train to Paris, an all-day journey that meant three meals with three children, Zellie, Leland, and me. Not a word was spoken all day by either Hayward child, which automatically shut my child down—it was like an infection. When we arrived in Paris, I had the ammunition I needed to reemphasize my appeal of the previous month. "I'm willing to take them back to America, I'm willing to put them in school," I told Leland. "I'll do whatever I have to do. When I say I'm willing, I don't want you to think that I'm doing this tremendous favor for you or that I'm doing my duty, or anything like that; it's just part of our life and I will do it. But I will not take the responsibility for people as disturbed as this into my own hands. We have to seek professional help. It's something *you* must do for them."

Unfortunately, there really wasn't time to take them to see a doctor. We arrived in America just as school was about to start. And even though I was urging Leland to get professional advice, I also suspected I could handle it on my own. I'd had success with my former stepchildren, Kitty seemed healthy; perhaps if I adopted the same formula—love, support, and attention—these children would even out. I decided that Leland and I should try and make their lives seem as normal as possible, which meant putting Billy back in boarding school and keeping Bridget with me. Thinking it would be better if she stayed in a family atmosphere, I decided to take her to California, where Leland and Kitty and I would be while *The Spirit of St. Louis* was being edited. There, I would enroll her with Kitty in the Westlake School for Girls.

I dispatched Bridget, Kitty, and the nanny to Los Angeles and stayed in New York with Billy to get him organized for boarding school at Lawrenceville, in New Jersey. Billy didn't want me to take him to school. I understood his feelings. I knew he'd feel silly among his peers if they saw him arriving with his stepmother and all his equipment in a chauffeured car. Things like that can make other kids hate you for the rest of time.

I agreed to let him make the journey alone under the condition that, as a special gift to me, he would go visit his mother before the school term started. He was reluctant to do this, but after a lot of begging and pleading and assuring him if it didn't work out, he would never have to do it again, he agreed. I sent him with the chauffeur, who waited for him and then brought him back to New York. When he returned, all he said was, "I'll never do it again."

I said, "Okay. A deal's a deal. And off to school you go." To school he went. And I breathed a sigh of relief that the summer had passed. Maybe, with Billy at boarding school and Bridget in school in L.A. and living with us, they would both outgrow their problems.

I was looking forward to being by myself when Leland rang from Europe. He was nervous about how things were progressing on the script for *The Old Man and the Sea*. Would I go down to Cuba where Peter Viertel was working with Papa on the screenplay and see what was going on? How I was to ascertain this I wasn't quite sure, but the idea intrigued me a great deal more than my much coveted need for solitude and the continuing problem of dealing with Leland's children. So off I went to Cuba, where I proceeded to get in all manner of trouble.

THE
BEGINNING
OF PAPA'S
LEAVE-TAKING

Ernest seemed in a very strange frame of mind when I arrived at the Finca. I assumed he was worried about *The Old Man and the Sea* becoming a film. Now that he could see the script taking shape, he was having misgivings about the project—or about the screenplay which Peter Viertel had been writing for six months. Peter's September 1 deadline had come and gone. From a distance, it appeared Peter was having problems.

Ernest had said as much. In a letter he wrote to me on August 8, 1955, he said, "I am on page 564 of my book. Work, like fishing, does not upset me at all. What is murder is having to have Peter f--- around with my book *The Old Man and the Sea* and have me f--- around with it too. That is what I should never have agreed to or gotten mixed up in. But I feel very detached about it now and all the geniuses can genius around at their own pace and I know one good old word, No, and how to say it in all languages or at least I have rediscovered this word."

This animosity toward Viertel was curious inasmuch as he'd been Ernest's personal choice to write the script of *The Old Man and the Sea*. They'd known one another for quite a few years and Papa had always adored him. It wasn't hard—Peter was funny, easy to be

At the Finca with Ernest.

with, and he had marvelous manners. Papa wasn't working on the script with Peter, but he was reading over his shoulder, motherhenning the project while he wrote his "Big Book."

I had known Peter Viertel in California. He came from a Hollywood background: his father was an Austrian playwright who directed movies in Hollywood in the twenties and thirties, and his mother, Salka Viertel, collaborated on several screenplays that were made into Greta Garbo movies. When he was about twenty,

Peter had achieved a skyrocketing, boy-wonder success with his
novel *The Canyon*, which was based on his childhood in Santa Monica. He wrote various screenplays (among them the script of *The
Sun Also Rises)*, and in 1952 he published *White Hunter, Black
Heart*, a not altogether flattering portrait of John Huston during the
filming of *The African Queen*, but a good book nonetheless.

Peter possessed classic tall, dark, and handsome looks; he was
extremely flirtatious and always had a string of admirers around
him. He had been married to a woman called Jigee, who was previously married to the screenwriter Budd Schulberg. When she met
Peter, Jigee was absolutely swept off her feet. And after *that*, she
was swept off her feet by Ernest, who, as Jigee had never been a
drinker, felt it his duty to teach her to drink. He taught her too well.
She became an alcoholic, and one drunken night while smoking in
bed she burned herself up. By that time she and Peter were estranged.

The day I arrived in Cuba, Peter invited me to go off for the
weekend with him and some friends to Varadero, a wonderful
Cuban resort with one of the most beautiful beaches in the world.
Whatever was bothering Ernest wasn't relieved by the prospect of
getting rid of Peter and me for the weekend. He stayed edgy and
slightly mean, and I kept away from him, because his wrath could
be so great. Though Papa had never thrown shots at me, I'd seen
him do it to other people and it was painful to watch.

Papa was a big man, and that alone kept you afraid most of the
time. He could have swatted you dead with one swat if he wanted
to. He had a way of narrowing his eyes when he was angry, or
ignoring you utterly. And then there were his words; always spare,
so that when they hit you they came twice as hard, with the velocity
of a bullet. In Spain once, Harry Kurnitz jokingly had introduced
himself to Ernest with a fey "How marvelous to meet you . . . I'm
Slim's Parisian lover." Ernest's little steel eyes bored into Harry,
and then he snarled, "Lonely work, isn't it?" Harry was leveled. I
felt terrible. I had learned that you just didn't want to tangle with
Papa when he was in one of his black moods.

So I went to Varadero. On Sunday evening, Peter dropped me off
at the Finca on his way back to Havana, where he was staying.
Whenever I visited Ernest and Mary, I always stayed in the little
house on the grounds, but before making my way to those quarters,

THE BEGINNING OF PAPA'S LEAVE-TAKING

I stopped off at the main house to check in with them. Papa was alone in the drawing room, reading. When I entered the room, he looked up from his paper and said coldly, "Well, you're back, I'm surprised."

I immediately understood. Ernest, who was naturally jealous and grabby about all kinds of things, was furious because I'd gone off for the weekend with Peter. Ernest was an absolute king in sniffing out a situation, and he instinctively knew that Peter and I had had a little dalliance.

Peter had intimated on several occasions in other cities at other times that he thought I was the Candy Kid. But I'd never taken him seriously. He was a notorious ladies' man. And while I'd always found Peter an attractive man, it didn't occur to me before I got down to Cuba that anything could happen between us. It was all aboveboard—go down to have peeks at the pages and see Papa.

But no sooner had I arrived at the Finca than I'd realized Ernest wasn't the only one in Cuba who was on edge. I was in a state of shock, terrified of what lay ahead of me, knowing that I had the responsibility of two disturbed children whose father was too deep into his work to realize what was going on with his family. That annoyed me. Clearly Leland didn't understand the severity of his children's problems—he was more anxious for me to check on the screenplay than he was for me to be with his children. And I was angry at myself for being slow to realize that my most important responsibility was to our children, Leland's and mine. By the time I got to Varadero and it became evident that something could happen between Peter and me, I took a "What the hell, Marybelle" attitude for three days, and thought I deserved it. I needed the escape.

The weekend was behind us, but at the Finca Ernest grew more and more difficult. He not only gave me my first taste of his irrational side, he began to show the craziness that was in him. There was no verbal abuse, but when he looked at me, his eyes became smaller, sharper, meaner. It was obvious he was pissed off. In conversation, he was cold.

And then he'd do a wild thing in the evenings. He'd come out and sit on the front steps of his house, which was across the courtyard from where I was staying, and sing or whistle "Greensleeves" or some sad romantic song. I'd pretend I was asleep. I'd lie there, trying desperately not to move or cough or breathe, and I'd think to myself, "Oh my God! If he ever walks in here, what'll I do? I'll scream and then for sure his wife will shoot me."

Between Papa and the whole thing with Peter, I couldn't wait to get out of there. As I counted the days until my departure, I tried to stay out of Ernest's way as much as possible. This wasn't hard in the morning—he wrote until lunchtime—and in the afternoon I just tried to make myself scarce. As Peter worked all day at his hotel in Havana, I didn't have to see much of him either.

The evening was the challenge. Usually, all of us—Papa and Mary and whoever else was around—would drive into Havana, meet at the Floridita bar, and then have dinner somewhere. Or Peter would come to the house during the day to work with Papa, and then we'd all go into town together.

On the day of my last night there, Peter came out to the Finca to work. I didn't see him or Ernest until the end of the day, when I came up to the drawing room of the main house. Ernest was talking with Peter, ignoring me. I made myself a drink and proceeded to read an old *New York Times* that was lying nearby.

Ernest, who hadn't made any move to clean himself up for the evening, was still barefoot and clad in his huge shorts. He always wore shorts that were too big for him. Or he pretended they were too big—he'd suck in his stomach so they'd fall down a little and you'd see how "thin" he was. Invariably, the shorts were held up with what Ernest called his Kraut belt, because he'd taken it off a dead German in the war.

On this night, Ernest waited until I was about to toss the paper aside. Then he undid his Kraut belt, sucked his stomach in, and let his pants fall to the floor. Frightened at what this display could possibly mean and terrified that Mary would walk in at any moment and find Ernest stark naked, I quickly buried my face in that old *Times*, studying it as if I were about to take a final exam.

Peter was as astonished as I was—thank God he was there. Finally, after what seemed like a long time, he said, "Oh, Ernest! Come on, Papa. Pull up your pants and let's get going. I'm hungry. Slim is starving. Let's go." And Ernest snapped out of it and got out of there.

I'm not sure what prompted Ernest to show everything. Perhaps it was simply the antics of a man who'd had a little too much to

With Miss Mary in Cuba.

drink and wanted to get my attention—a move to shock and challenge me. Papa had something going on in his head about Peter and me, and he thought our fling, if you could call it that, was something serious. The act had been meant to be a reprimand, but it was also an overture and the message was clear: If Slim's going to cheat, why not with Papa?

The final scene of this crazy week happened the next day, just as I was leaving. Peter asked Papa and me to meet him at the Floridita bar on my way to the airport so that he could give me what Leland wanted so desperately, the first pages of the screenplay. As Peter wished, Papa and I went to the Floridita, and Peter handed me a manila envelope. Ernest was beyond caring about the screenplay— he thought there was some skulduggery going on and he went absolutely crazy with rage.

"Goddamnit! All this behind my back!"

"It's nothing, Papa," Peter said. "They're the same pages you've got. Slim's going to take them to Leland."

"I don't believe you," Ernest said.

"Here, Papa, don't be so silly, really. You're making things awfully difficult for everybody," I said, hoping to God I was right. I handed Ernest the envelope and, of course, the pages inside were exactly the pages he had. The fact made him even more furious.

It was blessedly time to go. Ernest took me alone to the airport, leaving Peter in the bar to wait for Mary, who was to have met us but hadn't shown up. Poor Mary! How can I begin to relate how miserable a time she'd been having? At the best of times Ernest was sweet to Mary in the way you might be with a child. But when he was in one of his moods he dumped on her. While I was at the Finca, Ernest had become increasingly abusive to her—so rude, belligerent, and cruel it was painful to witness. The abuse was mostly in the form of a put-down. For example, she would be dressed to go out for dinner and he'd say something like, "Oh, are you going to wear that rotten dress, again?" Or he'd bring me into the picture. Once while I was there Mary and I walked into the drawing room at the same time, ready to go out. Papa looked up from his paper and said, "I like Miss Slimsky's dress." And then he just glared at Mary. It had never been easy for her to watch the attention that Papa paid to me, and so Mary and I conducted our relations at arm's length. She was polite, I was polite, but she didn't like me. I understood; I probably wouldn't have liked me either if I'd been in Mary's position.

I tried to keep things under control as much as I could, but with my silly reputation as one of the best-dressed women in the world preceding me, Mary had to feel uncomfortable. I always made an effort not to be too done up when I was around her, because she was, however you cut it, a badly groomed, unkempt woman.

Where was Mary on my last day in Cuba? As Peter later told me, she'd gone to the hairdresser that morning. She finally showed up in the Floridita bar a half hour after I had left, with her hair no longer its usual platinum blond. It was now several shades darker. Peter stared at her in disbelief, then asked, "What have you done?" Mary said, "I did what Papa told me to do. He wanted me to have hair like Miss Slimsky's, so I went to the beauty parlor and had it dyed her color."

Ernest, knowing that he'd successfully, if temporarily, slimified Miss Mary, managed to give me a conciliatory send-off at the airport. While waiting for my flight to be called, he said, "Miss Mary's birthday is coming up, and I want to give her a present. What she

202

With Papa and Mary.

loves is that bracelet you're wearing. I'd like to buy it from you and give it to her."

This bracelet was one I always wore. It had pine cones dangling from a thick gold chain. To Ernest, they were "ballroom bananas."

"Well," I said, "I obviously won't sell it to you. I'll give it to you as a present, and you do whatever you want with it."

He took the bracelet and gave it to Mary. Now Mary not only had Miss Slimsky's hair color, she had her jewelry. I can't imagine that this made her any happier. I never saw her wear it.

As for Peter Viertel? Well, that interlude began and ended in Varadero. The last thing I needed in my life at the moment, on top of everything else I had to deal with, was to start nurturing an affair.

Ernest's relationship with Peter deteriorated after I left. I don't know if it was about me or the script, but Ernest continued to behave strangely. He began to demand that they work on the boat, which, as he already knew, made Peter seasick—and if you got seasick with Ernest, you were a coward. He had this foolish theory that the reason you were seasick was because you were afraid of the fish. And a writer who was scared of a fish obviously couldn't turn out a good screenplay about one.

Once filming began, Ernest stopped picking on Peter and settled into a general dislike of the world at large. He had, from his point of view, good reason. Shortly before I went to Cuba in September, a camera crew had gone down to film action shots of giant marlin. Papa went out with the crew for the fishing, but they were unable to get adequate footage. The real filming with the cast and the director, Fred Zinnemann, was to start in the spring of 1956. Leland's opinion was that since the camera crew was having trouble getting live fishing shots, they would be better off using fake fish. Ernest hated the idea.

In a letter dated October 31, he appealed to me for help. "I love the picture very much and will work very hard on it with Freddy who is the first intelligent man with any delicacy and metier that I have met in a long time," he wrote. "I ask you, and I have not asked you many things or anything practically except not to blow the back of my head off, to use any influence you have with Leland Hayward, the man you love, to not plan to do it with miniatures, rubber fish, stale cuts, or other money-saving devices. I don't want to write and bother him when he has Lindbergh problems. Please give him my best. No picture with a rubber fish ever made a dime."

I don't blame Ernest. I understood Leland's position, but I remember thinking, "How on earth are they going to do the fishing sequences without a fake fish? But who's going to believe a fake fish?" How wrong I was. How wrong Ernest was. If he'd lived to see *Jaws*, he would have known how much money a fake fish can make.

But neither a terrifyingly real fake marlin nor a vibrant live fish was what *The Old Man and the Sea* needed; what it lacked was another point of view. I think Papa realized too late that Peter's script wasn't good enough. It's true that the script was not a great one. In Peter's defense, no screenwriter could have done a better job. *The Old Man and the Sea* wasn't meant to be a film. And that was Leland's error.

Instead of acknowledging this, Ernest became fixated on the idea that the film's success or failure depended on real footage of the fish. He wanted to see a beautiful fish jumping, surfacing, and then sounding.

Artists at play. L. to r.: Leland, Peter Viertel, Papa, and Gregorio, the Pilar's *captain.*

In April of 1956, Leland decided to appease Ernest by sending him along with the crew to Cabo Blanco, Peru, to attempt to film the marlin there. They gave up after two weeks on the boat with no fish sighted. In the end, stock film was used.

I wasn't around for any of the filming but I got enough information from Leland, Peter Viertel, and Papa to have a good idea of the silliness and unpleasantness of the experience. At one point, Ernest outdid himself: he dragged poor Peter and Leland, who also hated fishing, out to sea for a few manly days of trolling. Papa had this wonderful old man called Gregorio—he really was the Old Man—who ran the boat and cooked. This last was particularly important, because it was very hard to eat anything from Ernest's cuisine.

On this trip, Ernest had the good fortune to catch a sea turtle, an accomplishment that had to be celebrated by a lunch of turtle steak. Leland, who was an artist at cutting things up and worrying them around a plate so you'd think he'd eaten whatever horror had been served, managed to get away without swallowing any of this turtle. Peter, who still nursed the hope of pleasing Papa, dutifully ate it. Ernest just watched. And, of course, Peter got sick, giving Ernest the opportunity to tell me the whole story, months later, appending the inappropriate punchline: "That's what you get for taking a Jew with you!"

The anti-Semitism that critics have noted in some of Ernest's work wasn't there because artistic characterization called for it. That was Ernest. His anti-Semitism, never attractive, was exacerbated by his realization that although he'd gotten some money from the film, he had no control. He began to blame it all on the Jewish people involved. Doggedly, he would come to watch the dailies every night. For the director and cameraman, this is everyday stuff; for someone who's never seen rushes before, the film always looks dreadful. It's flat and empty and devoid of sound effects. Ernest would walk out of these screenings and say, "Well, it's just the worst shit I've ever seen. How can we stop it?"

In defense of the movie *The Old Man and the Sea*, Ernest never liked any film adaptations of his books. He only tolerated *For Whom the Bell Tolls*. What was clear in his growing disaffection with everything around him now was that the curtain was beginning to fall on his giant talent. His mind and his words had always been hard and true, like well-hit golfballs when they make that marvelous sound. His prose had drive and aim. But it was all falling away. The judgment, wisdom, and sanity that had attracted me and held me in their spell were all receding, vanishing as I watched.

BILLY AND
BRIDGET

Once again, I was in California, looking after children, children, and more children. Bridget was not doing well in the Westlake School. We were getting terrible reports from Lawrenceville about Billy, who was doing even worse. Finally, they threw him out. Billy had gone to New York on a weekend with some other boys, and one of the younger masters had given him some whiskey on the train on the way back to school. Another boy turned him in. Billy, with an unusual sense of loyalty, wouldn't tell where he'd gotten the booze, so they booted him. I had to go to New York, pick him up, and take him back to California, where for several weeks he simply lay around the house watching television. It was another defeat for this strange, uneven boy.

Billy wouldn't tell me where he'd gotten the whiskey, but I suspected there was more to the story. I finally said, "Billy, it's not dishonorable to tell where you got that booze. I know you didn't buy it, no one would sell it to you. Where did you get it?" He said, "I can't tell you." I goaded him, and he finally did tell me that it was from a master. "Well, you're not going to take a bath for that. The guy that gave it to you should be taking the rap." I made Leland call up the school and describe the circumstances—and Billy was reinstated.

In the spring of 1956, Bridget was accepted at Swarthmore College. That autumn, much to everyone's delight, she began at the prestigious school. Leland and I visited her several times that year. She seemed to love the place and her roommate. But soon she was living alone in her room. I asked her why, but her only reply was that she preferred to be by herself. We didn't think too much about it. She was a loner by nature and I assumed this was just part of her eccentricity.

At Christmas all the children except for Brooke gathered at our home in Manhasset. Bridget seemed to be making strides, Billy was as precocious as ever, and Kitty at age ten was doing her best to keep up with him and doing very well at it. It was on all fronts a happy family Christmas.

But on Christmas morning, Bridget didn't bound downstairs with the others to open presents. I finally knocked on her door, and asked, "Are you all right?" There was no answer, so I walked in. She was asleep. I gave her a little kiss and said, "Don't you want to have Christmas?" She said, "Not right now." So I said, "I'll tell you what we'll do. You keep sleeping, and when you wake up, we'll bring your presents to you." Hours later, she finally awoke, and each member of the family brought a present up to her. Then she went back to sleep again.

What we didn't know was that she was an epileptic and on Christmas Eve she'd had a seizure. After such a trauma, the length of time it takes to return to normal is equal to—or sometimes greater than—the length of time that you've been unconscious. And we thought she had the flu!

Leland and I went back to California in the new year. *The Spirit of St. Louis* was scheduled to open, and Leland was now in post-production for *The Old Man and the Sea*. One evening in late spring Leland and I were at the premiere of the Lindbergh film. In the middle—with Lindy somewhere over the Atlantic—Leland was called to the telephone. It was Lawrenceville, telling him that Billy had blown his reprieve; he'd been caught attempting to run away from school, apparently having decided that education was a waste of time and he'd be better off getting a job in the oil fields of Oklahoma.

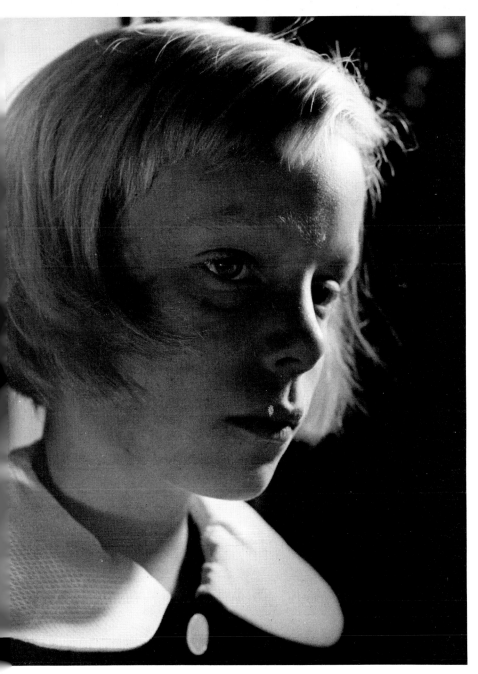

Bridget Hayward. (Photo by John Swope)

SLIM

By this time, Leland was tired of the Lawrenceville calls. There had been the television-set-in-the-room call, the smoking-on-campus call, and the trips to New York with visits to "21" that would end with Billy—playing the role of valued customer Leland Hayward—signing his father's name on the chit. And now this.

Leland stormed out of the theater, got on an airplane, and went to Lawrenceville. He took Billy straight to New York to see the renowned and controversial psychoanalyst Dr. Lawrence Kubie, who admitted him into Regent Hospital. Kubie never put a medical label on Billy's problem. To me, it was all unreal. The boy was precocious, with a very high IQ for which he had no channel. People with IQs as high as Billy's are often maladjusted. If his father hadn't been well off and if Billy had had to struggle a bit, I think his difficulties would have resolved. Instead, Dr. Kubie ended up sending this troubled and unruly sixteen-year-old to the premier psychiatric institute in the country at that time, the Menninger Clinic in Topeka, Kansas.

Billy stayed at Regent for a week or two until a space at Menninger opened up. Because he'd refused to see his mother and his father, Dr. Kubie decided he should, in that case, not be allowed to see anyone else. I flew in from California a few days after he'd been admitted. When I said I wanted to visit Billy, Leland said, "He won't see you. And besides, the nurses won't let you visit him. *I* can't even see him."

I was enraged that Billy was being treated as a violent person. I told Leland that, nurses or not, I would get in to see him. I went straight to the hospital, asked his room number at reception, and proceeded to the elevator. When I got to Billy's floor, I walked past the front desk without slowing down. The duty nurse said, "Where do you think you're going?" I said, "To see Bill Hayward." She said, "You're not allowed." I said, "We'll see about that." And I walked straight into his room.

Billy was glad to see someone he knew. He was *petrified*. "What have I done that's so wrong?" he said. "Why am I here? They've even taken away my clothes, my wallet, my watch, everything."

"You haven't done anything bad, Billy, but you haven't lived by the rules that you're supposed to live by, and this is all anybody can think of doing. I think it's a dumb solution, but we're in it now, so let's get out of it. I wish you'd see your father."

"No! I don't want to see him," he said.

"I want you to see your mother."

"No! I don't want to see her. I'll only see you, and I'll see Brooke."

And so, every day, I came to the hospital and I'd bring him hamburgers and other favorite foods, I'd do crossword puzzles with him on the phone, and mostly I tried to make him forget that he was, literally, incarcerated.

When a room became available at Menninger, I borrowed a friend's airplane and took Billy there. He refused to go freely with anyone else. I felt that since no one really knew the extent of the confusion and terror that was going on inside of him, there should be some extra protection for him. The night before our flight, I told the pilot, "Lock your cabin door. This child is not violent, but I don't know what he is. Let's not take any chances. I'll have a male nurse with me who will look like a flight attendant, and he can bring Billy his Coca-Cola or whatever he wants."

I knew Billy was terrified of going to Menninger. He imagined it as an old-style loony bin. To keep him from overreacting, I arranged for the Menninger attendants, who would be meeting us at the airport in Topeka, to be dressed like civilians rather than white-coated guards. And I had them drive a civilian car, not the usual ambulance. We arrived at the clinic without a hitch.

Leland was waiting for us at Menninger, having taken a commercial flight. He hoped that Billy would want to see him. When Billy and I arrived, we were met by Billy's doctor, who led us into a small reception room. Leland waited outside as I chatted away, trying to make it all seem as ordinary as possible—as if Leland routinely traveled to Topeka.

At an easy point in the conversation, the doctor casually asked Billy if he'd like to see his father. Billy declined. While Billy was being given a tour of the clinic, the doctor kindly suggested I come back the following day with Leland for a second try.

Before I left that first day, I put my arms around Billy and gave him the biggest hug I could. He gave me a big hug back. We looked into each other's faces, both filled with unspilled tears—his puzzled, hurt, and terrified, and mine, I would think, like a melting wax mask. There was absolutely nothing more I could do to help the boy.

SLIM

He turned once to look at me before I closed the door behind me. "See you tomorrow, kid," I said, "I love you."

As I waited for Leland to join me, the full impact of what had just happened crashed over me. The drive from the clinic to the hotel with Leland was impossible. I wanted to be the saviour, the mother, the bearer of the anodyne that was going to make everything right for everyone else. But all I could bring to this traumatic and sad situation was the sort of steadiness that a stabilizer brings to a ship in dirty weather. I had to appear level, soothing, and secure so that Leland, who was torn in half over Billy's problems, could get comfort from me.

I held Leland, but there was really nothing I could say to reassure him. We returned to Menninger the next day, hoping that Billy would see his father before we went back to New York. This time, the doctor wanted a conference with us. "Mrs. Hayward, I'm sure you read the list of things that Bill is allowed to have," he began. "He's allowed to have a cigarette lighter, but a gold lighter is a little much, especially when it's one given to him by Frank Sinatra. He has been proudly flashing it about."

"But, doctor, that's not *his* lighter," I said. "It's *mine*. I thought I'd lost it during the trip. Bill must have lifted it from my purse on the plane."

The doctor said he would ask Bill to give it back to me.

I said, "No, I'd rather get it back myself. The less public embarrassment he has, the less work for you, doctor."

I went to see Billy in his room. "Well, how is it?" I asked.

"It's all right. Strange, but it's okay, I guess. How long will I have to be here?"

What kind of an answer could I give? I felt that anything I said would sound like a cliché, so I just said, "As long as you need to be. The duration of the stay will depend largely on you; it's a matter of cooperation, a matter of giving yourself to the doctor and learning to trust him. It's a matter of telling the truth. You're a very bright young man, and a moment will come when things become clear to you. You'll be back with us long before you expect."

Then I took out a cigarette and asked him for a light. He casually took out my gold lighter, lit my cigarette, and handed me the lighter without comment. I thanked him, put it in my handbag without comment, and that was that. I guess he had wanted something that would give him identity, and nothing at hand was more glamorous than a gold lighter from his friend Frank Sinatra.

After we'd gotten through this moment, I said to Bill, "I'm going to ask you for a great big present. Will you see your father?"

"I don't want to," he said.

"I know you don't, but will you see him for me?"

Billy agreed, and Leland came into the room. Their reunion was awkward, touching, heartbreaking. You could see how much they loved one another and how grateful they both were that at least one barrier had been eliminated. Somehow, they made a kind of bridge toward each other.

The trip back to New York was quiet. I was conscious of the extreme agony that had suddenly inhabited Leland. For Leland, who always had a physical youthfulness about him, now looked his fifty-five years and a bit more.

Billy had been at Menninger for about a month when we got the telephone call telling us he had run away. This was not easy to do, but Bill's imagination and his daring were so original that I dare say he's one of the few people who ever got out of there. He had taken one of his few personal possessions that he was allowed to have at the clinic—a pair of cuticle scissors—and cut, wire by wire, the screen that protected his window. He got out, then stole a car and drove to Corpus Christi, Texas. We had cops and Pinkerton men all over the country looking for him. Luckily they found him and brought him back to the clinic. It all sounds a bit dramatic, but you didn't know what Bill was capable of doing. He would steal if he had to. If he got hold of a gun, he'd shoot if he had to.

I knew it was wrong for Bill to escape from Menninger, but I have to admit I was filled with admiration that he pulled it off. I thought it was the most glamorous getaway, almost like the Great Train Robbery. Years later, I asked him, "How the hell did you know where to go?" He said, "I memorized the town coming in with you in the car."

Bill had run away because he was afraid that he would never be able to join the Army—his ambition was to be a paratrooper. I assured him that a lot of people had gone through life without being in the Army and he had to get well before he could do anything. For Billy, that would mean three years at Menninger.

One incident stands out during that gray time. Frank Sinatra

Leland and Billy.

hung around our house in California a lot. It was no big deal—he'd
walk in at six o'clock and say, "I've come for a drink," and I'd look
up from my reading or letter writing or whatever and say, "Okay,
you know where the bar is." Frank was very sweet to Billy that
year, and when Billy was in Menninger, he wanted to do something
for the boy who used to joke with him in our living room. I told
Frank about the cigarette lighter, and he was so touched he offered
to visit Billy at Menninger.

"That's terribly dear," I said, "but I can't give you permission to
do that. First of all, he's not my son, and even if he were, the
doctors make the final decision. But if you really mean it, if you
really want to do it, let me call Topeka and see."

Frank said he'd like that, so I called Billy's doctor. And he said,
"Well, if it could happen, I think it would be marvelous. Bill talks
about Frank Sinatra as though they were Boy Scouts together, and

214

I don't think anybody believes him. So it would be a very good thing."

And I said, "If he decides to come, it has to be arranged so that he arrives in the airport and a car goes to the airplane, so nobody sees him. I don't really want to take out an ad that Leland's son is in a cuckoo hospital."

"I understand," the doctor said. "I'll get it all arranged."

I called Frank and explained to him. He couldn't have been more enthusiastic. "I'll be there," he kept saying.

The visit was scheduled for a Sunday. I was home in Manhasset all day, waiting to hear how it went. In the late afternoon, just as I was about to call Menninger, Billy's doctor phoned me. "Where *is* he?" he asked.

I said, "Where is who?"

He said, "Mr. Sinatra."

I said, "He's with you."

He said, "No, he's not. And we haven't heard a word from him, and Billy's sitting here waiting."

I didn't know what to do. I called various hotels in Kansas City and asked if Sinatra was there—though I knew that, if he had been registered, they wouldn't have told me. After a few calls like that, I rang Betty Bacall, who had, since Bogart's death, become very close to Frank. I said, "Betty, where is the Dago?" She said he was on his way to Kansas to see Billy. And I said, "But it's now three hours after the time he should have gotten there. Can you try and find out where he is?"

An hour later, I had to call Menninger to tell Bill's doctor what Betty had found out—Frank wasn't coming. On his way to the airport, he'd stopped in a bar to have a drink, and never made the plane.

Frank called me the next day. "Slim, I don't know what I can do," he said.

I said, "Frank, you've already done too much."

I didn't think Billy could stand one more indignity, but he survived. He eventually left Menninger and became a paratrooper. There were many fragmented, listless years for Billy. But in his early forties, at last Billy found the right outlet for his extraordinary mind. At forty-five, he graduated from law school, passed the bar exam on his first try and won his first case in court. His success makes me doubly happy because I know that he knows everything turned out all right.

While Billy was at Menninger, however, Bridget, who was nearly nineteen, knew there was something wrong with her and that it was too big for her to handle. Once again, Dr. Kubie was called in for consultation. For Bridget, he suggested the Austen Riggs Foundation in Stockbridge, Massachusetts. One night we got a phone call —not from Menninger, as we'd grown to expect, but from Riggs. Bridget had had a seizure, and they had rushed her to Massachusetts General Hospital, where she was put into the psychiatric ward.

Once again, I was horrified at the treatment a stepchild of mine was getting. Bridget wasn't violent; how could they have put her in with people who were? I immediately called Dana Atchley and begged him to get her out of there. He said he'd try. When he called me back, he had big news. Apparently Bridget had had *several* seizures at Riggs. She'd been transferred to Mass. General not only to be put under observation but so she could have tests done. These tests proved to be inconclusive, and Bridget returned to Riggs, where she remained for a couple of years. She was treated for her emotional problems, and she felt safe there. Because of her obsessive need for privacy, she knew that Riggs was a haven where she could suffer her seizures in relative solitude among people she trusted.

Bridget's epilepsy wasn't authoritatively diagnosed until 1960. Eventually, it led to her death—when she was twenty-one, she overdosed on her medication. By that time, I was no longer married to Leland and, cut off from the inside story, I grieved in private. Still, nearly thirty years later, the mere mention of Bridget's name creates a hollow sound in my heart. She was, for me, the most unusual child I've ever encountered—she was like a nymph, a cygnet.

One incident in particular always conjures up those feelings about her. It dates from our first meeting, when Leland took me to see his children for the first time. We arrived shortly before their bedtime, a moment when children are sometimes singularly lucid. I was wearing a big, black, circular taffeta skirt. This little golden child came up behind me and picked up the back of my skirt, so it made sort of a train. And she said, "You're the bride! You're the bride in black!"

Bridget with Doris Stein at the eighteenth-birthday party Leland and I gave for her at Romanoff's.

Bridget had no idea I was going to marry her father; none of the children did. A chill went up my spine. And it was in those few seconds that I realized I was dealing with a child unlike any I'd met before. She was not of this earth, that sprite of a girl.

TRU

The friend people always ask me about—even more than Hemingway—is Truman Capote. I could almost sum that friendship up with one memory. Once, when Truman started a rumor that was blatantly untrue, I told him it was immoral to make trouble where there was none. "Never mind, Big Mama," he replied, in that high, wispy voice. "You just wait and see. And if you wait long enough, it'll all come true." And it usually did.

When I think back to our twenty-five-year friendship, I see only what I think is the truth; and as amusing as that story was along the way, it becomes, at the end, a bitter tale, with nothing but heartbreak, mistrust, and betrayal.

I met Truman in the early 1950s at Diana Vreeland's house at dinner. It was no surprise to see him in that rarefied setting—ever since the publication of his novel *Other Voices, Other Rooms*, in 1948, at the age of twenty-four, Truman had become the darling of New York society and a frequent fixture in the salons of the Upper East Side. It was inevitable that he would, in time, get around to meeting me. Typically, he avoided the possibility of rejection by asking a powerful woman to make the introduction.

With Truman in Madrid. (Photo by Leland Hayward)

Like everyone else who met Truman in those days, I was enchanted by him. He wasn't just bright, he was riveting—and so shrewd a conversationalist that, when he led with his vulnerabilities and quirks, you couldn't help but take an instant liking to him. A few days later, Truman moved to cement our friendship at lunch. He followed this up with an invitation to tea. Then we arranged to have a drink. Before long, I was seeing him on a regular basis.

Anyone with a little time on her hands would have done the same. This funny-looking, dwarflike figure with the fey southern accent was, you quickly learned, no oddity to be collected casually and then discarded; in any social situation he was a tremendous asset. In the middle of the morning, instead of breaking from his writing to walk around or make tea, he would reach for the phone. He never identified himself; he didn't need to.

With Truman at the airport en route to Russia.
(Photo by Leland Hayward)

"Big Mama," he'd say, "you're going to have lunch with me today."

"I can't, Truman, I have a lunch date."

"Cancel it!"

"I can't."

"Yes, you can. Listen to me, Big Mama, you're *going* to have lunch with your little Trueheart."

And because you knew you were going to have a much better time with little Trueheart, you did as you were told.

My friendship with Truman was mostly limited to the city. He did come to the country occasionally, but he always stayed with Babe, his new adored friend—and he really did adore her. Although he lived very simply, there were few things Truman loved better than wallowing in luxury provided by others.

Although we lunched and dined often, I didn't have a sustained bout with Truman until the winter of 1958, when Sam Spiegel, the film producer and a great friend of mine and Leland's, invited Truman, Cary Grant, and me to go to Russia with him. Sam had been invited by the Russians to show three of his films: *Bridge Over the River Kwai, On the Waterfront,* and *The African Queen.* In a hands-across-the-tundra gesture, the Russians would, in return, show Sam some of their films.

With Truman and Sam Spiegel in Paris en route to Prague.

In 1958, few Americans had the opportunity to visit Russia. Avid traveler that I am, I didn't want to postpone this trip—particularly when I considered the cast. I knew that Leland, who was a dream about my wanderlust tendencies, wouldn't object. In all our years together, he'd only put his foot down once, when Ernest Hemingway asked me to join him and Mary on safari. I had wanted desperately to go, until Leland said, "There's going to be an accident with a gun, and when the smoke clears, Mary will be looking puzzled and you'll be dead." That sounded just about right, and I didn't go.

This time, with Leland's blessing, I set out to visit the Kremlin, to see the Bolshoi Ballet perform, and to ferret out any undiscovered Fabergé enamels. The trip quickly became more about culture than shopping; the only Fabergé I saw was a miniature golden train in the Kremlin Museum.

Any trip, no matter how fascinating, can sometimes be uninteresting if you're with the wrong traveling companions. But it was non-stop hilarity to be with Cary Grant in a place where he was totally unrecognized. If people stared at him, it was only because he was one of the world's best-looking men. He kept raving to me about how much he loved the anonymity and how it had been years since he could enjoy himself without crowds of autograph hounds outside his hotel. But all this ended the night we went to see Ulanova dance Giselle. Someone from the British Consulate came up behind Cary and said, "Oh, Mr. Grant, if it's not too much trouble, I would love to introduce you to my daughter. She thinks you're wonderful, and we would love to have your autograph." A great smile of relief appeared on Cary's face; in the end he was, for all his love of privacy, still a movie star.

After our ten days in Moscow, we were bound for Leningrad. Sam and Cary flew, but Truman and I decided it would be much more adventuresome to take the Red Arrow, an overnight train from Moscow to Leningrad. We reserved the very best accommodations on the train: a stateroom with an upper and lower berth, a little loo enclosed in a box, and a washstand.

It was rugged going, to say the least, but with Truman, it was all a lark. He ignored the negatives and focused completely on what was fascinating. In this rickety, primitive, and freezing stateroom,

Truman visiting Hamlet's ghost at Elsinore.

Truman and I had a ball. We ate, we drank our vodka, and we laughed our way shooting through the bleak Russian night.

From Leningrad, we came back to the West via Copenhagen. Sam and Cary peeled off from the group and went ahead. Truman and I decided to stay on for a few days. We settled into the Angleterre Hotel, which seemed like Versailles after twelve days in dreary Russian hotels, and set about arranging a visit with one of his literary idols, and mine, Isak Dinesen. He had visited her once before at Rungstedlund, her home in the country; apparently he had been a great success, for she was happy now to invite him to tea.

Her house on the Baltic Sea was pretty and simple, set on an open piece of land. A lady ushered us in, and there, seated like an ancient Mandarin, was the Baroness, tiny, fragile-boned, and exceedingly frail. Her face was skeletal; the life was entirely in her eyes, which were two jet black fires. They bored into you, almost devoid of pupils or expression.

I sat in silent fascination, just listening to Truman and the Baroness. At one point, as they discussed a particular writer's work, she said, "There are really only three elements to write about—air, fire, and water—and that particular piece [whatever it was] doesn't have enough air, enough space, enough *sky*. I don't think it's really all that good, do you, Mr. Capote?"

When Truman and I were leaving, Baroness Blixen asked if there was anything she could do to enhance my enjoyment of her country. "This will sound very, very trite and very American," I said, "but what I would love to have more than anything is a copy of *Out of Africa*, with a dedication."

The following day, I did indeed receive a copy inscribed "To Nancy Hawks, in memory of her visit to Rungstedlund, Best Wishes, Karen Blixen." The name was wrong, but no matter, I was thrilled all the same. A day later, I received a second copy. This time she wrote, "To Nancy Hayward, in memory of her visit to Rungstedlund. 'He who makes no mistakes, seldom makes anything.'" The delicacy and thoroughness of her manners impressed me almost as deeply as her writing.

By then, Truman and I had spent three weeks together traveling —an eternity to spend with a man who's not your lover. But Truman was so protective of me, so gallant, that he became dear to me in a new way on this trip. We were having an enormous amount of fun. He'd slip into shops when I wasn't looking, reappear, and say, "Here, Big Mama, I bought this for you." And he'd offer up some little trinket.

At one point he slipped a little jar of lip balm into my hand that he called "ooey-gooey." And he said, "You must wear this. It makes you more kissable."

I said, "Do you wear it?"

"Of course I do," he said, feigning umbrage. That was Truman's childlike side coming out, the part of him that loved to find wonder in the tiniest things. This quality was not only delightful, it was a spur to further delights; you could respond to it. That Christmas, I gave Truman a course of Erno Laszlo facials. To him, that was the most marvelous gift in the world. "Oh, I love the *pampering*," he told me. "And the *smell!* And the black *room!*"

On our last night in Copenhagen, we had dinner and decided to go to bed early, as we had to rise at dawn to fly back to New York. Truman escorted me back to my room. Every other night, we kissed one another and separated. On this night, he said, "Now, Big Mama, you get undressed, get into bed, and then I'll tuck you in."

We went inside. He sat in a chair while I disrobed—I felt as though I was getting undressed in front of my daughter—and he watched the cold cream and the fifty strokes with the hairbrush, and all those female preparations. I climbed into bed. Then he came over, tucked me in, and kissed me on the forehead.

"Thank you, Truman," I said. "That was dear."

"Sleep well," he replied softly, "because I love you very, very much."

I said, "I love you too, Truman."

And then Truman fixed a long gaze on me and said, "No, you don't."

"Don't talk like that—of course I do!"

"No, no, no. You don't. No one loves me. I'm a freak. You think I don't know that? I know how difficult it is for people to adjust to what I look like and how I sound when they first see me. It's one of the reasons that I'm so outrageous. I don't think anyone has ever loved me—maybe Jack [Jack Dunphy, Truman's lover for many years]. But not many other people. I'm an *object*. I'm a *centerpiece*, not a figure of love, and I miss that. There's not an awful lot to love."

"That's nonsense," I replied. "You love whom you love."

Truman shook his head. "Sometime, Big Mama, imagine what it's like to be me. When I walk into a room full of people who don't know me, I always do something silly instead of walking into a room straight. If I just walk in, I'm this funny, sawed-off fellow with a high voice, and it's hard for people to accept me. But if I come in and say, 'I don't want to sit with the boys, I want to sit with the girls,' everybody giggles and everybody's more comfortable. I do that on purpose to make it easier for people to be around me because then *I'm* easier and the whole thing works better."

There was no self-pity in Truman's voice. This was the truth as he knew it, and in the silence of the foreign night, it was a truth I couldn't deny. But to acknowledge it was not to diminish Truman. Just the opposite. In this hotel room, my compassion for him deepened. I had always viewed Truman as a wonderful, entertaining companion, but I suddenly saw just how perishable this odd little creature was, and he evoked in me a combination of love and pity—love for the giant who lived inside, pity for the dwarf that held the giant.

I began to remember trips I'd taken with him. His presence did require a strange adjustment and readjustment, even for someone as close to him as I was. Once, I recalled, after Leland and Truman and I had been in Spain for the Feria, we flew to Paris and checked into the Ritz. We agreed that we'd go to our rooms and rest and bathe, then meet in the Cambon Bar at nine o'clock for a drink before we went out to dinner. At nine, Leland and I walked into the bar. There sat Truman. The shock of seeing him again—though we'd been apart for only five hours—was overwhelming.

Now I understood why. When you were remembering his witticisms, he seemed like anyone else. But when you looked at him and listened to him being funny, you had to start at the beginning and get used to this curious physical presence all over again. The waiters would be looking askance, the rest of the customers would snicker behind their menus—and you'd walk in, standing tall, and give him a kiss, knowing that once you got past the shock, you'd be back in a close, comfortable friendship.

*Truman
and
friend.*

In all the years I knew him well and saw him regularly, the need for this readjustment never went away. You had to start at the beginning every time. When you said good night or goodbye to Truman, it was a full stop.

I think Truman was wrong though when he told me that no one loved him. Many people did love Truman. Truthfully, I don't know whether I loved him or not; I never trusted him, and that makes love difficult. He used to say, "You *never* confide in me, Big Mama." I'd always say, "That's right, honey, I don't. Because I don't trust you." I always figured that if he was telling me things that other people told him in confidence, then he was bound to be telling others what I might have revealed to him. And if he didn't think my story was good enough, he'd embellish it. My overriding aim with Truman was, therefore, not to be his source or his subject. Early on in our friendship I decided not to believe most of what he told me.

Babe, on the other hand, took in every word as though it were the Gospel. I remember her describing Truman's apartment: "Slim, it's incredible. He's taken all the plaster off the walls and he's exposed the brick." She described a marvelous room—which, when you saw it, was nothing but a cellar. But anything Truman said to Babe, she swooned over. I once told Babe I thought it was a mistake to tell Truman every confidence. She didn't understand—until the end. Because, right up to the end, Truman was a rewarding friend with a boundless appetite to be at the source.

He could also, with equal lack of notice, show extraordinary kindness and generosity. In 1961, he bought a little condominium in Verbier, Switzerland, and he and Jack Dunphy went there to spend their winters. Jack ran the house and skied; Truman worked on *In Cold Blood*. I was in between marriages at this point, so I decided to spend a few days with them.

One morning, Truman brought coffee to my bed and asked if I would like to read the first quarter of *In Cold Blood*. Flattered and delighted, I snuggled down in my bed and read what was to be the first of four installments published in *The New Yorker*. I was absolutely bowled over. I kept putting my head out the door and calling, "More, more."

"That's enough for now, Big Mama," Truman finally said. "What do you think of it?"

I told him the writing was exceptional and his technique was staggering, that this was far and away the best thing he'd ever written. It was so intelligent and yet so compassionate. And beyond all that, it would make a marvelous movie.

At this stage, it hadn't occurred to him that the story of a couple of killers in Kansas had movie potential. And he was quite surprised I could think this so early in the game. But Truman was a money player, and he quickly turned his attention to the opportunity at hand.

"How do you go about selling the film rights to a book like this?" he asked, quite innocently, I thought.

"You get an agent. I don't know if you're far enough along to start negotiating, but I'd think you are."

"Good," he said. His eyes glistened, the sure sign of a scheme being hatched. "Why don't you do it?"

"Truman, I don't know *how* to be an agent."

"You were married to the best."

"And I learned a great deal. But this is an important property. I'd be scared to death to take it on."

This didn't deter Truman in the slightest. "You can do it, Big Mama. And just think what it would do for you."

"What do you mean?"

"Well, if you're my *agent*, and you and I have a *contract* together, every *trip* you take, every *book* you buy, *everything* you do is tax-deductible because you'll be a bona fide businesswoman. You can write off a *great* deal of expenses, and you'll get ten percent of whatever the book sells for, which will make life easier for you financially."

Truman had me there. Without a husband, I wasn't as financially secure as I'd been in the past. And this was a gesture so kind, thoughtful, and generous I really couldn't refuse.

I was, however, rather terrified of going into the marketplace to start selling such a property. Fortunately, the offers came right in, and I was soon turning down very substantial sums for 1961: $250,000 from Twentieth Century–Fox, $300,000 from Frank Sinatra. Though the book was still unfinished, I believed in it to such a degree that I was certain if I held out long enough Truman could get a million dollars.

In the meantime, Truman kept pecking away at the typewriter, draining his gut out little by little. By the time I received the second installment—which was even better—I'd married Kenneth Keith and was living extremely comfortably in London. In these circumstances, I decided it was immoral of me to hold on to the film rights of the material.

I didn't want Truman to take my withdrawal the wrong way, so I said that I was now too far removed from the movie world to do him any good. What he needed, I told him again, was a really hot, tough, professional agent—Swifty Lazar. It took some doing, but I convinced Truman that if anyone was capable of getting him a million dollars, it was Swifty.

Truman finally agreed, but only under the condition that if Swifty sold the movie rights I would still get a percentage. I don't think Swifty was too pleased about this little clause in the contract, particularly when he succeeded in getting Truman a million dollars for the movie rights. By this time, however, everyone on both sides of the Atlantic knew of my involvement.

From morning to night, all I did was get calls from friends telling me to make sure Swifty paid me. Even Leland called and said,

"Nan, don't let that little bastard get away with anything. Because if it weren't for you, he wouldn't have the property to sell." In the end, I was badgered by so many people that I got very rigid and, though I'm no operator when it comes to money, I told Swifty he was going to have to pay up.

Swifty had a different idea. He suggested that I go to the jeweler David Webb and pick out a bauble worth seven or eight thousand dollars. He would buy it, have his wife bring it to me in England, and we'd be square.

I said, "Swifty, I think we're talking about a jewel worth twenty-five thousand. And that would be a very sensible solution except that Truman says take the cash and Leland Hayward says take the cash, so that's what I'm going to do."

Swifty grumbled, but he ponied up. Many were thrilled—Swifty Lazar writing a non-deductible check is not a common spectacle. But by the time I'd paid American tax on the money, it really wasn't worth the aggravation.

The money and fame that *In Cold Blood* brought Truman were even less useful. Celebrity slowed him down and distracted him from his calling. And although Truman rich could be hugely entertaining, he wasn't nearly as captivating as Truman thinking and working. There was a great stillness in him when he was writing, and I felt I could almost see past his armor into his soul.

There was, when he was working, an order to his life. He would rise very early and, in that tiny spider penmanship of his, work all morning. He'd break just before lunch and have a Bloody Mary or martini; after he ate, he would nap for a couple of hours. He would get up around four-thirty and make himself another martini, which he nursed as he reworked what he'd done in the morning.

Truman used to tell me he never touched that day's writing again, but then again he told other people he rewrote, rewrote, and rewrote. I don't know. What he always used to say was, "What I do, it's like making a mosaic. I move words around for their weight and their color until I know that it's a perfect line. And then I don't touch it anymore, I leave it alone."

Once Truman finished working, he might have one more martini before dinner. He'd have quite a bit of wine with his meal, and get a little loaded. But around midnight, no matter how good the company, he tapered off, made his good nights, and went off to re-

Truman in his better days. (Photo by Leland Hayward)

charge. Glamorous though his life was then, it had a routine as
regular as a factory worker's.

It was when Truman was idle that he managed to get himself into trouble. He would drink too much, and his forays with men he called the "vice squad" were more frequent. In the years I knew him, Truman was careful to feed the dark side of his soul in private. Though his straight friends knew he wandered at night, we never knew the details.

In the winter of 1970, when Truman took a house in Palm Springs, his cruising finally got the better of him. He had started the ill-fated *Answered Prayers*, his "big book," but writing took second place to a new obsession—a relationship with a man called Randy McKuen. Truman always told me he picked Randy up in a cruise bar; his biographer, Gerald Clarke, claims they met when Randy came to repair Truman's air conditoner. Whatever the case, Randy McKuen was indeed an air-conditioning repairman. Because he had a wife and two children who lived somewhere in the Midwest, he needed a second job as well, so in his spare hours he worked at the airport, pumping fuel into the tanks of private planes.

That winter when I arrived in Palm Springs to stay with Truman, I was immediately introduced to "this wonderful man who I know you'll adore." No chance. Randy was the nearest to nothing of anybody I've ever met: a dim, mothlike creature who was nothing more than ordinary. Still, he had some appeal that made him the center of Truman's life for one full winter, spring, and summer.

Truman was not only hopelessly in love with Randy, he had big plans for him; he intended to include Randy in his social life. Randy was to make his debut at a dinner given by one of the grande dames of Palm Springs. At first, luck was with Truman. When it became known that he was bringing a "Mr. McKuen," the society matrons went wild, assuming that Truman was bringing the pop poet Rod McKuen. Instead, they got Randy, whose brightest conversational topics were compressors, condensation, and power failures.

Truman should have known right then and there that Randy was out of his element. But he persisted. He wanted his beloved swans —Babe Paley, Marella Agnelli, Gloria Vanderbilt, Lee Radziwill, and me, among others—to feel about Randy the way he felt about him. If Randy had at least an idea of Truman's talent or position, we might have understood. But he didn't even know that Truman was a writer of tremendous stature. It was a Pygmalion scenario for Truman, who was desperate to expose this unfortunate man to the wonders of the rich.

No, Truman's blindness was worse; his adventure with Randy was about the greatest degree of non-smartness in Truman's misbegotten love life. For once Truman had supplied Randy with a new wardrobe, had his teeth fixed, and generally polished him up, he decided to take him on a grand tour of Europe. This trip included a boat ride on the Agnelli yacht, a weekend in London with Lee Radziwill, and another with Kenneth Keith and me at our country house in Norfolk—all very high-grade stuff. They got as far as London before Randy came to his senses and decided that the life Truman led wasn't for him.

When Randy flew back to California, he left behind a bereft, crushed, and love-lorn wreck. As intelligent as Truman was, he was totally myopic on this issue. He couldn't understand why Randy jumped ship.

I said, "Well, *I* can understand why he left. He's uncomfortable, he's in over his head and he knows it. You're talking about people he's never heard of. How could he have been anything but miserable?"

"I just wanted to bring him to your house," Truman moaned, "because you're so nice, and I know you would've been nice to him."

"Of course I'd have been nice to him. But he wouldn't have been any *happier* in a grand house in England than he was on a grand yacht in the Mediterranean."

I urged Truman to come and stay with me anyway, but he was too devastated, and he made his way back to New York. Those who cared about Truman were relieved that this affair was finished. But we knew he'd paid a huge price. Shortly after his visit to England, I went to New York and spent a lot of time with him; Truman barely noticed. He carried Randy's picture in his pocket, and would take it out continually to look at it. He'd sit by the hour, rereading letters Randy had written him. He was like a lovesick schoolgirl.

His friends, fearful that he would try to knock himself off, rallied around. In those unprotected and mournful weeks, he never tried to kill himself, but he did expose aspects of his character that he'd previously kept well hidden. That was how I came to realize that something had snapped in Truman—that he was doomed. From this time on, Truman never loved anyone as wholeheartedly as he had Randy. Now his partners reflected his self-destructive streak; they were, from what I know, of a rougher, more dangerous cut.

Add idleness and boredom to heartbreak and, in Truman Capote, you got viciousness. For a long time we didn't see it as such; his stunts, though increasingly brazen, were still funny. Like the lunch he gave at the Colony. It was after Leland and I had split up and Leland had married my English successor, Pam Churchill. One morning, Truman rang me and said, "Big Mama, you *have* to come to lunch. You're going to have a *wonderful* time. It's going to be a *fascinating* lunch. I'm *not* going to explain it to you—it's a *surprise*. Just be there."

So I went. The table was elaborately decorated and every lady was given a gardenia. "How nice," I thought. And I wondered: "Who's coming?" Then Marella Agnelli, an old friend, walked in. No surprise there. Babe Paley, my best friend, arrived next—nothing unexpected in that choice. That left one empty place at the table. Clearly, the mystery guest was the fascination factor.

At this point, with perfect Hollywood timing, the final guest entered. She was none other than Pam Churchill, the new Mrs. Leland Hayward. Very clever of Truman not to tell me the guest list! Pam took her seat, and then we sat there, like hooked fish, gasping for air. All of us, I'm quite sure, were thinking the same thing: What possessed Truman to host such a vicious little lunch?

But Truman's wickedness didn't stop there. Midway through our meal, who should enter but Gianni Agnelli, husband of Marella and former "close friend and protector" to Pam. As if he'd suddenly remembered something important, Truman turned to Pam and said, rather loudly, "Where's Leland? I asked him, too."

"Leland decided not to come," Pam replied.

I couldn't resist a shot. "He showed very good judgment for once," I said, looking directly at Pam.

In another setting, a remark like that could have started a catfight. Not here. We played through every barbed gambit Truman served up for his own amusement, avoided multi-leveled topics, and got all the way to the coffee without a scene. Two sips into my demitasse, I suddenly had a hair appointment, someone else remembered an early manicure, and we all graciously said our goodbyes.

"You're a devil," I told Truman on the way out. "A true devil."

"Well, did you have a good time?" he asked, with that little mischievous twinkle in his eyes. And I thought for a moment and had to admit that, in spite of the inappropriate cast, I had a great time. Only Truman—whose charms were so irresistible—could have given a cozy lunch that included the woman my husband left me for, one of her former lovers, and his wife, and still make it an entertaining occasion.

Then there was Truman the liar and Truman the ultimate shit-stirrer. He called me in London one day from Verbier in a panic and said, "Oh, Big Mama. You have to help me. I'm in terrible trouble. I've just sent a telegram to Gloria Guinness."

"That doesn't seem too extraordinary. What did it say?"

"It said, 'Darling Gloria, isn't it a shame about Pam?'—and that's *all*. I have to think of something very quickly, because Gloria will cable back wanting to know what terrible thing could have happened to Pam."

"Oh, Truman . . ."

"Well, it's so *quiet* in Verbier and I was so *bored* that I decided to stir up a little something."

Truman knew how to hook his friends. Instead of leaving him to invent his own explanation, I was all ideas. "We know she can't be pregnant, that's for sure. I'll work on it and get back to you." I should have kept out of it, but I did come up with an idea I couldn't resist sharing. So I sent Truman a telegram—it was the medium of choice for this particular prank—which read, in its entirety, "How about clap—as in applause?" Truman adored it.

Truman liked to cite higher authority whenever possible. I once asked him who his guide was on the subject of troublemaking. He wrote back: "Like dear St. Julian, I find salvation mingling in the lives of others." What he didn't acknowledge, though, was the lethal poison that ran through him while he was doing it. I knew he was a troublemaker, I knew he was a snoop, but, like everyone else, I thought he was armed with nothing more than a penknife. In fact, it was a dagger.

If the dagger was sheathed during most of our friendship, it was because women like me had an odd fascination for Truman. It's strange, given his personality and extraordinary gifts, that he should have been so obsessed with the trivia of the prominent. My only explanation is the one he later gave—that he was gathering material all along in order to become a latter-day Marcel Proust.

So, when he set out to write *Answered Prayers*, he must have believed he was creating a great work that would make his reputation for the ages. With an ambition that overreaching, his friendships were secondary. They would have to be sacrificed—at least temporarily. But once his literary permanence was established, his friends would return.

As for his friends, we were poor psychologists. We cited years of knowing the shining side of Truman to wash out our less happy encounters with his lying, gossiping, and troublemaking.

That was our mistake. Though we certainly knew Truman was a genius as a writer, we had let him all the way in; to us he was simply our very talented friend. That was, at worst, a social miscalculation. It was, however ignorant, a well-intentioned mistake. And it was private.

Truman's mistake was not.

"She was indeed a lady—Lady Ina Coolbirth, an American married to a British chemicals tycoon and a lot of woman in every way. Tall, taller than most men, Ina was a big breezy peppy broad, born and raised on a ranch in Montana."

That's part of paragraph number five of Truman's Waterloo, "La Côte Basque." And that's me. Me and me alone. He couldn't have been describing anyone else. Not only had he used my persona, he had made me the narrator of the damned thing.

"La Côte Basque," as some of the world now knows, was published in 1975 as a short story in *Esquire*. In Truman's plan, it was to be a section of his "masterpiece," *Answered Prayers*. Its notoriety, however, was more immediate. What Truman had done was "invent" a character named Ann Hopkins, who resembled in every detail the extremely well-known Ann Woodward. As you'll recall, Mrs. Woodward was a showgirl who married into one of America's most prominent families, only to shoot her husband, at near point-blank range, because, she said, she thought he was an intruder. No one believed her story, but because her mother-in-law stood up for her, she got off. Not, however, in Truman's version. The day after she found her own shabby portrait in his roundhouse hatchet job,

Truman putting his hex on the world.

Ann Woodward swallowed a truckload of barbiturates and died.

Even before Ann Woodward did herself in, the phones on the Upper East Side were humming. I, happily divorced from the English tycoon, was sitting in my living room blissfully unaware of Truman's treason when I got a call from Babe.

"Have you read Truman's piece in *Esquire?*" she asked, in a very un-Babe-like rush.

"No."

"Well, get it and read it and call me back."

An hour later, my jaw was on the floor. I couldn't believe that I'd

237

been so duped. I couldn't believe that Truman would use his friends in such a destructive and evil way. I was furious and hurt.

The word got back to Truman very quickly that a few people weren't too pleased. Shortly after the story's publication, John O'Shea, the man Truman was living with at the time, rang me and said, "Truman is very upset."

"Really?"

"Yes, he understands you don't like the piece."

"He understands correctly."

"You don't think that person is you, do you?"

"Well, who else *could* it be?"

"Pam Churchill, of course. He thought it would make you laugh."

"I'm sorry, but Pam doesn't bring to mind the picture of a pure western kind of cowgirl. It's a photograph of me. I *can* read, John. And even if it were Pam, it wouldn't make me laugh, John, because Pam has extended as much kindness and generosity to him as the rest of us. She doesn't deserve the piece either."

"Don't you think it's well written?"

"No, I don't think it's well written. And I never want to see, speak, or hear from Truman again. I've lost my friend, and I'm sorry."

That was that. I saw Truman—New York's too small a town to let you avoid anybody—but I never spoke to him ever again. And neither did Barbara Paley.

In the face of the impact of "La Côte Basque," I felt a deep sense of disloyalty. Truman had borrowed my mouth to spill out all the stories that he had either heard from other people or conjured up by himself. I had been exploited; now I was embarrassed. The disappointment I continue to hold against Truman for what he did to me and my friends—the people whom he so desperately sought to populate his life—made it impossible, then and now, to feel anything for him but disdain.

He did make advances to renew our friendship. He sent me a telegram when I was in Sydney, Australia, traveling with friends. The cable read: "My dear Big Mama. I have decided to forgive you. All my love, Tru." I was, I must say, enchanted by the daring tenderness that was in that missive, and my instinct was to answer it. On my friends' advice, I did not. So the break between us after the *Esquire* piece was final.

In friendlier times. (Photo by Van Williams)

Perhaps if the work were better, I would now be feeling a mellowing toward Truman. But "La Côte Basque" was most certainly not like reading Proust; it was more like a surgeon doing an operation with garage tools. It's as though Truman, having lost his scalpel and sutures, said, "Pass me the wrench." His delicacy, his finesse, his exquisite way of setting up his effects—there was none of that here. His finely honed style had been replaced with something else. The best you could say about this crude rendering was that the author surely had a strange, indomitable courage.

But forget the writer. Think, for a moment, about the man. Consider it from any angle you like, you still can't argue that a man of Truman's intelligence wouldn't know the effect his story would have on the people he'd profiled.

And so, when Truman Capote died on August 23, 1984, I felt nothing. For me, he had died nine years before.

SPILT
MILK

In October of 1958, a year after Humphrey Bogart died, Betty Bacall realized that it was time to start her life moving again. So she did two things to change her lot: she decided to go to Europe, and she asked me to fly over with her. An innocent desire, an understandable request. Why didn't I say yes right away?

I told myself I had just taken too long a trip and didn't want to see my suitcases again until the end of the month. I was to accompany Leland on a business trip, but the business couldn't have been more pleasant—Leland and I were going to Munich so that he could negotiate with Baroness Maria Von Trapp for the rights to her story. Leland sensed it could be a nice hit for him; I don't think even he dreamed the Baroness's story would grow up to be *The Sound of Music*.

So Leland was his best, most expansive self when we talked about Betty's request. "She only wants a week of your time. Considering what she's been through, how can you say no? All she's asking is for you to leave a week ahead of me. I'll meet you both in Paris and you and I will go on to Munich."

Put that way, I couldn't refuse. So Betty and I went to Madrid, where we spent a wonderful week together. When I left her, I could

My instructions to Betty Bacall on how to restructure her life. Bottoms up! (Photo by Leland Hayward)

see that Betty's plan to put her life back on track was going to work out. What I couldn't see was that our chummy little trip had set the stage for my life to fall apart.

To tell this story accurately, let me backtrack for a moment to insert a crucial detail into the seamy and deceptive tale I am about to unfold. Before I left for Europe, I got a call from Babe Paley. "My sister Betsey is sending me Pamela Churchill for the weekend," she said.

These two lines say everything to a small group of society insiders, not much to others. Let me do the geography: Betsey Whitney,

241

Babe's sister, was the wife of Jock Whitney, the newspaper publisher who was then the American ambassador to Great Britain. His great friend Pamela Churchill, about whom more in a minute, was leaving her base in Paris to spend a week in New York. Had the Whitneys been in town, they would have welcomed Pam at Greentree, their home in Manhasset; as they were in England, Greentree would have all the warmth of a deserted castle. So, thought Betsey, why not give Pam the cozy experience of a weekend with Babe and Bill?

If Babe was less than enthusiastic, she had her reasons. Great lady that she was, she knew that the arrival of a single guest from abroad carried with it certain obligations. She would have to give Pam a little dinner party in the country on Saturday night. She would have to get Pam some theater tickets for one night in the city —and, on top of that, she was honor-bound to find Pam an escort. Babe, who wasn't wildly fond of Mrs. Churchill, didn't want to go to any more trouble than she had to, so she asked me if I would mind—as I was going to be away that week—if she borrowed Leland for one night to take Pam to the theater. Without even a thought I was more than happy to help Babe out of her jam. But that, perhaps, was because I had met Pam exactly once, at Babe's house, just before I left for Europe.

Consider: Thirty-nine-year-old, English-born Pamela Digby Churchill had been divorced from Winston Churchill's son Randolph for a number of years. In that time, she had not been idle. She had been allied with, coveted by, and underwritten by many powerful men—Elie de Rothschild, Gianni Agnelli, Prince Aly Khan, Stavros Niarchos, Aristotle Onassis, Jakie Astor, Averell Harriman, and Edward R. Murrow, among others. Rich and powerful men were, in short, her career.

But although Pam Churchill had captivated most of the rich men in Europe, there was one prize that eluded her. Men supported her, they gave her a lot of things, and, when their romances with her were over, they came to Paris to visit her as friends—all considerable achievements. They just weren't available for marriage. Across an ocean, knowing her only by reputation, I assumed Pam Churchill had reconciled herself to her situation. And so I told Babe that I saw no problem if Leland were to take Pam to the theater with them.

And that's when all my troubles began in earnest. After a hilarious week in Madrid, Betty and I went to Paris, where I was to meet Leland. No sooner had we arrived at the Ritz than the concierge handed me a flurry of messages from Pam Churchill. "Mrs. Churchill's car is outside for Mrs. Hayward's use," "Mrs. Churchill wants Mrs. Hayward to call her. She's planned a dinner." And on and on and on.

All this attention was very odd to me. Why her sudden interest in Mrs. Hayward? Well, I thought, she's just trying to be hospitable, returning the favor I'd done her by loaning her my husband. Then Pam topped herself—she invited Betty and me to her sumptuous apartment for a quiet supper. The conversation was all girl talk, but it was, in its way, extremely pointed. "Are you happy in your marriage?" Pam asked at one point. I stupidly said something like "Well, no marriage is perfect . . ." and proceeded to tell her, in carefully chosen words, that although I deeply loved Leland, she might have the better set-up. A woman in Pam's position has the advantage of living alone, with all the freedom that implies, and yet she doesn't have to worry about her finances, doesn't have to keep house for her man; really, she doesn't have to put up with all the tedious things that come to define most marriages.

From this provocative start, we were moving on to even more intimate chat when the butler came in and announced a cable call for Mrs. Churchill. Pam excused herself and left the room. Betty and I immediately leaned in and began to wonder which tycoon was calling. We knew it had to be a big shot—this was 1958, remember, when people didn't make trans-Atlantic calls at the drop of a hat. It never would have occurred to me to think that the man on the other end was my husband.

A few minutes later, Pam re-entered the dining room and breezily said, "It's amazing how clear those cable calls are. You know, you used to talk on the phone to Europe and it sounded like the ocean was between you. Your voice would go up and down, you could almost hear the waves of the Atlantic. But this was just as clear as if I was calling you from the next room." With that, she turned to Betty. "Is there anything I can do for you tomorrow?"

Betty said she was leaving Paris in the morning.

Now Pam focused on me. "Can I do anything for you?"

"No, Leland is arriving tomorrow," I said.

SLIM

She took that, it seemed, as a neutral fact, for she went on to say that she had planned a little dinner for Leland and me and she hoped we would come, and oh, by the way, after dinner she had tickets for a play that, she felt, would be amusing for Leland to see.

The following night, Leland and I joined a dinner party of about twenty people at Pam's apartment, and then went off to the theater. In the car, she sat next to Leland; at the theater, she sat with him again, while I languished two rows ahead of them. After the show, she took all of us to a nightclub, where she had a twirl around the dance floor with Leland. My only question about this evening was financial: Who was picking up the tab? It didn't occur to me to wonder why Pam was providing all this for us.

The next morning, Leland and I went off to Munich, where he was his usual devoted, adorable self. And why not? The Baroness Von Trapp was amusing, eccentric, and, in the end, as eager for a hit as Leland was. I had to admire her negotiating techniques. At their first meeting, Leland offered her 5 percent of the show—not bad considering the composers would be Rodgers and Hammerstein, the book would be by Lindsay and Crouse, and Mary Martin would play the Baroness. "Well, I'll have to think about it a little bit," she said. At teatime, she returned with her answer. "You know, Mr. Hayward, whenever I have a puzzle in my head, or a decision to make, I always pray to the Holy Ghost. And I prayed to the Holy Ghost, and the Holy Ghost says ten percent!" And she got it. And everybody got rich. Except me. Pam ended up with the producer's shares.

We returned from Munich feeling so victorious that I settled back into my routine and forgot about Pam Churchill. It's often said that marriage is a series of peaks and valleys; if so, the last five years of our marriage had been mostly valleys. More often than not, I felt I was an underpaid nanny saddled with troubled children. Every time the phone rang, it seemed, it would be the Menninger Clinic calling to say that Billy Hayward had run away, or Stockbridge announcing that Bridget had had a seizure, or a tearful Brooke recounting the usual troubles in a young marriage. And during this period, Leland was having a very difficult time in his career—his life wasn't always *Mister Roberts* or *South Pacific*. Leland was, beneath the surface enamel, the patina, a very emotional, very fragile man, and his failures were beginning to wear on him.

244

SPILT MILK

If Leland were alive today, I'm sure he could tot up his share of grievances, too. I wasn't always easy to live with. I traveled too much on my own. In the first three years of our marriage, I was forever half-pregnant and lying in hospitals recuperating from miscarriages. And I'm a somewhat moody creature by nature. Between my deep black moods and my tendency to go for the sarcastic conversation stopper, I wasn't always adorable.

But as 1958 ended and I began my forty-second year, the time in our marriage when Leland and I were silently saying "This is the most tedious life imaginable" seemed over. We dealt with the children with less stress, entertained old friends, and thoroughly enjoyed the holidays; we were feeling good. In February 1959, when I decided I needed to spend a week at the Main Chance health spa in Arizona and lose a few pounds, Leland couldn't have been more supportive.

Nothing in Leland's behavior while I was away suggested that my absence had initiated the endgame of my marriage; he called three times a day. But when I returned home on Saturday, I hadn't gotten my coat off before he announced that we were going into the city the next night for dinner. "Sunday night?" I said, with a look of mild astonishment. It wasn't the distance—we were only about thirty-five minutes from the middle of Manhattan, and very often we'd go to the theater and then drive back home to the country. But whenever possible, we tried to avoid going into the city on a Sunday night.

"Well, I've accepted a dinner for us," he said, "and I'd like very much for you to go."

"Whose dinner?"

"Pam Churchill's. It's small, and I've said we'd come."

I stiffened. "Well, I don't want to go into town to have dinner with Pam Churchill. I'd rather stay home, look at my garden, and eat my own cook's food."

"If you're not going," Leland said, "I'll go alone."

With that, I knew I'd better go. I pulled myself together, and in we went to Mrs. Churchill's apartment in the Carlton House that was on loan from some benefactor. And the first thing I noticed when I walked in was that the room was filled with a certain kind of white rose that Leland had always sent to me. Restraining my rage, I walked over to Pam and asked her where she got those roses.

"Oh, someone sent them," she said.

I thought, "I know *exactly* who sent them," and shot Leland a look which read, "You sonofabitch." But I still wasn't taking the liaison very seriously; I thought it was some kind of joke. Ernest Hemingway used to tell me that I had a built-in, self-starting, automatic shit detector. Well, this invaluable mechanism was shut off at the moment when I needed it most.

At one point in the dinner, Pam turned to Leland and said, "Oh Leland, darling, would you be an angel and fill the ice bucket? You know where the ice is." Once again I thought, "That doesn't sound right." But I didn't muse on this evidence long; it didn't occur to me that anyone could take Leland away from me. When a man tells you that you're the stars and the moon and that you mean the world to him—and he tells you this for thirteen years—you believe him. I was blinded by my bogus sense of security.

This was, indeed, blindness mixed with an equal part of complacency. But there was some support for this myopia and self-satisfaction. Billy and Bridget were making great progress at their institutions. And Leland finally had an enormous hit, *Gypsy*. Truly, in that spring of 1959, it felt as if the mist of trouble that had surrounded us for so long was finally beginning to lift.

Buoyed by what I took to be a brightening future, I proposed to Leland the trip that was to be my final undoing—a real man-and-wife vacation, the first holiday in a long time that wasn't either at Menninger, Stockbridge, or the Shubert Theater. This time, we'd go somewhere alone, somewhere far away, where no one could call us to say there was something wrong with a child, or that the grosses had fallen off and it wasn't worth putting the play on the road, or the show was doing so well it had to be put on the road with a company that needed to be put together instantly. This trip would coincide with our tenth wedding anniversary; it was my ambition that it would put us back to square one.

For this honeymoon, we decided on brief stops in Paris and Madrid, and then on to Venice, where we had booked an apartment for a month at the Gritti Palace. But a week before we were to leave, Leland announced that business obligations forced him to postpone his departure. He suggested that I go ahead to Paris, and see some of our pals and he would meet me in Madrid.

The point of the whole trip was to do everything together, but

The incomparable Betty Bacall au naturel *on our trip to Madrid together.*

Leland was so insistent that I followed orders. And had, for my compliance, a very strange week in Paris. Harry Kurnitz and Martin Gabel squired me all over town, taking care of me, seeing that everything was all right, as if I were some sort of frail little flower. One day I ran into Yul Brynner in a restaurant. He came over to my table and knelt at my feet. It was so strange—I felt like the King of Siam to his Anna. "My darling girl, is there anything I can do for you?" he asked. "Anything in the world you want that I can provide, I will."

I couldn't imagine what this peculiar behavior was about. I said, "I don't need anything. I'm fine. I'm flying to Madrid tomorrow, and Leland's meeting me there in a few days, and then we're going on a long holiday together."

What I didn't know was that there was a master plan ticking away

With Papa and Betty in Málaga.

like a time bomb. And in this instance, the wife was really and truly the last to know.

I arrived in Madrid and there, awaiting me, was a message from Leland saying he had to postpone his arrival for the better part of a week because he hadn't finished casting the second company of *Gypsy.* A week passed. Leland called to say he would be further delayed because he couldn't leave Bill Paley, who was having a lung operation. I pointed out that Bill had a wife and children for this purpose; there really was no need for Leland to clutter up the hospital hall. But Leland insisted he had to be with his friend. I couldn't quite figure it out. I knew Leland was fond of Bill, but I didn't know his devotion was so total. Still, I didn't question his sincerity.

So there I was, going along with everything, and having, if truth be told, a pretty good time. Betty Bacall was making a film in Granada, so I went and spent a couple of days with her. Ernest was in Málaga for a week or so with a cuadrilla of friends, following the mano a mano between the two great matadors of the day, Luis Miguel Dominguín and Antonio Ordóñez, which resulted in the book *The Dangerous Summer.* At this point he was staying with his dearest friends, Bill Davis and Bill's wife Annie. Betty, who had wanted to meet Hemingway ever since she made *To Have and Have Not,* suggested that we join them. So off we went.

Papa watching me take off for Madrid.

Long experience had taught me to take Miss Mary's temperature immediately; this time, I knew from the moment we arrived that she wasn't too pleased. Not only did she have me to contend with, but I had one of the world's most provocative, witty, and lively women in tow. And that was when Betty wasn't working at it. Here in Spain, invigorated by sun and fresh air, she was looking as handsome as a golden palomino. Any man would fall for her—and Papa did.

Give this to Mary: she didn't crack until our last night in Málaga. We went to dine at the Davises', where we spent a long time at the table, chatting, making jokes, and consuming a lot of rough Spanish wine. No one really noticed when Mary excused herself.

After ten minutes or so, Mary returned. She walked over to Betty, who was seated beside Ernest, and held out two closed fists. "Which hand do you want?" she growled.

Betty, always up for some fun, missed the hostility completely. "I'll take that one," she said merrily, and pointed to the left hand.

Mary turned it over and slowly opened her fingers. In the palm of her hand was a bullet. "That is for anyone who moves in on my man," she said.

There was a deafening silence for what seemed like the longest minute on earth.

"Betty," I said at last, "I think we'd better be going."

Betty readily agreed. I can only imagine what ensued after our departure.

That scene stands out in my mind now, but then it was a mere incident in a vast sea of dramatic moments. For after another three or four days in Madrid, Leland finally turned up. And we had quite a reunion.

On my own in Spain, I'd had plenty of time to think about our marriage and what this trip could mean for us. I had rationalized it perfectly in my head. We had invested much in our marriage, we had been through much—ultimately, it had to stand us in good stead. It's not only the good times that serve to keep a marriage together; the cataclysms also bring two people closer.

This was, in retrospect, a terribly naive logic.

I was primed to share these revelations with Leland. But as soon as he arrived, he immediately went to sleep. When he woke up, late in the afternoon, I ordered his breakfast and opened the soft-boiled egg as I'd done for the last ten years. Then, before I could start, he got right down to business.

"I think we should have a talk," he began, in much the same manner of the maid who says, "I'd like to speak with you a moment, madam. I'm quitting." He proceeded with what sounded like a fairly rehearsed monologue. "I want our marriage to survive more than anything else in the world. But I think in order for that to happen, we should cancel the trip to Venice. I think we need to take a sabbatical from one another for a few weeks. Why don't you go to Biarritz, I'll send Kitty to you, and I'll go home and finish my work, and then we'll take another look?"

I said, "That doesn't make sense to me. If you think the marriage is in trouble and you're thinking about mending it, that's not the way to do it. You mend it by being together."

But he wouldn't see it that way. We talked in generalities for a while, going in circles until I understood there wasn't any logic to

Leland's position. That's when I began to smell a rat. And that's when he confirmed my suspicions.

"Oh, by the way, I think I should tell you, because if I don't, Truman or some other gossip will," Leland announced. "I've taken Pam Churchill to dinner a couple of times."

I'd found the rat. "Well, now," I said, "that should have been your opening line."

"It wasn't the most important thing that I had to tell you."

"Oh, yes it is. You've just dropped a building on me. But let me tell you something. It is not very original of you, but if you want to have a love affair with Pam Churchill, there's nothing I can do to stop you. But whatever you do, for your own protection, for your own dignity, don't marry her. You don't have to. Nobody *marries* Pam Churchill. Gianni Agnelli didn't do it, Elie de Rothschild didn't do it, Edward Murrow didn't do it. Why should you?"

At this point, Leland became very defensive. "I'm not going to marry her! What are you talking about? What I'm trying to do is make the marriage that *we* have survive and be healthier than I think it is right now. You know the only woman I've ever really loved with all my heart and soul has been you . . . is you. I can't imagine my life without you."

This huge speech—the same one he'd told me over and over since the days of our courtship—was delivered with his accustomed sincerity, but this time I didn't believe a word of it. The only thing I heard was the terror within me saying, "You're facing the world alone now, get used to it."

"I think I'll take a walk," Leland said. "I need some air."

I said, "I can well imagine that you do."

He left me in the sitting room of our suite at the Ritz. When he returned, forty-five minutes later, I said, "I hope it was a clear phone connection."

"I knew you'd say that."

At this point the doorbell rang, and into the room came about $500 worth of white flowers.

"These, of course, are from you," I said.

"Yes. You see, I wasn't on the phone, I was at the florist."

"Don't play with me like that. We're much too grown-up, we've been through much too much."

251

After we'd acted out this scene—and because I couldn't believe it was actually happening to me, it really did feel like a scene in a play—I took a bath and cried my heart out in the bathtub. All I could think was, "Why doesn't he tell me the truth? What's going to happen to me? What's going to happen to my child?" I was in a total state of shock.

The next morning Leland, with deliberate and smooth moves, prepared himself for his trip to Paris and then on to America. I sat in the hotel alone, completely totaled, not knowing what to do or where to go next, functional only to the point that I could shiver, shake, and sob.

I had been refusing all calls. I couldn't, after a few days, refuse Sam Spiegel's. Apparently Leland and Sam had flown out of Madrid on the same plane to Paris, and Sam learned from the horse's mouth what was up. As it turned out, he knew a great deal more than I did.

"Get on an airplane and go to Barcelona," Sam ordered. "My boat is there. It's yours—the whole crew, everything. Go anywhere you want, take anyone you want or take no one, but it's yours. I won't be using it for two weeks."

I thought about it a little bit, and accepted the offer. But by the time I reached Barcelona, I regretted my decision. Alone on a boat —how morbid! I felt fully capable of getting so depressed that I'd jump off. So I stalled; before embarking, I checked into the Ritz in Barcelona for a day. Inevitably, Sam called.

"I don't think you should go alone," he said.

"There's not much I can do about that."

"Yes, there is. I'm downstairs. And I have two lovely girls with me!"

Apparently he'd picked up two tomatoes and brought them along. Well, what the hell—at least they didn't know me. I stayed in my cabin all day, brooding, weeping, and carrying on, and only made an appearance for dinner. But I wasn't coming to terms with what had happened; I was completely delusional. Like a bereaved widow who thinks her husband is going to return from the dead, I'd convinced myself that Leland had told me the truth. He wasn't going to marry Pam Churchill. As everybody else had done, he'd have the walk-out with Pam, and then he'd get over it and return to me.

Giving myself this glimmer of hope, I composed what I thought was an irresistible cable to him: "Think twice before you do this.

We've put so much of ourselves into this marriage, and it's at the place where it can go wonderfully forward."

Sam was going ashore to send some cables about business and make a couple of phone calls, so I asked him if he'd send mine. When he returned, he gave me back the cable. "I read it and decided not to send it," he explained. "You can't send a cable unless you can read it to the man, and spell it for him. Besides I won't let you put yourself in that position." Then dear Sam enlightened me to the bitter facts. "Slim, everybody in the world knows Leland's going to marry Pam. She's told everybody, and he's told everybody."

"Nobody knows this but you and me," I insisted.

"Not true," he said. "Everybody in your world, my world, his world, and her world knows it."

I thought back on what had happened: various kind gestures, the sudden and unusual concern that my friends in Paris had shown for me. Harry Kurnitz, Martin Gabel, Yul Brynner—they all knew Leland was going to marry Pam. Once Sam laid the grim facts in front of me, I knew, too.

I couldn't save the marriage. Mrs. Churchill had moved in with such stealth that she was, by now, completely in control. For she had, in addition to the usual charm, a skill most people lack—a genius for long-range planning. Like a brilliant chess player, she knew her moves way in advance. She knew both where to place herself and how to maneuver you into a position where you couldn't intrude on her plans. And so her mission had been completed long before I'd even begun to realize what was happening.

There is a touch of irony to all this. Maggie Sullavan had made the mistake of leaving him alone too much. I'd done the same thing. Pam understood what we hadn't: Leland was a man who liked being taken care of. If you did that, you could get anything from him.

I was shattered, of course. The dominant reaction, however, was anger. I was livid that Leland never had the guts to say to me what he should have—that he'd fallen in love with Pam and was going to marry her. The truth would have hurt no more than what he told me. I was going to be swept away in any case.

And, yes, I was angry with myself. I understood Leland's wanting to have a walk-out with Mrs. Churchill. With auburn hair and a flawless English Rose complexion, she was certainly attractive, but her success wasn't based on beauty. She was famous for her ability to make even a casual dinner partner think he was the smartest, most interesting, most important man she'd ever met.

It's hard, if not impossible, to feed a man's ego for ten years. It's easy, in contrast, to get restless, to feel trapped. You tell yourself there's nothing wrong with a harmless flirt or fling. Man or woman, you sometimes need an escape from marriage. Leland did—and I did nothing to let him know, in advance, that he could do that and still be loved by his wife.

This may sound odd. But if you have any conscience or spirit or soul or goodness in you at all, you help a mate get through his troubles. Maybe in a different marriage, I could have had that compassion. Unfortunately, I'd been drawing on a dwindling supply of it for a long, long time; and when all you can do, over and over, is sympathize with sick children and a beleaguered husband, you stop, at some point, thinking about them and start wondering where you're going to get some relief.

I'm not to going to lie. I wandered on a few occasions. I think Leland probably did, too. He always said he didn't, and I always said I didn't. And that's correct—any fool who tells the truth deserves what he or she gets. That kind of infidelity is no threat to a marriage. It's just an entertainment, an itch you want to scratch. It doesn't have anything to do with loving someone.

The way I feel, right now, is the proof. I never stopped loving Leland. Even his death wasn't, for me, a reason to blunt my feelings. The fact is, I still love him. In a crazy way, even our divorce was a testimony to the strength of our love. At the maddest that I was, the most furious, and the most angry, we never stopped being friends.

And there was a lot to be furious about.

When I returned from Europe several months after the separation, I went to our house in Manhasset and learned from my cook that Pam had been in residence. Leland vehemently denied it—but there, on furniture and paintings, were red stickers that Pam had planted to indicate which treasures she wanted Leland to get in the divorce. Even then, I didn't hate Leland. I didn't hate him when I had to get the toughest lawyer in town to fight for my fair share, or when Leland had the balls to ask *me* to sit out in Nevada for six weeks so he could get a quick divorce and marry Pam pronto. We just liked each other too much to give one another up all the way.

Although I went on to marry Kenneth Keith and move to England, Leland and I still saw one another. In my new marriage, I kept an apartment at the Pierre Hotel and was in the position to afford the luxury of flying to New York once a week for a manicure, if I chose. I never came for such a frivolous reason, when I flew over it was to visit Kitty at school. I took a flight that got me into New York in the afternoon. No sooner would I arrive at the Pierre than the phone would ring—and it would always be Leland. How he knew I was there, I'll never know.

"Nan?"

"Hay! How are you?"

"Fine, fine, love to see you."

"Well, I haven't even gotten my breath. Where are you? I'll call you back."

"You can't, I'm in a phone booth. Right around the corner."

"This is where I came in. Always in a phone booth on the corner."

"Can I come up to say hello?"

He'd zip over to the hotel and, five minutes later, he'd be talking about the children or his work. By then, he'd stopped smoking and stopped drinking because he'd been diagnosed with pancreatitis. But each time he came to see me he looked sicker and sicker. At one point I asked him how sick he really was. He shrugged and said, "Well, I'm pretty sick, I guess. But it's nothing so serious that a hit wouldn't cure."

Although he was low in the last couple of years before his death in 1971, he was still darling. At the end of his life, when he was too sick to visit, he'd call me on the phone or send me messages from the hospital through Brooke or Billy. I never saw him in the last year of his life, but only because we both sensed the pain would be too great.

When I knew Leland was dying, I wanted to get away from New York. So I called Claudette Colbert, who had been very close to Leland and me over the years, and asked if I could stay with her in Barbados for a week or so. Three days after I arrived, Kitty called from New York to say that Leland had died. Claudette was nearby as I took the call; she knew, without hearing the news, what I was hearing.

With Claudette, in 1975.

I'd been prepared for this call. But preparation is meaningless in that situation. I hung up, deeply shaken. Claudette, a woman of great kindness and compassion, took me for a long walk on the beach, staying ten paces ahead of me, never intruding on my private thoughts, well aware that I had never gotten over the break-up of my marriage to Leland—and never would.

Yes, I had made a life for myself. I'd had a beau, remarried, divorced, and was now living happily alone. But in the end, when I lost Leland, I lost the best part of my life.

In Nassau in happier days. A very nice picture of two people who liked each other an awful lot.

ALONE AGAIN

I'd never been left before. All my life I had walked away from men; no one had ever walked away from me. I either got out before they could reject me or before I could get bored. But in the novel condition of abandonment, I went back to Madrid after my boat trip with Sam with my spirits touching bottom and my brain literally unable to figure out what to do next.

Everyone in my world knew what was going on, so I was given the kind of support that meant a lot later on but didn't really penetrate at the time. Only two contacts stand out in my memory of those confused days. One was a telephone call from Ernest in which he talked to me like a boxing coach: advice, commiseration, comfort, and love all couched in fight language, along with the reassurance that he would always be in my corner. The other was a cable from Spoleto, Italy, where Jerry Robbins was choreographing a ballet for the Spoleto Festival of Two Worlds. The cable simply read: "Move over, Lady Brett. Why don't you come and be with me? Call me."

When I called Jerry, he'd heard everything from the usual town criers in New York. He instantly knew what to do with me. "Tell the concierge at the Ritz to put you on an airplane to Rome, and have him cable me what flight you're on. I'll take care of the rest. Just don't stay there by yourself."

At this point, I was putty in anyone's hands. I numbly followed Jerry's instructions. And soon found myself in Spoleto, installed in the sweetest little apartment, where you could only take a bath at six o'clock because at five they built the fire under the water tank. "I have to work all the time," Jerry said, "but you can stay in the theater with me, eat every meal with me, and never leave my side. If that's what you want to do."

That was just the beginning of his kindness. Once Jerry had finished his work in Spoleto, we rented a car and drove all over northern Italy. We stayed in funny small hotels, stopped at quaint restaurants, looked at beautiful things. We were on a safari to hunt down every Piero della Francesca we could find, and we saw quite a few of them. The trip was a great comfort, as if the world had reached out to put its arms around me.

It was Jerry's tender and abiding friendship that got me through the most miserable time of my life. My trip to Italy was, however, only a temporary cure. I was fine as long as someone was holding my hand, but the minute I was alone I fell to pieces again. I returned to Madrid and met up with Ernest, who took time off from his mano a mano research crusade through Spain to spend a couple of days with me, and look after me.

Ernest was going to the Feria in Pamplona, a place I'd wanted to visit for a long time. He volunteered to take me, but despite my frame of mind I could see what a disaster that would be. I felt going to Pamplona with Ernest would end up the same way Leland felt my going to Africa with Ernest might end. Mary would surely put a sword through my back.

What Ernest didn't know was that I'd already made arrangements to go there with someone else. Through my crisis I not only felt defeated, failed, inadequate, but for the first time undesirable. I was in desperate need of reestablishing that I was a woman who was still a viable, believable, attractive female. You can't talk yourself into that; someone else has to do it. Back at my headquarters—Madrid—I'd met a Spaniard who'd taken a shine to me. I had already agreed to go to Pamplona with him.

The Feria de San Fermin in Pamplona is a rollicking event. It's seven days and seven nights of non-stop drinking, no sleep, and thousands upon thousands of people thronging the streets, jamming the cafés, watching the running of the bulls in the morning, and the corrida each afternoon. Basket case that I was, I jumped right into the madness. I drank a lot, I rode the Alguacil's horse down the streets of Pamplona. There's a picture of me in a dress, on the horse of the Alguacil—the man who enters first into the arena, rides straight across the bullring, stands under the box of the presidente, and is thrown the key to the bull cages. The rider wears a hat with feathers. In the picture, I'm on his horse, in his hat.

I did manage to meet up with Ernest. He was happy to see me until he caught sight of my traveling companion and then he was unnerved, furious that I would dare to go to Pamplona with anyone but him. I could see that Ernest was on a steady diet of too much drinking, which invariably resulted in truculent behavior. I left the Spaniard behind one night and accompanied Ernest to a restaurant where we ran into David and Jennifer Selznick who were sitting at another table. David had made *A Farewell to Arms* and Ernest felt about the movie the way he felt about all the screen adaptations of his books—he simply thought it was a piece of crap. He was right: it was not a good film. Upon catching sight of David, Ernest went wild with anger, shouting across the room, "I'm going to kill him! Sonofabitch! He ruined my book!" I managed to restrain him from going over to David and turning the table over on his head or something equally aggressive. At which point Ernest forbade me to go over and say hello, accusing me of being a traitor if I dared to disobey his orders. I set him straight on this point very quickly—I told him they were close friends of mine and I would do anything I pleased. At that I marched over to David and Jennifer with the usual warm salutations.

Ernest might have been crazy, but in Pamplona he was also king. He would walk into the bullring and the crowd would scream, "Olé, Mr. Papa, olé, Señor Papa!" Once, he entered the bullring before the parade of the matadors. The gate opened, and Papa came out and walked the full way around the ring, behind the barrera, to the sounds of screaming, cheering people. Ham that he could be, he loved the celebrity of it all. It was the last time I saw him as I had first known him.

Papa came to visit me in Biarritz after that, but his illness had

*At the bullfight
in Pamplona.*

*With Papa
in Pamplona.*

really taken hold and he was distracted and unlike himself—swinging between depression and madness. In general, I missed the next two years of paranoia, disintegration, and longing for death. We spoke on the phone, he wrote, but on his side there was more evasion than communication. Toward the end, when he was at the Mayo Clinic, I wrote to him: "Friends with as much going for them as you and I have had all these years should not let that friendship go. And I'm not going to allow you to let it go. This is to tell you that I think about you all the time, I'm concerned about you, I hope they're finding out what the trouble is. I'm your Miss Slimsky, just like I've always been."

Mary called me one day to say he kept that letter in a drawer beside his bed. He would take it out and read it three or four times a day. She asked if I would do her a great favor and talk to Ernest on the telephone. Of course I agreed. She explained that they would make the call to me only if he was in a "good frame of mind." There were no guarantees. I was by the phone on the appointed day at the appointed hour, but the call never came.

Many times I think about a promise Ernest made, but couldn't keep. Once when we were at a bullfight in Aranjuez, Ernest turned to me and said, "You know, Miss Slimsky, I can promise you one thing. You and I will spend the end of our lives together. We always should have been together. And we will be together in the end."

I laughed. "Papa, that's impossible. You have a wife and she's good to you. I'd make you a terrible wife, we'd end up hating each other!"

"Well, that's the way it will be," he told me. "I promise you."

For all the warning, the end took me by surprise. In July of 1961, I was summering with Kitty on Cape Cod. Shipwreck Kelly and his daughter, Victoria, had taken a cottage next to ours. One afternoon, Ship sent the girls off on a treasure hunt. And then he sat me down and told me that Ernest was dead. Ship was a great prankster, but I knew this was no joke.

"How?"

"Slimsky, he killed himself."

When he said that, I believed him completely. I had always maintained that nothing could kill Ernest but Ernest himself. Airplanes couldn't do it, disease only slowed him down, he walked through wars. The only immunity he didn't have was from himself, and now that he had finally been defeated by his demons, I felt bloodless and numb. As the news became known and the broadcasts began to deliver additional details of his suicide, the numbness was replaced by acute pain. The world didn't have two Ernests in it; a big part of my life was gone, and I knew it.

But in 1959, my future seemed more problematic than Ernest's. After the marathon of fatigue-making jollity at the Feria, the Spaniard drove me to Biarritz, where I'd decided to settle for the rest of the summer and have Kitty come from New York to be with me. The Spaniard was beginning to wear on me. Though his determination was fierce, I quickly saw that he was not for me.

I arrived in Biarritz shaky and scared. Six weeks had passed since Leland left, and aside from wondering how I was going to live without this man whom I loved, I was asking myself an even bigger question: How was I going to live at all? I had never been on my own. I'd been looked after by my mother, Howard, and then Leland. If I wanted something, I said what I wanted and I got it. If I wanted to go someplace, I called an office and told a secretary to arrange it. I had no idea of what it meant to do things myself.

Beyond the emotional part, there were practical worries. I was terrified about money because I didn't know how much I had or what it meant or how much I could use. On top of that I had the full, total responsibility of my child.

I had to face the ordeal of telling Kitty. I knew it would be devastating for her because—as her own father was nonexistent in her life—she'd come to regard Leland as her father. She called him Pop and had even gone so far as to call herself Kitty Hayward because she didn't want to be the only one in the family with a different last name. Leland put her on a plane and as luck would have it, an old friend from my Hawks days, Jayne Wrightsman, shepherded her to Paris, where we would stay overnight before going to Biarritz.

It always seems that in times like these an incident occurs that will provide you with a ray of light, a kind of strength, a clarity that you hadn't been able to grasp before; and through the incident it becomes possible to take the reins of your life and go forward. For me, the strength came in the form of my daughter.

Kitty arrived at the hotel with her little valise. "Leland the brave" obviously hadn't told her, but in that perceptive way that children have, she sensed something was wrong. Of course all she had to do was take one look at me and know that this was not the same mother who'd kissed her goodbye two months earlier.

I sat and watched her unpack her tiny, girlish belongings—wondering how I was going to break the news—when she pulled a Cartier box out of her suitcase and said, "Here, Mother, this is something from Pop."

In this box lay a string of lapis lazuli beads with a card that said: "These beads are blue like your eyes and my heart. I will always love you. Leland." In the face of what he was planning to do, I didn't know then and still don't know now what to make of that gesture.

When I finished reading the card, I completely broke down with dear little Kitty watching me. Finally she asked what was wrong. And in the simplest, most uncomplicated way possible, I said, "Lelee and I are getting a divorce. He's met someone else who makes him very happy and I hope I will meet someone too, but I've got you and he hasn't, and that's a big advantage."

Her only response was, "Oh." And she walked out of the room and into the bathroom. I followed and stood watching her, though she didn't know I could see her. She brushed her long brown hair for quite a while and finally she stopped, came back into the room, and with absolute confidence said, "Mother, we don't need him, we can get through this by ourselves. We'll be fine without him."

Those words were chilling, coming from the mouth of a thirteen-year-old child, and yet so loving. Here was my daughter in the throes of adolescence with a wisdom and fortitude that I completely lacked. I began to think back to the time when my grandmother had died and I had become the mother and my mother became the child. Leland's leaving was Kitty's loss too, and in the long run maybe harder on her than on me. Now, in her short life, she'd already suffered two heartbreaks—a real father who ignored her, and Leland who left her—these are scars that don't mend easily, if at all. It was a brave thing for a young girl to swallow her pain and give her mother this kind of love and support.

The words of Ernest, Jerry, Sam, and many others had meant a great deal to me, but there was something in what Kitty said that gave me the grit I needed to pull myself together. It made me realize that no matter what happened there was this creation—Kitty—

Mother and daughter.

whom I'd raised on my own, without any help from her father and without much help from Leland, and she was beautiful and strong and kind. If I could create that by myself, then surely I needn't be terrified of being on my own. Thirty years later, Kitty is the same kind of daughter she was then.

THERE'LL ALWAYS BE AN ENGLAND:

Sir Kenneth Keith

There's one thing I used to pride myself on. I always married for love. I thought I loved Hawks. I knew I loved Hayward. The third time around, when I married Kenneth Keith, there was no love involved. It was purely a cerebral decision—I thought I needed to be married—and Kenneth was the ideal prospect. But ideal prospects rarely make ideal husbands.

When I returned to New York after my tumultuous summer, I settled into a life that autumn of 1959 with someone I met in Biarritz. Ted Bassett was darling and totally inappropriate, but he came along at just the right time. He single-handedly pieced together my shattered ego and never left my side for three years.

Bass was a catalogue of exterior attributes. He was fun. He was adventuresome. He had strange, wonderful good looks. He was a graceful athlete, a brilliant gamesman, a real gent, a very good backgammon player and an excellent bridge player, which is how he really made his living. And he was the best dancer I ever danced with.

He wanted to marry me, but as much as I adored him I knew that if I married him, I wouldn't adore him in about five minutes. Be-

Bass.

cause he was, in the end, a lightweight—a gambler, a do-nothing, a playboy. The time I spent with Bass was like being on a three-year summer vacation. At the end of summer you say, Vacation time is over, let's get back to work, let's learn or accomplish something.

Bass never had those larger ambitions. His days were spent getting himself all dressed up neat as a pin, looking very chic, and going off to his office—that meant the Racquet Club—to play backgammon all day long for thousands of dollars. He traveled with the

267

seasons, from New York to Palm Beach, then on to Deauville and Biarritz, and St. Moritz in the winter, always in the main watering place where, he believed, he was *supposed* to be at that particular time of year.

In Spain, during a Bassett summer when I was single, I was at one of those great groaning lunches that Ernest's friends Bill and Annie Davis used to give in their garden in Málaga before the bullfight. Extraordinary they were. Always more than enough of everything—places at the table, food, and guests. I sat spooning away at my white gazpacho (no American can make it properly, we don't even get the red one right) and nibbling on blood-red ripe tomatoes and figs still warm from the sun. From behind me came a pair of cool hands covering my eyes. A voice I knew so well said, "I would know the back of this head anywhere in the world." I looked around into Leland Hayward's big china-blue eyes in his daughter's— Brooke Hayward's—face. A wave of affection went through me. Both of us felt an immediate realization of how much we both meant to each other; the bond had only increased with the years.

As much as I loved Brooke—and we are still warm, loving friends today—seeing her was like a blow to the heart. For to see her was to see Leland and to be reminded of everything that was not happening in my life. I knew I had to put an end to this idle life with Bass, and I knew I had to get out of New York.

Since the summer of 1960 there were now two Mrs. Haywards in New York. I didn't want to run on the same track anymore. I was tired of mutual friends having to decide whether they should have Leland and Pam or me for dinner. I was usually the one who got disinvited. And I was tired of the dumb life I was leading with Ted Bassett.

To make a clean break, I took a small flat in London for the months of May and June. My plan was to be alone, to read, look at some art, and reflect. I was, I said, looking for a quiet time.

Enter Kenneth Keith.

Shortly before I took this trip, Ann, Lady Orr-Lewis, an English friend of mine who was staying with me in New York, arranged a blind date for me. She wanted very much to go to the theater with John McClain, a jolly, funny man who wrote theatrical reviews for the old *Journal American*. But she had a previous date with an illustrious single young banker from London. Would I stand in for her? All I had to do was to go and see the opening night of Jason Robards in *A Thousand Clowns* with this man, and then, after John had written his review, he and Annie would meet us at "21." Not much disaster possible in that scenario; I agreed.

My date came to pick me up. The maid let him in and showed him the way up to the drawing room. And the oddest thing happened—as I heard him coming upstairs, it ran through my mind that maybe my destiny was climbing those stairs. You just never know.

Kenneth Keith appeared. He was big and quite good-looking in a totally English way: pale blue eyes like two drills and dark brown hair that was slicked back with English men's pomade. He was beautifully tailored and obviously rich—and I couldn't understand one single word he said. He sounded as if he had marbles, mush, and a lot of steak and kidney pudding in his mouth. I might as well have been talking to the Ayatollah.

We made enough sense for me to give him a sandwich and a drink, and then we went off to the theater. Later, at "21," he asked what I'd like. I said I'd arrange it, and told the waiter to bring me a baked potato and the whole can of caviar and I'd take what I wanted. Kenneth's head sort of snapped back and landed in a stunned position. In England, apparently, a lady doesn't order caviar on the first date; but I heartily scooped up about three ladles of the stuff.

However taken aback, he was interested enough to come all the way up from Wall Street the next day to give me lunch at the St. Regis. Though he was too solid a character to flirt, he was nice and bright, and told me he'd been divorced for some time and he had a fifteen-year-old son and daughter who were twins. He told me what he did, none of which I understood. All through lunch I kept saying things like "Would you please go back three paragraphs to the word 'partridge' and then go on again, because I didn't understand any of the last part."

This language barrier was one we never conquered. He used to say, "I don't know why you have trouble with me. The Prime Minister can understand me." Harry Kurnitz, who I thought was the funniest man alive, told me after he met Kenneth, "That man you're married to should have subtitles flashed across his vest!"

Kenneth was then chairman of a very important British merchant bank called Philip Hill Higginson, which eventually became Hill Samuel. He was obviously a fair-haired boy, and at forty-six, very young to have had such astonishing success. To most women in my position, he would have been a catch to be cultivated, pursued, and snared. But once he was gone, I forgot about my promise to call him when I got to London and take up his offer of a weekend at his country house—really, I forgot all about the boy banker. Instead, I went off to Spain to the Feria in Seville, and ended up in Madrid to stay with my friends Aline and Luis de Romanones.

One afternoon I was sunning myself by their pool when I was called to the phone. Because I was now planning my escape from Ted Bassett, no one knew where I was except my lawyer, who had to know how to reach me in case Kitty might need me.

As I went into the house to take the call, Luis said, "I'll bet you any money you want that you'll marry the person on the other end of the phone."

"You're crazy," I said. "What if it's a woman?"

It was Kenneth Keith.

"How did you find me?" I asked.

"I have my ways. I can do just about anything I want if I set my mind to it," he said.

"Well, it was nice of you to call. What do you want, boy banker?"

He was inviting me to a special dance in Norfolk at Holkham Hall —the home of Lord Leicester. Would I come to his house for the weekend and be his date? And oh, by the way, could I come for dinner at his flat in London the night I arrived?

Although my little flat was just across from his rather grand one in Eaton Square, Kenneth picked me up in his Bentley. We had a pleasant two-minute journey to his marvelous apartment. We had a drink, we chatted, we had dinner, and he brought me home. Nice. But not exciting.

Then a kind of courtship started. I began to get little presents, the first of which was—the standard English wooing present—a black crocodile handbag. Then he asked if I would come for the weekend. "You've asked me for the weekend of the Leicester party," I said. "Don't you think two in a row is a bit much?"

"No, I don't. We'll take my plane up."

This was sounding better and better.

The Wicken, Kenneth's country house, is a lovely old brick house with a cellar from Roman times. Many of the buildings date back to Thomas Coke, the first Lord Leicester, who had the property at the end of the eighteenth century. The main structure was a small "manor house" (as opposed to a "great house") that had been built at a later time over the ancient Roman foundation. It has a beautiful situation on a rise of soft, rolling open land, the horizon uninterrupted for five or six miles. There are walled gardens, vast lawns with every blade of grass pointing in the right direction, and noble trees planted in the eighteenth century by Capability Brown. To see it for the first time in late spring—the time when England is really at its best—took my breath away.

But what struck me the most, once I'd seen my room and unpacked and strolled around the house, was how impersonal it was. English country houses are noted for their cozy, lived-in feeling. When they're right, the rooms are filled with furniture and objects that each have a history and a story of their own. Inside the Wicken, though, there was very little. The first evening I was there, I asked him how long he had rented the house.

Kenneth looked at me like I was some sort of halfwit. "What do you mean, rent it? It's my house, I was *born* in it."

"I can't believe it," I said. "There's not one personal thing in it. There isn't a book or a photograph anywhere. And where are the flowers? There isn't one thing in this house that makes me think it's anything but a summer rental."

That is, when you think of it, quite a feat. To Kenneth's credit, what I did notice when I first saw the Wicken was a great sense of order and love. Kenneth did love the Wicken more than anything else in the world.

It was on my second weekend at the Wicken, after the dance at Holkham, that Kenneth asked me to marry him. I've never understood why people always propose to me so soon after they've met me. After two marriages that started in this way, you'd think I would have expected a sudden proposal from the delivery man, but Kenneth's offer caught me by surprise. As much as I wanted a change, I wasn't so sure this was the kind I had in mind. I told him I'd just finished with a marriage and was trying to get away from another fella; I just didn't think I wanted to belong to any one person for a while.

Kenneth was undaunted. Back in London, he asked me out for

dinner every night. On one of these occasions, he announced that he'd chartered a yacht. "Good for you," I said. "Bon voyage. When are you leaving?"

"It's for you *and* me," Kenneth replied. "It leaves from Ville-franche, and we'll sail around the Mediterranean and get to know each other."

"Well," I thought, "why not?" I wasn't married, and although I wasn't so sure I even liked this man, I was pretty adventuresome in those days. The worst that could happen would be that I'd abandon ship if things got too bad.

Our first stop was Monte Carlo, where we encountered my old friends Doris and Jules Stein at the bar of the Hôtel du Paris. Doris waved me over. "My God, Slim, what are you doing here?"

"I'm with Kenneth Keith."

"But, Slim, do you know who he is?"

"I'm sailing around with him. I should."

"Jules, Slim is with Kenneth Keith. Isn't that wonderful?"

Before Jules could weigh in with his approval, I thought I'd better drop what I considered a bombshell.

"I'm not so sure how great it is," I said. "He wants me to marry him."

"What? That's wonderful!" Doris said, as Jules nodded agreement. "Marry him, you've got to. He's one of the most important men in England. He's going to be knighted. It's just sensational. You must do this."

Still unconvinced, I left Monte Carlo with Kenneth and sailed down to Corsica. As we were cruising along, sunning ourselves on the aft deck, the conversation turned from general talk about money to the stunningly specific. "How much money have you got?" he asked.

"I don't know," I replied.

"What do you mean, you don't know?"

I said, "I don't know."

"Well. How much do you spend every year?"

"What I need to spend. Sometimes I spend more than I've got and sometimes less. But I buy what I want. That's all I understand about money. And that's all I want to know. I own my house, my kid's in school, if I want an expensive dress, I buy it."

"I think we ought to go to New York and get all those things straightened out," Kenneth said calmly, "so we can get married."

"I haven't said I was going to marry you."

He said, "Well, you are."

I could then understand how he'd gone so far in business at so young an age. He was a Sherman tank. He'd run over his mother, he'd kill his children, he'd do anything to get where he was going. He was so positive, and such a salesman, that it hardly mattered that I never officially said yes; overriding every objection was his refusal to hear no. Kenneth was soon saying, "I think we ought to announce it to the press when we get off this boat."

I said, "I wouldn't think of doing that before I've talked to my daughter and told her first, face to face. And you should not do that to your children, either."

"Camilla and Alastair are easy, it's just a phone call."

I said, "Well, my child isn't easy, it's not just a phone call. And I'm not that kind of parent. I hope you aren't either. I'll be going to New York."

This certainly gave me an inkling of the kind of relationship he had with his children. But he did listen to my advice and call them.

Kenneth thought he should accompany me to New York. I wasn't sure if it was because he believed I might not return or because he was anxious to find out about my financial status. Judging by the way he behaved about my income after we were married, I assume it was the latter. Anyway, he came with me. I got Kitty out of boarding school to tell her the news. She thought the whole thing was too romantic for words. I told her I didn't know how romantic it was but I hoped that she would like him; and I added that he had a daughter and son only a year younger than she.

Because Kitty took it so well, I began to feel that maybe it was the right move after all. Although I knew this important man wasn't going to provide a wonderful, joyful, tonight-is-the-opening-of-*South Pacific* kind of life, I also knew that he would be good and steady, had enough social status to reinstate Kitty and me to some place of dignity and position, and that he would give me the freedom to find things that interested me. That was not the best of recommendations, but you think twice about those things when you're a single, grown woman.

My decision was calculated; so was Kenneth's. The difference was that for Kenneth the decision wasn't out of his character; he'd resigned himself to a life without love. I was, in a sense, a jackpot beyond belief. I was decorative, I possessed social grace, I had tremendous acquaintanceship with all kinds of people he didn't know, I was financially independent and I could run a good, proper house.

And so we closed the deal.

We were married in London on June 22, 1962, with Kitty as my maid of honor. Kenneth's children didn't attend because they were still at boarding school. After a small, attractive lunch given by my friend Mrs. Gilbert Miller, we flew off in Kenneth's airplane to Paris for a few days. Once on the plane, my heart filled with terror as we sat, side by side, alone in the cabin and spoke not one word from takeoff to landing. In Paris, Kenneth was unsure, unhappy, and probably filled with the same misgivings as I was. He was, however, very generous, and went on a buying spree, bringing back some beautiful surprises.

It was in Paris that one of my reasons for marrying Kenneth backfired. After our wedding, Kitty and her best friend, Hopie Putnam, embarked on one of those grand tours on which a Count of no accounts was taking a few teenagers on a trip around to the grand palaces, cathedrals, and museums of Europe. The first stop on the tour was Paris. They arrived when Kenneth and I were there, and had lunch and dinner with us every day.

On our last day together, I told Kitty that we had to decide whether she should go to school in England or Switzerland. A cloud came over her face. Then, summoning her courage, she announced that she had no intention of going to any school except Westover— her present one in America. I was absolutely crushed. It had been such a dramatic step for me to be leaving my own country, my friends, and a life I knew and understood to go and live in a land with total strangers. I thought having Kitty nearby would ease the transition; though she was sixteen, I felt as if I was losing my baby. Luckily, Kenneth rose to the occasion and convinced me that I'd be doing Kitty no favors by forcing her to leave America.

Despite the bridge Kitty made, our honeymoon was a flop; when Kenneth and I returned to England, we were still in the same awkward state. God knows Kenneth tried to get through this. Every morning for the first week in London, my breakfast tray was adorned with a loving note and another trinket from Schlumberger.

A few weeks later, Kenneth astutely suggested that he give a cocktail party in order to introduce his new wife to his friends. Given the circumstances, I was most enthusiastic about this event. I had no decisions to make about it, though, because the house was run wonderfully by the butler, Mordecai, and his wife. I did take a peek in the kitchen at one point on the day of the party, and was amazed at how little preparation was going on.

I soon found out why. By the time the guests had assembled, there were ten people in the drawing room, including us. To my surprise, they were all business associates—with their wives—from Philip Hill Higginson.

Panic came over me. "What does this mean? He must know more people than this. He's lived here all his life. Either he was desultory in arranging this little wake, or he's public enemy number one."

Both conclusions were right. When I came on the scene, Kenneth was one of the most prominent men in England, but he was certainly not one of the most popular. He'd hurt a lot of people on the way to his gigantic success, and instead of soothing them afterward, his charmlessness compounded the hurt. So he was isolated—and destined, apparently, to remain so.

At the time, I didn't know that he was also experiencing a terrible business battle. As the head of Philip Hill Higginson, he'd recently bought the Erlanger Bank, run by Leo d'Erlanger, a much-loved man of the financial community whose family had come from France a century ago. As a result of this merger, Mr. d'Erlanger was thrown out. The running of the new entity was way beyond the gifts and talents of Leo d'Erlanger, who was by this time quite old, but I always felt Philip Hill Higginson had been hasty in asking d'Erlanger to go. Mr. d'Erlanger was bothered by the decision and made that quite known, but the person who really fanned the flames was his wife Edwina, a fellow American and a formidable woman.

Two months into our marriage, we were asked to a very grand dinner party—the first invitation we'd received as a couple. About an hour before we were to go, I was in my bedroom with the hairdresser when Kenneth walked in and announced that we'd been disinvited. The host and hostess had also invited the d'Erlangers

At the benefit performance of Charlie Chaplin's The Countess from Hong Kong, *for the Jules Stein Eye Hospital in London. L. to r.: Charlie Chaplin, Mrs. Jules Stein, and me, the chairperson of the event.*

and when the d'Erlangers had discovered that Kenneth was coming, they'd made their apologies. The hostess decided that Leo d'Erlanger, as the older man, should come; Kenneth was expendable. It was then that I realized that Kenneth's problem with the d'Erlangers was also my problem. Edwina d'Erlanger was well placed socially in London. She was adored by the English and the Americans and was in a position to make our lives miserable. If I didn't get to work and make a life for us, I sensed I was going to live a very unpopulated existence.

There was another surprise awaiting me. For an outsider, particularly if you're American, England is a very difficult country. Of all the countries I've ever been in, it is the most unfriendly to the expatriate, and by a wide margin. If I didn't know this before I married Kenneth, it was because, on my brief visits to England with Leland, I was surrounded by a lively theatrical group. But Kenneth's environment was the complete antithesis of Leland's. No one in his set was much impressed by a gregarious gal from Monterey. The fact that I can make friends easily, that I'm malleable, well mannered, and well informed, is hardly worth beans in England. The social structure is locked in. I soon learned I was condemned to live solely in Kenneth's world.

This world was a solid, traditional, huntin', shootin', fishin', upper-class life. The myth of impeccable English manners comes into play here. I remember in the early days of our marriage going to cocktail parties, walking into a room of sixty people and not meeting one person who was willing to make contact. My idea of good manners is that if you're the hostess and you've invited some-

Kenneth Keith at his country estate, the Wicken. (Photo by Horst)

one new in the community, you make an effort. You take several minutes to walk her through the room and introduce her to a few people. In England, you're not introduced to anyone unless your husband knows a lot of people in the room—which mine didn't.

But even if Kenneth had been wildly popular, I would have been at a deficit for years and years. The English really aren't interested in talking to you unless you've been to school with them or to bed with them. As I didn't fit into either of these categories, I spent a lot of time standing in corners, staring off into space.

Then there were the dinner parties—mostly for business. That was definitely the hardest work I've ever done. Seated between two gentlemen, I'd be forced to talk to the man on my right during the fish course, then to the man on my left during the meat course. Because I didn't know either one, I'd have exactly the same conversation with both of them.

Every time, that conversation went like this:

He says, "How do you like living in England?"

I reply, "Well, I like it very much. It's very new to me, and I'm finding my way around, but I'm enjoying it immensely."

"Where do you come from?"

Now, he knows full well what all the answers are going to be because he's read every single word in the press about me. So I save him the full story and give him a one-minute answer.

Now we're in trouble. We're at the point where I might ask: "What do you do?" But if he tells me, I'm not going to understand anyway. So there's a silence. Then he says, "Do you enjoy the shooting at the Wicken?"

"Well, not really, because I'm not allowed to shoot. I mean, I'm allowed to shoot, but I'm not a good enough shot to shoot with the men. Still, I love having the guests and the people, and I love the whole process, and it makes Kenneth happy so it makes me happy."

I have now consumed the first mouthful of fish. And you have to go all the way to the tail.

After dinner, I'd be led into the drawing room with the other ladies, where we'd sit in a little knot and talk about the maid or the children or have a tiny bit of gossip. Forty-five minutes later, the hostess calls the gentlemen to join us. And, finally, the evening expires.

I knew after a few months this sort of social life would never do.

I'd be dead by the time I was fifty. If Kenneth expected me to conduct a dinner party like this in our home, he was with the wrong girl. Dinners they were. Parties they were not; there was nothing party about them. Nobody was doing what he or she wanted to do. It was like an absurd parlor game.

I had to widen my circle of acquaintanceship. In London, I went to the Tate Gallery and volunteered my services; I was put on the fundraising committee, I didn't complain. With a lot of diligence, I began to meet people. In the country, my aim was to renovate the Wicken on every level: redecorate the rooms, improve the food, give it a climate of fun and gaiety so people would want to come there. Kenneth, to his credit, let me do just that.

Improve the Wicken I did, with the exceptional help, taste, and wisdom of the interior designer Tom Parr of Colefax & Fowler, who guided us through the restoration and additions. My problem was with the staff. The work hierarchy and the routine of progression had been so long established that this American interloper with her revolutionary notions about having a log fire burning in every room, flowers on every table, and things to read on every night table was met with very stiff backs. These backs did not unbend when I replaced Mrs. Willis, a cook who could create miracles of total destruction. There was a lot of sniffing and an intense study of the shoetops when I offered my suggestions. But with Kenneth's backing, I was able to make quick and constant improvements.

I didn't make too much of Kenneth's support. He encouraged me because he hoped I'd be happy, but he also helped me because of the Wicken itself. In my day, its 2,500 acres were systematically farmed—for profit, of course, but without ever losing sight of the fact that the land was primarily kept for shooting game.

Kenneth had a rigid and elaborate shooting life. Though the house was filled with guests every weekend from September until January, they didn't come because they were friends. The whole thing is built around shooting itself—how good a shot you are and how good the shoot is. The choice of guests is carefully made, based on who has the most pheasant or grouse or partridge. If a man accepts your invitation to shoot, the chances are good that he will ask you to shoot with him, which is what the whole system is about. So your house is filled with a lot of people you never see otherwise and who offer little in the way of stimulation or amusement.

SLIM

When I arrived, the dinner parties in the country were no better than the ones in town. Kenneth was looked upon by the locals of Norfolk as the catch of the century. It took them a long time to get over the fact he'd married an upstart American. There were very few people with whom I could converse and have a good healthy argument. And the man at your side was usually looking at you with crossed eyes because he was thinking about whether the fifth pheasant that came in from left to right on the afternoon drive was hit by him or the man opposite him.

Some of the rituals of the shooting life were, I knew, impossible to change. That simply was the English way. But by improving the house, the food, the staff, and the atmosphere, those shooting weekends became more tolerable for me.

On an ordinary weekend of shooting we would cater perhaps one hundred and twenty meals. Let us say there are ten people staying in the house, including Kenneth and me. Often two or three guests will have brought their own servants. Guests very often bring their own loaders with them, or a chauffeur who is also a loader, or the other way around. It was up to me to feed those people and to put them up as well.

If there are ten in the house, that usually means there are five guns, as only the men shoot, except in rare cases. I never saw a woman shoot with the men, but they sometimes do. As seven guns are required for a normal shoot, you have to ask two local people to fill out the required number. They also bring *their* loaders and wives (free lunch).

Let me explain what I mean by a loader. Each man shoots with two guns. He fires two shells from the gun in his hand and either hits or misses, then gives the gun with the spent shells to the loader in exchange for the other gun which is loaded, unlocked, and ready to fire. If it is a good, well-attended (by birds) drive, this maneuver can happen many times during a single drive. The loader carries the ammunition, the guns, the shooting stick and all the impedimenta that is required. He can be very important, as it is his business to see that the shooter always has a loaded, ready gun in his hands.

There was a separate kitchen and dining room for their care and feeding. Beer or lager was provided for them and the beaters. There

In my new domain. (Photo by Horst)

are usually about fifteen to twenty beaters. They are somewhat retarded villagers who walk through a field wearing yellow slickers, carrying sticks and thrashing away at the ground ahead of them as they walk in a loose flank across a cut grain field. Their mission is to frighten the bejesus out of the poor birds hiding there, so that they will rise and fly, unsuspecting, directly over the guns which have been strategically placed to decimate them.

There would be three people in the main kitchen: sometimes a chef that I would import from London with a couple of helpers, and later on Rose Mordecai, who was always the best. There were usually three men in the dining room. There were three or four local ladies who came in to make beds and generally tidy up, and a couple of washers-up in the pantry.

Mine was one of the few houses where one did not have to give breakfast orders the night before. In many houses, one is asked the night before what you would like for breakfast and what time. And if you wanted a cooked breakfast (as opposed to raw?). That puzzled me a lot in the beginning. I eventually found out that it meant anything more than tea and toast. One egg is a cooked breakfast. In my house you could call the kitchen from your bed and order what you wanted when you wanted it, rather than making a commitment which either left you starving for two hours because you had awakened too early or, worse, awakened you from a sound sleep in order to be given an undercooked egg, cold toast, and cool ecru coffee. It was a big breakthrough in country house amenities.

The gentlemen are brought their tea very early, before or while they dress. They attire themselves in their shooting suits—short pants and long stockings—and then come down to the dining room for breakfast. Women are not really welcome at that meal. If they are intrepid enough to show up, they must do so in silence. Breakfast for the men is a big meal laid out on the sideboard: always two or three kinds of eggs, bacon, ham, sausages, grilled kidneys, grilled tomatoes, one hot cereal, several cold ones, tea, coffee, toast (cold), buns, and whatever else I could think of to make it a little snappier than the last place they had been.

They all then foregather in the courtyard. The shooters and the loaders board jeeps, Land-Rovers, station wagons, and all available rolling stock, and are then delivered to their place for the first drive. There are usually three or four drives in the morning and two after lunch.

The ladies wander down as they rise, and very often go to the last drive before lunch. There was always a car at the front door waiting to take them into the field so that they could have some fresh air and feel that they had participated a little bit in this very manly sport.

Then they would all come back for lunch. At the Wicken a shoot-

A breather on the moors at Phones, Scotland.

ing lunch was a set menu which was unchangeable. No matter what innovations I might want to make, the shooting lunch was the shooting lunch, and it was not to be changed one iota. There was always steak and kidney pie or pudding, the difference being that the pie has a flaky crust and the pudding a suet crust—hardly a crust, more like a chewy white blanket. Always Brussels sprouts, potatoes, salad, and ham on the sideboard, Stilton cheese and glasses of fresh celery on the table. Always sloe gin at the end of the meal, and it had to be passed clockwise around the table, as with port. To thrust the decanter across the table to the chap with the empty glass? Never—never! Unforgivable manners. Best of all was dessert: some apple concoction—Brown Betty or deep-dish pie—or tiny little mince pies so small they could go one or two to a customer. You dug a little hole in the top crust and poured in a taste of sloe gin. How good that was! One began to feel that life wasn't so bad after all.

This procedure took an hour or so, including the before-lunch

Bloody Marys which I made by the gallon and Mordecai the butler handed around. We worked out a system so sophisticated, so graceful and so well timed it was as if the drinks came out of a tap.

Directly after lunch, the men loaded themselves back into the cars, jeeps and wagons for the last two drives. These were done with dispatch and a no-nonsense seriousness. It had to be finished at least by three-thirty because of course night was falling. Back to the house for tea. Another swinish great meal of scones, crumpets, grilled bacon, lobster or sardine sandwiches, cake, cookies—anything that was costly they got and ate. And always the same exchange: "How would you like your tea?" "As it comes." Well, it comes out of the pot dark brown. "As it comes" really means with a bit of hot water, a dash of milk, and three sugars.

The men then find themselves chairs in the drawing room or the library, where they cover their faces with the London *Times* and go to sleep until they are nudged by Mordecai, who reminds them: "It is time to change for dinner, sir." "I will just have a whiskey and soda before I go up." They change quite quickly and are back in no time for their very dry martini before dinner. The ladies appear, dressed to the nines, and dinner is served.

I would entertain them after dinner with a movie so that I wouldn't have to spend too much energy on conversation with the non-bridge players, and one by one they would peel off and go to bed.

That crew of people would leave on Sunday after lunch, and very often there would be a second day's shooting on Monday for guests arriving Sunday night, which meant that the house had to be changed like a Holiday Inn. Bed linen, towels, bedroom flowers—everything had to be done over after we got the weekenders out.

It was all done smoothly and marvelously well, mainly because of the fantastic executive ability of Mordecai the butler and his wife Rose. They are probably the nicest people I have ever known, and also the most professional. They truly made my life in England bearable. None of it would have been anywhere near as good as it turned out to be without Mordecai's brilliant managerial talent. Eventually, Rose took over the kitchen and, with a couple of helpers, provided certainly some of the best food in England.

It did give me some satisfaction to be able to do it. It was more like a challenging game of solitaire to me than a domestic tour de force, I suppose, because I really didn't give a damn whether the cast got the point or not, and many of them didn't. I got the point, and I knew it was as good as could be done. The Baron Edmund de Rothschild said it was the only house he had ever been in where shooting boots were cleaned between the morning and afternoon drives. And indeed they were, while we were all at lunch. I never knew who did it, but no doubt it was Mordecai himself, in between courses.

I certainly enjoyed our own shoots more than other people's. Being a guest is a lot harder work than being a hostess. The worst thing that you can do is go grouse shooting. It's complicated and uncomfortable. It is either very cold or very hot or very wet, always buggy, and very far away. I went to two grouse shoots, my first one and my last one. They were separated by two years, during which time I recovered from the first one.

It was given by Kenneth's uncle Alec Keith. He was a strong, erect, imposing man who, when I met him, must have been in his middle seventies. He was king and emperor of a property called Chesters, a vast hideous Charles Addams house near a town called Humshaugh in Northumberland. Uncle Alec had a grouse moor not too far from where he lived, and Kenneth was delighted to have been asked, as Uncle Alec sometimes came to shoot with us (the system at work).

There was a gray, grim discomfort about the place, and a gloom that enshrouds that part of the world. It was one of the most unhappy houses I have ever been in. Legend had it that when Uncle Alec was a dashing young country gentleman he had fallen in love with a local beauty, and one evening, being more than usual in his cups, had decided to pop the question. Somehow between the fog and the grog, he got her confused with her sister and popped the question to the wrong lady. She of course accepted and he, gentleman that he was, was stuck with her for the rest of his life. That unfortunate lady was Aunt Daphne. She looked like a tweed sculpture. Her face, her hair, her costume, her legs—especially her legs —and even her shoes looked like gray heather tweed. She did two things very well. One was to make pincushions which were admired during the cocktail hour, and the other was to walk. She would go out on the moor with Alec and walk the whole day through like a beater or a hound. No jeep lift to the next drive for her. She strode across that treacherous terrain as though it were a lawn.

Kenneth's twins had briefed me on some of the Chesters house rules. The most important was to be sure to steal something from the sideboard at breakfast, because if you didn't you might not have anything to eat until 2:30 in the afternoon, and that could be very skimpy when you got it. Taking their advice, I left the dining room that morning after breakfast with pockets stuffed with bananas and peaches and a few crumbled biscuits that I hoped would get me through the day. I climbed aboard Uncle Alec's jeep and off we went to the moors.

You drive for a long time and when you arrive at absolutely nowhere, you stop and get out and take off, walking across the moor to your assigned butt. The moor looks smooth and lavender and endless. You start to walk across it. You then realize that what you are looking at is heather. You don't walk on heather. You walk on what is underneath the heather, which, as it turns out, is a series of surprise potholes that occur when you least expect them. By the end of the first twenty minutes, I was limping, in severe pain, and complaining bitterly, mostly to the loader, who I felt would not report me for poor conduct in the field. I was loathing it and it had hardly started.

I felt as though I had just scaled Anapurna when we arrived at the butt which had been designated to Kenneth. A butt is a little hole in the ground that has rocks all around it and on the inside too. It is large enough to hold the shooter and the chap who is going to load his guns. There is no room for a dutiful wife, or an admiring girlfriend, or a small child. Even the dogs are not allowed in the butt. They had to sit outside, like me.

I was shown to a rock outside the butt. The loader handed me a thick, dark-green plastic envelope on which I sat, weeping, with two dogs, also weeping. And I was told to keep my head down! At any cost, don't show your face. If the grouse sees your face, it will turn around and fly away. This news did not help my ego an awful lot. I obediently did as I was told, by now in a fury of colossal proportions. I could not understand why I had been brought on this torture trip if I wasn't even allowed to watch the damned birds fly

over. I smoked constantly in order to envelop myself in a haze that
I hoped would ward off the mayflies and mosquitoes who, by the
way, were as big as the grouse and, unlike the grouse, were fascinated by my face and hands and ankles and anything else they could
reach.

As a very fine mist started to fall, the loader came to me and said,
"Pardon me, but may I have that envelope you are sitting on?"
"Why?" I asked. "Well, it contains Mr. Keith's rain gear. It is in
that envelope." So I gave it up. Out came rain trousers that went
over the other trousers and a jacket that went over the other jacket,
and a kind of Baggie that went over his hat.

That left me with nothing to do but take off my macintosh jacket
and sit on that, before I realized that I had made a puree of my
illicit lunch that I had so carefully stowed in its pockets. The loader
tried to placate me and the dogs—all of us crying—by tossing the
dogs a biscuit and me a lemon sour ball, while the three of us
endured the glares and curses of the shooter: "Bloody damn
women! Bloody damn dogs!" And that was only the first drive, the
beginning of one of the blackest days of my life.

After hours of this purgatory, we were finally offered lunch in a
little stone hut with a dirt floor and a smoking fireplace on some
distant moor. I, of course, went straight for the whiskey. And Aunt
Daphne said to Uncle Alec, "She's not supposed to drink it now.
It's for later. She can't have it now." I simply looked at Kenneth
and said, "I am going to drink it now and I am going to drink your
share and her share or I am not going one more step. This is the
most barbaric pastime ever conceived by man, and if I do any more
I am going to do it drunk."

After January, when the shooting season ended, there were many
weekends at the Wicken when there were no guests. The winters
were long, cold, and dark. I would read or play solitaire. In the
spring and summer, I adored working the same hours as Billy the
gardener, a dear man who, at the beginning, knew about as much
as I did; we learned together and had great joy in bringing seedlings
to flower.

Those weekends after shooting season were the times I could
have a non-English cast and import my own friends. Claudette Colbert and her husband came a few times. Rosalind Russell came.
The locals couldn't quite deal with the American and her Hollywood

cronies. They referred to Roz as the "film actress," as though both words were four letters.

And there were English people whom I adored having. Sir Solly Zuckerman, now Lord Zuckerman, who was responsible for all the scientific warfare during World War II. Julian Melchett—and his wife Sonia—who was one of the brightest people in English politics. Or Cecil Beaton.

That last invitation was met with disapproval. Kenneth wasn't interested in having one of his country's most distinguished men for dinner. He simply "didn't want that pansy in my house." Which always mystified me. I mean, in England how can you tell who is and who isn't? But with persistence I managed to get Cecil and a few others who were off Kenneth's track into the house.

No matter what I did, the drive to the Wicken every Friday night with Kenneth was made in total silence. Not only wouldn't he talk, he wouldn't let me listen to the radio. We'd get into the car about four in the afternoon and make the three-hour drive to Norfolk, a bump of land that sticks out into the North Sea like a wart on the right side of England. I think the next solid piece of land is probably the North Pole. It is such an alienated part of England that I always felt better traveling back and forth with my passport.

Kenneth appreciated the way our houses were run and the effort I made to widen his scope, but he grew competitive with me. He realized very shortly into the marriage that if I wanted to run a dinner table, I could do it without him. He once told me rather plaintively, "When we give dinners and you're way at the other end of the table, I always see the people around you laughing and carrying on. You loosen them up and they enjoy themselves. I find myself wishing I was at your end instead of mine." He knew I could make the conversation go where I wanted it to go, and make people talk about what I wanted them to. That drove him a little crazy; England is, as Englishmen say, a man's world. Every morning he would get up in the flat in London and go to his bathroom where the toothpaste had been squirted onto the brush by Mordecai. I would hear him making strange noises, as if he were a baritone doing breath exercises, warming up. One morning I walked down the hall—and there he was, standing stark naked in front of his bathroom mirror, with his foot up on the washstand, making the sounds he was going to

Mr. and Mrs. Irving (Swifty) Lazar at the Wicken.

make when he gave his orders that day. To my amazement, he rehearsed his personality.

Could Kenneth be funny? Terribly, but only when he didn't know he was being funny. He never joked, and he never got my jokes, which made me lonelier than lonely. In the beginning, I used to tell myself it was because we were from different cultures and countries. But I knew that wasn't true; I could have a hell of a good time with David Niven, Cary Grant, or Laurence Olivier. Kenneth was just serious stuff.

In this, history repeats itself. In many ways, Kenneth was like

My walled garden at the Wicken.

North face of the Wicken.

The Wicken.

Howard Hawks, incapable of real love or emotion. He had a nascent tenderness, but he didn't want anyone to see it. He compensated by being tough, tough, tough.

The real bone of contention, however, was money. As I lived in England and was married to an Englishman, I was British-domiciled. This meant that once I paid American taxes, whatever was left of my income came to England and went on top of Kenneth's income—which put him in a 99 percent tax bracket. This drove him so wild that he refused, in all the years we were married, ever to pay a bill of mine.

After a few years, he devised a scheme to lower his tax bill. It was simplicity itself—I wasn't to have any income. Which didn't sit too well with me. The thought of being at this man's mercy for every penny I needed was too horrible to contemplate. Once I declined that idea, he came up with one better. Why not get a Mexican divorce and not tell anyone? I told him, "Honey, if we're divorced, that's it. I'm gone."

It's hard enough to negotiate about money with someone you love, but when it's someone you don't, it's next to impossible. I really didn't think I wanted to go through with these discussions. Maybe a divorce—a real one—was the answer. I knew I'd live in different circumstances: there wouldn't be the cars and the airplanes and the servants, but I didn't really give a damn about that.

We decided to go to New York and have lunch with my lawyer, Abe Bienstock, to discuss the money business. Kenneth had what he considered a great solution. The details are unimportant. What matters is that I sat and listened, and then I pushed back my chair, got up, and walked out of the office.

I went back to my apartment in the Pierre Hotel that I owned and paid for and that Kenneth used. The phone was jangling as I came in. It was Abe. "That was the most brilliant piece of negotiation I've ever seen!"

I said, "It wasn't that at all. It's exactly what I think about Kenneth's solution. And by now I feel so cold about it, I don't care whether it works or not."

He said, "Well, just let me tell you what happened. You left, he left, but he was back in fifteen minutes with a completely different set-up that's very advantageous to you. I advise you to take it."

I said, "Well, I'll think about it." And I eventually accepted it.

But things were never right after that. If they were ever right before. There was always tension over money. My money. And there was really no way it could be eliminated from our life.

I think that Kenneth saw me as always crouched for takeoff. He felt that any moment now I'd run for the train. After I finished my restoration of the Wicken and made it really first-rate, he said to me, "I'm so glad I waited for you to come into my life before I redid this house, because now it is everything I've always wanted it to be. You've done a wonderful job. I love it. I'm proud of it, and I'm grateful to you. One thing, however, I hope you don't leave me until you do the drawing room."

Again, the old question: Why did I stay? And, once again, the answer is familiar. Because, when his brother Michael died, Kenneth cried. For the first time. Just as Howard Hawks had told me that he threw up on his way to the set every day, Kenneth told me something about himself that moved me—it bought Kenneth a few more years of marriage. And there were just enough bright moments to distract me and make me think it might all work out. Most of these were provided not by Kenneth but by his family. I loved his children and I enjoyed the same kind of relationship I'd had with all my other stepchildren. Kenneth, I knew, loved them very much, but treated them in the upper-class English way—as if they were miniature adults. From the time they were little, they were farmed out to boarding school; when they came home, there was no display of parental affection.

The first time I met Kenneth's children was when I arrived at the Wicken as the new Mrs. Keith. Kenneth, Kitty, and I had flown up to the Wicken, not only so that I could meet Camilla and Alastair but also so that the staff could meet the new lady of the manor. Awaiting me at the Wicken's airfield were these attractive and appropriately nervous teen-aged twins. We politely shook hands and made our way to the cars that were waiting to take the five of us and our luggage. To break the ice, I turned to Alastair and said, "You look old enough to drive, why don't I ride with you?" Without batting an eye, he hopped in one of the cars and off we went. The drive was more or less made in silence with such standard questions as, "Are you enjoying your summer holiday?" As we approached the long gravel driveway that led up to the house, I could see the staff in their uniforms, lined up like soldiers waiting to greet me.

Up to this point Alastair had been driving at a snail's pace. Suddenly he decided to step on the gas—and we drove through the garage door and right into the wall.

A look of horror swept the poor boy's face. It read: "Father's going to kill me." For some reason the whole thing struck me as comical. I proceeded to have an uncontrollable laughing attack, during which time I managed to say, "I thought you knew how to drive." "No," he said. And he started to laugh. It was definitely an icebreaker. Alastair was right about two things. His father was angry. And, as Alastair later told me, "Slim, when that happened, and you laughed, I knew Camilla and I were safe."

The first improvement I made in Kenneth's life concerned Camilla and Alastair. Our first dinner together as a family was like attending mass. As we worked our way through the first course, there was nothing but silence and the intermittent clank of the silverware against china. Kitty and I looked at one another with great discomfort and started chattering away to keep the ball in the air. The twins were amazed, but they continued to eat with their heads down, and once they'd finished everything on their plates, they neatly placed their cutlery correctly in the middle of the dish and waited in silence until their father decided to say something. Which he didn't.

Afterwards, I said to Kenneth, "That was the dreariest dinner I've ever been to. Don't you people *talk?*" "Not until we're finished with our food," he said. I told him that would have to change because I talk all the time. And it did change. Along with actual conversations during dinner, I also instituted the revolutionary practice of decorating the house at Christmas and celebrating holidays in a traditional family way. The children were agog. In these small ways, by bringing a bit of life and jollity to the house, Kenneth began to enjoy his children.

Another highlight for me was Frank Keith, Kenneth's father. He was a gentleman farmer—a breed that only England seems to produce—a sensitive, erudite, and elegant man. He was marvelously dressed, and ran his house as well as you can possibly run a house. Even though he was in his late seventies, he was also the best shot I've ever seen.

When I came onto the scene, Kenneth hadn't spoken to his father

Christmas at the Wicken. L. to r.: Kitty, Alastair, and Camilla.

for quite a few years. He wasn't too eager to talk about him and all I was ever able to glean from our conversation was that his father was a neurotic and strange man, though Kenneth was never able to back up that characterization with fact. Everyone in the Keith family was scared to death of Frank, including Kenneth, who never seemed terrified of anyone.

One evening, a few months after Kenneth and I were married, we were having dinner with his brother and his brother's wife, and I said, "I don't think it's right that we've been married for four months and I've never met your father." All three of them just sat there like stones. "Obviously, none of you is going to introduce me to him, so I'll go by myself." At this, they found their tongues. They said, "You wouldn't." I said, "Yes I would. Just tell me how to get to his house."

A few days later, I carried out my threat. The proverbial ancient butler answered the door to the mysterious woman who'd arrived unannounced. "I'd like to see Mr. Keith. I'm the new Mrs. Kenneth Keith," I explained. "Just a minute, madam," he said.

The butler disappeared, to be replaced by a wonderful-looking old man. "I'm Kenneth's new wife," I announced, "and I think it's high time we knew each other."

Frank Keith looked me over. "I'll say one thing, you're a fine figure of a woman!"

"Well, *that's* the way to start. I hear you have a marvelous garden. Would you show it to me?"

And he walked me through the garden, served me tea, and gave me some 1912 port.

I asked Frank why Kenneth didn't speak to him. He said, "I don't know, it's something about money, and Kenneth is very strange about those things." I assured him I knew all too well how strange Kenneth was about money.

I invited Frank for lunch the following Sunday, which he reluctantly accepted. Kenneth was also reluctant about seeing his father and rather surprised to hear he had agreed to come. I told Kenneth he was going to behave and be sweet because I knew from my own experience with my father that it would be better for him in the long run if he mended some fences.

Frank showed up at the appointed time in his green Jaguar with his corgi, George—he'd had twenty of them in his lifetime and they were always called George. I greeted him at the driveway, brought him in, and said to Kenneth, "Your father's here." All Kenneth could say was, "Well, I'll be damned." The lunch was a success; they began to get on and make a relationship again, for which I gave myself full credit.

Father and I became good friends. I would often dine with him alone. He was bright, eager for an intellectual argument that didn't have to be won, infinitely more stimulating than Kenneth. And he was fun. The two of us would potter in the garden together, jabbering away about plants; he'd give me plants and I'd give him plants. He was great fun to buy a Christmas present for. He'd say, "Oh, I will never wear that dressing gown, it's too grand." I'd say, "That's not too grand for a man like you."

At one point, he asked me to read *The Forsyte Saga*, warning me, "There'll be lots of things in it that will remind you of this family." He marked the section in his copy that he particularly wanted me to see: the part about Irene and her relationship with the father. It was his way of saying, "You've brought a lot of brightness and happiness into a life that didn't have any in it."

Being American, I always felt, throughout my marriage to Kenneth, as if I were watching an English play or reading an English novel. Many of the people were the stock characters we've all seen or read about. Kenneth, for instance, was a musical comedy Englishman, a Colonel Blimp. His father was the typical distinguished country gentleman.

And then there was my beloved Mordecai, who was a butler out of central casting if there ever was one. Mordecai is his surname; his given name is Edgar. But as is the English tradition, the butler is always called by his last name, and his wife Rose was called Mrs. Mordie. Mordecai had a searing wit and a keen perception of things

My beloved Mordecai and John Ringling North (seated).

as they are. There was nothing fake or phony about him. He began his career as a boot boy at Hatfield House, the very, very grand house belonging to the Marquis of Salisbury. It was here that he met Rose, who was an upstairs maid. They fell in love, married, and Mordecai got promoted to Lord Salisbury's valet.

He used to regale me with stories of when he was being trained as a butler at Hatfield House. The best was how he was taught to set a table. Each setting had to be in a straight line—with the glass directly above the knife. After the table had been set, the head butler would come in with a long stick. He'd place it along the row of glasses, and if the stick touched one, woe to the servant who had set that place. Mordecai did everything that way when he came to work for Kenneth. He was one of the great professionals. But more than that he was a terrific human being, and so was Mrs. Mordie.

As the Friday evening journey up to the Wicken with Kenneth was so dreary, I most often chose to precede him by car with the Mordecais in the morning. They would pack a picnic and stop halfway at the Newmarket Downs to give the dogs a run and have our lunch. Our picnics were easy, but proper. They used paper plates and plastic cups and cutlery. I used china and silver. Their napkins were paper, mine was linen. The only thing that was the same was the food. Although we shared so much with the running of the house and we really had a deep, warm friendship, never in all those years were bounds overstepped on either side. It was a marvelously controlled relationship. Sometimes when I would talk about Kitty or my many stepchildren, Mordecai would want to tell me about his children. He'd say something like, "Well, my son in Australia . . . ," and then suddenly stop, stiffen, and remember that he was the butler, after all.

I used to love to make Mordecai laugh in the middle of a sticky, formal dinner party. He'd stand at the head of the table and watch everything like a hawk. I would purposely say something that would convulse him, and he would have to leave the room. I'd hear him roar with laughter in the kitchen, "Rose, do you know what she just said?" And then he'd return with impeccable composure.

Mordecai had been with Kenneth for quite a while before I arrived. Kenneth once told me his greatest fear in getting remarried was that Mordecai might leave him. But we immediately hit it off. He loved how I wanted to make the Wicken a proper house and he was largely responsible for helping me achieve it. The sense of pride he took in it matched mine: he always referred to the house or rooms in the house as "our house." Once, a houseguest—the foreign minister George Brown, to be exact—being unused to breakfast in bed, spilled it all over everything. Mordecai came to me shattered and shaking. "Madam, someone has ruined the linen in *our* best guestroom."

I don't know what I would have done without Mordecai and Rose. I was closer to them than I was to my own husband. They nursed me, taught me, and cared for me during those trying ten years with a devotion I've seldom had in my life.

There were things I enjoyed. Because of Kenneth's position in the financial world, I was able to have experiences that would have been denied me otherwise. The trouble was that I didn't have anyone to laugh with me as I hacked and stumbled my way through all the traditions, habits, and ritual ceremonies that are England. I'll admit that following the same rites and practices year after year, century after century, is what makes England so charming a country. Not to be moved to tears at the Trooping of the Color on the Queen's Birthday, for instance, is impossible. I attended it with Kenneth the year the Welsh Guards—his regiment during World War II—did the honors. The ceremony is performed in total silence, except for the sound of the horses' hooves against the pavement. Not one horse makes a mistake, not one horse relieves himself on the sand—it's just magic. The Queen makes her procession from Buckingham Palace down the Mall on horseback, and rides onto the parade ground in front of all the government buildings. She rides a horse of unique calm—I always thought he was on Valium. He approaches the entire ritual with total equanimity. He never rears or does anything wrong. Then the troops form around the edge of the parade ground. Her Majesty leaves the formation and reviews the regiment all the way around the U. The sight is breathtaking!

Most of the world has read about or seen photos of the Trooping of the Color, or the Royal Ascot Races, or the Henley Regatta, but there are other more obscure ceremonies that I attended. Like Swan Upping. Would you believe that all the swans in England are the property of Her Majesty, the Queen? Every year a swan feast is held in London at a beautiful building called the Fishmonger's Hall.

SLIM

It has a marvelous dining hall with smaller rooms off to the sides where, if you're among the favored few, you're invited in for a glass of sherry with the presiding royal. In my case, this was old Princess Alice, the Queen's aunt. You have your little slug and then you stand in an oval with the other guests, and the royal personage slowly walks past and the women curtsey and the men bow. Then you go to the dining room and are seated with grand placecards and thus begins an incredibly long and rather hateful meal. But there is a wonderful moment when, to the flurry of a bugle procession, four men in white smocks carrying crooks, supposedly the keepers of the swans, walk into the room. They are followed by four chefs holding over their heads a gigantic silver platter that bears a reconstructed cooked swan, feathers and all. The guests stand as the swan makes its way down the center of the room and returns to the kitchen. You're then served cooked swan, which is cut up into small, gray pieces that taste exactly like what swans eat—mud.

Another mesmerizing event was dinner with the governor of the Bank of England. You go to the official building on Threadneedle Street in the City of London. There to greet you is the entire staff, from the doormen, elevator operators, to footmen and butlers. And they're all wearing black knee britches, black shoes, white stockings, and gorgeous pink coats. Not hunting pink, but strawberries-and-cream pink. It's the smartest livery anywhere.

And then there were bigger moments, like Kenneth's knighthood. We were at Blenheim, staying with the Duke of Marlborough, when Mordecai called to say a letter had arrrived and he thought Mr. Keith should see it immediately, and he would drive it down to us. The letter was from Prime Minister Harold Wilson. It said that the Queen wished to consider Kenneth for the Birthday Honors—that is, for knighthood—and would he wish to accept the honor if she so deemed?

When you receive that letter, you're not supposed to tell a soul about it until the Birthday Honors are published in the newspaper. Then you are instantly called "Sir" and "Lady"—you don't wait for the official investiture at Buckingham Palace to use the title. As it happened, Kenneth and I were in America when the Birthday Honors were announced. All my friends were excited and ribbed me, calling me "Lady Slim." I couldn't take it too seriously.

Back in England, however, the first time Mordecai spoke to me,

With Alastair, Camilla, and Kenneth in front of Buckingham Palace after Kenneth was knighted by Her Majesty.

he called me "Milady." I took a deep breath and asked him not to talk to me like that. "I have to," he said. "You're Lady Keith, and I'll have to call you Milady for the rest of our life together." I thought that was pretty silly. But, of course, you get used to it quite quickly. For a while, you begin to think it's quite ring-a-ding-ding, but it's just a very sensible way of handling political paybacks; in this case, for service to the financial community.

A few months later, there was a ceremony at Buckingham Palace and we went with Kenneth's children. I'd never been to the Palace before. You drive into the courtyard, get out, and go up a long flight of stairs, bordered on one side by a mirror. At the top, you go through two or three rooms. And then you're in the Throne Room.

I thought it would be much more ornate. It was, in fact, simple

301

and spare. There were rows of chairs for the families of the recipients with a balustrade to separate us from the Queen. She appeared in a simple Alice blue frock and a jewel. The ceremony was sensible and businesslike. A man stood beside the Queen and told her the name of each recipient, as he or she approached. Kenneth knelt in front of her, bowed his head, and she touched each of his shoulders with a sword. "Arise, Sir Kenneth," she said. And that was it.

A knighthood is a shrewd way of rewarding good works. In America, you have to give a man an ambassadorial appointment or set him up with a concrete contract. The English approach is not only more economical, it has dignity and meaning. You don't have to be an Anglophile to be impressed by it.

In the end, though, nothing changed for me. Kenneth was happier —that is, he was more arrogant. And so the great honor didn't make me more eager to preserve the marriage. And when I got right down to it, I simply didn't like Kenneth. I didn't like anything about him. With my eyes wide open, and knowing that, I had married him. I made the same mistake a lot of women make: you think you can change your man. I thought I could soften him, civilize him, create a life for him that would attract interesting people—and thereby make him agreeable. To some degree I accomplished that, but I hadn't been totally successful; he was still an unlovable chap.

The main difficulty, I suppose, was that Kenneth never really understood who and what I was. He had been brought up in a rigid "There'll Always Be an England" atmosphere and was bound by the many customs and the arrogance of its upper class: "stiff upper lip" and "don't blub in public"—mores with which I had little in common. In the beginning of our marriage he had tried hard to figure me out, because he couldn't understand why I attracted more friends than he did, nor could he comprehend my philosophy that *some* part of life had to be fun. But somewhere along the way he stopped trying to find out who I was.

One evening near the end of our marriage, as we were dressing for dinner, he came into my dressing room and watched as I finished my preparations. He studied me for a long time, then said, "You know something, Slim? One day I'll get the cut of your jib." The archaic nautical expression brought a smile to my face. I said to him, "I do hope you will, Kenneth, because if you do we'll have a much better life together. The difference between us is simple: I must be free. If I'm confined by tradition or ritual, I get restless and itchy, and I want to escape. I've always been able to think whatever I want to think, and deal with the consequences no matter what."

His was a lifetime of indoctrination about what's right, what's accepted, and what isn't, so I never knew if he understood what in God's name I was talking about. I'm quite sure that right up to the end of our marriage, my "jib" remained a total mystery to him.

The decision to leave came like a bolt of lightning. I was taking the train back to London from the Wicken on a Monday afternoon. The train pulled into the station at Ely, one of the towns along the way. I was in a compartment alone, watching the people leaving and boarding the train. My eye caught a young couple embracing each other on the platform. The girl then entered the compartment next to mine, leaving the young man to wait until the train left the station. I could no longer see her, but I continued to watch him as he raised his right hand to his lips. His arm then lifted in a soft gesture toward her and he mouthed the words: "I love you."

With a flash of realization, I knew that such a moment did not and could not exist in my life. There was no love in it. If I stayed, I would wither and die. I knew then that I had to leave England.

A few days later, we were back in the country. It was Friday evening. Kenneth was in his bathtub, I was across the hall in mine. He called over, "How would you like to be the wife of the chairman of Rolls-Royce?"

"I don't think I would," I called back. "Have they offered it to you?"

"Yes. Do you think I ought to take it?"

"I think you'd be wonderful at it. It's a business you know nothing about, and your curiosity and brains would bring a lot to it that they haven't got. It would be marvelous for you."

"So, you'd like it, then?"

"No, I wouldn't like it," I said.

"What do you mean?"

"Well, I won't be here."

"What are you saying?"

"I'm going home. This is no place for me. We're not making each other happy, we're just treading water."

"When did you decide this?"

"A few days ago, but it's taken me to this moment to tell you."

We said no more. He got out of his bath, I got out of mine, and we dressed for dinner as we did any other Friday night.

My decision to leave was as cold as my decision to marry him. The next day, we walked through the whole house so that I could show him what was mine and what I was taking. He kept saying over and over, "I think you're making a great mistake."

"Well, perhaps," I admitted. "But it's my mistake. I think I *made* a great mistake. I didn't mean to, I'm sorry it worked out like this. I admire you a great deal, I love your children, I love the garden, I love the gardener, I love the butler, I love the cook, I love it all. But I don't love you any more than you love me, and it's killing me. I'm drying up, I'm getting like a dusty old paper flower, and I just don't want to let that happen."

He quietly walked out of the house and into another building on the property—his office. From there, the king of the final word telephoned our interior designer, Tom Parr. "I've decided that Slim should go back. She's going to take her things with her, and you'll have to replace them all. I want you here next week." That's as much as he did.

The day I was to leave, he didn't go to work. As I was leaving for the airplane, I went into his study and said, "I'm leaving, Kenneth —I'm not mad at you, I don't hate you. I just think we should stop wasting each other's time. You have a chance for a much better life than you can have with me. And let's hope that I will have the same."

I shook his hand and walked out of the room. He did not follow me. At the front door of the flat I found Mordecai and I said very simply, "Mordecai."

"Milady, how can you do this to us?"

"I'm not doing it *to* you, I'm doing it *for* me. Please understand that. I couldn't have lived these years without you and your wife. I love you and I'll always love you."

I put my arms up around him and kissed him. Nobody had ever done that to him. Tears came to his eyes.

"I'll take you down to the car," he choked.

"Please don't."

"But I've always taken you down and put you in the car."

"Never again. Now we stop."

I got in the elevator and the door closed.

EPILOGUE

It has been twenty years since the elevator door closed on my life in England. I have been home in my own country in New York, the city I love, for the greater part of those years. If I had a good time before, I have had an even better time since. It serves little here to report my day-to-day existence, for that account would read like a social column spliced with a travel piece and published in a medical journal. There have been wonderful moments with valuable, cherished friends, and there have been difficult times, sick times.

I am very good at living alone. It is what I do best. I consider solitude, although it is expensive, one of the greatest luxuries that life has to provide, and I enjoy it to its fullest. My mind is well enough furnished to think on things a great long while; being alone and thinking on them has become my selfish eccentricity.

On these pages I have told about many of the good things that have happened to me and some of the bad ones, but I have held a few things back. I don't believe in appearing totally naked in public. "The secret of being a bore," said Voltaire, "is to tell everything." In any event, when I let the reel of memory run free, the good times prevail.

EPILOGUE

God blessed me with a happy spirit and many other gifts. What I was not blessed with I went out and got. Sometimes the price was too high, but I have never been much of a bargain hunter.

What matters most, it seems to me, is what one is left with at the end of the day. It's not the celebrity that matters, it's the substance: small happenings, good things to eat, an unexpected bouquet of flowers, the sun on my back, the image of my daughter's beautiful face, listening to Mozart in the dark, the bright wonder of first love as vivid and shining now as fifty years ago. These are like personal and very precious private treasures turned over in one's hands and shown to almost no one.

If I can be called lucky, it is in my memories that my luck lies. Mostly I dwell on the children in my life. Brooke, Billy, Camilla and Alastair were, at times, a passel of wild little numbers, all flying in different directions at once, blaming everything they could on everyone else—often, as children tend to do, on their parents! But the time comes when children become people, real people. And the pleasure that this gives is immeasurable. To be included in their lives at all is bank night at the movies with two sets of china. I only wish that I hadn't been for so many years one continent, sometimes two, away from my Hawks stepchildren. But they're a part of me as I am part of them.

Kitty, my own true child, remains what she has always been— the center of my existence. Her accomplishments and facilities astonish me. I have great admiration for her integrity, her diligence, and most of all, her taste. The only asset for which I'm entitled even partial credit is her astounding beauty. What she has become feeds me and persuades me that the whole process of mothering is a very worthwhile procedure. From this pinnacle of time I don't remember much about life's terrors, physical or emotional. Growing old in the long run has brought me peace and has made me understand the value of hard-won contentment.

Regrets? What I regret are the things I didn't do and the people I missed. I regret not going to Africa with Ernest Hemingway when I could have. I wish I had known Willa Cather and Edith Wharton. I would love to have had lunch at the Algonquin Round Table once and heard Dorothy Parker throw a line or two in person. And I regret not hearing a Toscanini performance.

There are people in my life I wish I'd known better. And those I wish I'd never met. And I suppose I sometimes long for some big good-looking man to walk in here and just watch over me.

What's to be said about a life? Do you thank the people who made it, who contributed to it? I do. Those who still remain close by, those who have left forever, and even those who have just plain left for whatever reason. I thank them all, for they have given me much. They are part of the woman I am. Even with all the confinements of age, that strong current of freedom that has always run through me and charted my course still, for good or bad, pulses in my veins. I am truly my own person, and that's enough.

I've more than made it. My life has been a feast, and I don't intend to push back my chair just yet.

INDEX

(Page numbers in *italics* refer to illustrations.)

INDEX

INDEX

INDEX

INDEX

INDEX

INDEX

319